RICHARD DOYLE

THE
ARTIST AND THE CRITIC
SERIES

Volume 2

Richard Doyle
Wood engraved portrait

RICHARD DOYLE

by
Rodney Engen

CATALPA PRESS LTD.
STROUD, GLOS.
1983

"The Cadi's Daughter", from
The Book of Ballads, *1849.*

Published 1983 by
Catalpa Press Ltd.

Copyright © *1983 Rodney Engen*

Designed, produced and printed by
B.P.Hawkins Ltd.
4 London Road, Stroud, Glos.

Bound by Braithwaites of Wolverhampton

ISBN 0 904995 05 4

ACKNOWLEDGMENTS

The task of assembling research materials over the past four years has been made easier by a number of interested collectors of Doyle material, of whom my greatest thanks must go to Mr Michael Heseltine, whose Doyle collection must rival many public museums. His enthusiasm for this biography and forthcoming centenary exhibition of Richard Doyle's work at the Victoria and Albert Museum, has been my greatest spur and inspiration. At the V & A Mr Lionel Lambourne's constant interest and assistance, with his staff, has been much appreciated. I wish to thank those institutions and their staffs who freely provided manuscript materials: Huguette Pidoux, Keeper of Manuscripts, Bibliothèque Cantonale et Universitaire, Lausanne, for copies of the invaluable Lewis Lusk biography and Doyle family letters; Houghton Library, Harvard University; University of Texas Humanities Research Center; Osborne Collection, Toronto Public Library; Mr Brooke Whiting of University of California Library for his assistance during my visit to Los Angeles; Lola Szladits of the Berg Collection, New York Public Library; Mr Robert Wark of the Art Gallery, and staff of Library of the Huntington Art Gallery for opening their collections to me; Mr C.A.Ryskamp, Director of the Pierpont Morgan Library, for permission to use the Doyle letters in their collection; Mr J.F.Russell of the National Library of Scotland for manuscript material; Mr John Wilson of John Wilson Ltd. for generous copies of Doyle letters in his possession; the staff of the British Library and manuscript department; British Museum Prints and Drawings Department; Ashmoleon Museum Oxford; Fitzwilliam Museum, Cambridge; National Portrait Gallery, London; National Gallery of Ireland; Mary Anne Bonney of the Punch offices archive; and Mr David Brass of E.Joseph. Numerous private individuals have taken an interest in this biography, of whom my thanks must go to Mr Justin Schiller for bibliographical material; Professor Thomas B.Brumbaugh of Vanderbilt University; Mr John Thompson; Mrs Penelope Fitzgerald, who had originally planned a Doyle biography herself; Mr Ruari McLean; Professor Robert Martin; Mr Robin Griffith-Jones of Christie's; and finally the kind hospitality of Lady Bromet, daughter of Sir Arthur Conan Doyle, for her help and interest in this book and the accompanying exhibition.

The photographs used in the book were taken mostly by Miss Joanna Smith, who deserves my special thanks for her efficiency and skill. Others were supplied by Sotheby's Belgravia, Victoria and Albert Museum, National Portrait Gallery, National Gallery of Ireland, Huntington Art Gallery, British Museum and Christie's. Special thanks must go to Mr D.L.Laird of the Airlie Estates for photographing the portrait of Blanche, Countess of Airlie, to Lord Ogilvy for permission to reproduce the painting; to Miss Jane Fowles, Librarian of Longleat House and the Marquis of Bath for permission to use the painting of the Old Library, Longleat.

Finally thanks are due to Mr Ian Hodgkins for his belief in the project, and to my editor Shaun Hammond for his dedicated work on the manuscript.
Rodney Engen
London 1983

CONTENTS

Dick Doyle as Dick Kitcat
Victoria and Albert Museum.

I

The Astonishing Dicky Doyle

1824 - 1843

o the biographer, a family of famous artists is a fascinating phenomena, for whatever form its members chose for their art, they all share a common ancestral tie. In the case of the Doyle family, which gave five prominent figures from the world of art and literature to the English-speaking world over a brief three generations, it is tempting to search for some universal strand which linked them all. Why should John Doyle, the Victorian head of the family, his artist sons Richard ("Dick"), James, Henry or Charles, or their revered nephew Arthur Conan Doyle share a common desire to express themselves so successfully? In the words of Arthur's most famous creation, Sherlock Holmes, "Art in the blood is liable to take the strongest forms". It was certainly a perceptive remark, which echoed the Doyle family's devotion, above all else, to its ancestry and its religion. Wasn't Sherlock Holmes intensely proud of being a descendant, through his great uncle, of the famous French history painter Horace Vernet? So too the story of John Doyle, the remarkably successful artist HB, his talented sons and their nephew is a tale of devotion to their past.

John Doyle was, from an early age, a remarkably resilient and talented artist. Born in Dublin in 1797, into a family of prominent Irish Catholics, he endured the genteel poverty of his family with a characteristic air of pride. He learned how his father's ancestors could be traced as far back in Ireland as the fourteenth century, how in the seventeenth century they were granted large estates and their own coat of arms, emblazoned with the appropriate "Fortitudine Vincit" under a crown and stag. Soon afterwards, however, the family's fortunes turned. They suffered for their religion, were dispossessed of their lands and property and John's father was forced to set up business as a silk mercer in Dublin. There he raised his two sons, John and James, to share his devotion to their past, to the family religion and name, just as his father had done.

When John Doyle showed a talent for drawing, his father encouraged him in numerous ways. He was sent to learn landscape painting under the ex-patriot Italian, Gaspare Gabrielli, as well as miniature painting at the Royal Dublin Society's school under John Comerford. He quickly developed a sharp eye for detail which he combined with a love of horses to produce portraits of such influential horsemen as the Marquis of Sligo and Lord Talbot, the Irish Viceroy. His success among such important patrons led to a series of six prints depicting "The Life of a Race Horse", 1822, and more importantly, the ambition to leave his homeland for the challenge of life as an artist in London, that mecca for all aspiring provincial painters. He consulted his young wife, Marianna Conan, who shared his religion and could in fact trace her ancestry further back to the Dukes of Burgundy. She agreed to the move, although the uncertainty of their new life together now that she was married, must have given cause for second thoughts. But in the end, she believed in her husband's determination to succeed in a new country, especially when he firmly declared he would never return to his native Ireland, despite the recent improvement in treatment of his fellow Catholics there. He believed in his birthright; but he also believed in a better life for his family. And so the twenty year old artist gathered together his meagre inheritance and left for London. He took with him poignant reminders of his family's once prosperous past: pieces of seventeenth century plate, a sixteenth century mortar and pestle for grinding home medicines with the Doyle crest embossed on its side, and a painting said to be by Van Dyck which he refused at all costs to sell.

The first few years in London were filled with sacrifices and severe disappointments as John struggled to find his artistic footing. His greatest enemy was his quiet, unassuming manner which isolated him from prospective patrons, and his

bids for public acclaim suffered "for want of connections".[1] Having inherited the austere, aloof nature of his father, he presented the image of a thoroughly polite gentleman whose reserve could occasionally be broken in the company of such exalted social circles as those once surrounding Byron, Sheridan and Walter Scott. Gradually his artistic friends admired his "disinterested modesty", which was so refreshing in the age of opulence and ostentation in Regency London. But when he attempted to support his wife on his painted portrait miniatures, his efforts brought only domestic upheavals for his growing family, which was forced to move house four times in less than ten years.

By 1832 the Doyle family had grown to seven children, five sons and two daughters: the eldest son James William Edmund, born in 1822, Richard born in 1824, Henry Edward born in 1827, Charles born in 1832, and Francis (who

John Doyle
Pencil and chalk drawing by his son Henry.
National Portrait Gallery.

died about 1840), as well as the daughters Adelaide (who also died young) and Annette. They were a considerable strain upon their father's ambitions to become recognised as a portrait painter, and for some years he had waivered between painting portraits for the London galleries, private commissions, as well as his favourite sporting subjects. He painted in a succession of small houses rented in London's artisan districts, firstly in Berners Street, then for two years south of the Thames in Lambeth. Eventually he joined the struggling painters and engravers in the Euston and Somerstown districts of the city. It was not, however, until 1825 that the first signs of recognition came, when his first painting, "Turning out the Stag", was accepted for exhibition at the prestigious Royal Academy. It was followed the next year and until 1835, with a succession of portrait paintings of "Ladies and Gentlemen"; all clear bids for lucrative new patronage by a competent if uninspired new portrait painter.

The domestic trials of caring for a large family in each new house, while her husband painted and drew in whichever room was free, soon took their toll on Marianna Doyle. She had been a devoted mother for over ten years, but her poor health, which was a constant worry to her husband, eventually proved fatal sometime after the difficult birth of her last child, Charles in 1832. It was a tragic loss to the family, and a bitter blow to John Doyle, who was plunged deeper into a sense of responsibility for his growing family.

Fortunately his career showed signs of a breakthrough, not in the portrait painting commissions he half-heartedly sought, but as a result of the lithographic portraits he had begun to produce, "drawn merely from reminiscence". He drew the Duke of Wellington on his charger, and the Duke of York, and both prints were very popular and sold in large quantities. He also attempted small portrait paintings of noted politicians like George Canning, and the Prime Minister Robert Peel, then a suitable subject since he had secured the Catholic Emancipation Act in 1829, when Home Secretary. His drawing of the young Princess Victoria in her pony phaeton was also much admired. But it was the drawings, which from 1827 onward became more political, that earned John Doyle his reputation. To preserve his objectivity, and maintain what he regarded as essential artistic

distance from his subjects, he refused to sign his drawings with his name. Instead he adopted the signature "HB", a combination of two js and two ds placed above each other, and jealously guarded his anonymity until his retirement in 1851.

The Political Sketches of HB, as they were known, were issued at regular intervals, usually once a month during parliamentary sessions, from 1829, published in book form in 1841. These gentle, dignified jabs at prominent political figures were a refreshing change from the more outrageous political cartoons of Gillray and Rowlandson which the English public had come to expect in political caricatures of the day. So great was HB's following, that *The Times* printed a key to his drawings, as did McLean in the 1840s, so there could be no doubt where the amused HB was pointing his carefully aimed and disapproving pencil. For over twenty years John Doyle produced his admired lithographs, which totaled about a thousand prints and made HB a household phenomena.

By 1840 he had earned enough to move his family to the more fashionable address of 17 Cambridge Terrace, Hyde Park, which became the Doyle family home and centre of a very closed, yet inspired world of famous artistic and literary visitors. Here John Doyle never discussed his work. To his children he was the "Guv'nor", or "Lord John" (although they never addressed him in this way). As the fame of HB grew, he became obsessed with preserving his anonymity. His drawings were first drawn on the heavy lithographic stone then collected by a messenger in a special closed carriage to insure absolute secrecy. He never allowed his children to discuss his work, or kept examples of published drawings in the house to incriminate him. When he went out in public, he was the "quiet, silent unsuspected frequenter of the lobby and gallery" at the House of Commons, noting generally from memory the details of his subjects. Later he used his memory like a detective, slowly piecing together clues, mannerisms and details to recreate a clear impression of his next victims. These he arranged around favourite themes. They were generally preoccupations, like a scene from the classics or a fairy-tale, like Cinderella, recently read to his children, and sometimes a current play with his political subjects as actors. There were versions of his friend Edwin Landseer's popular anthropomorphized paintings, and occasional hints of a preoccupation with the spirit

"The Harpies Attacking the Daughters of Pandarus (after Flaxman)", HB Political Sketch No.903, published 15 July 1848. Depicts Bentinck, Disraeli, Lord Stanley as harpies attacking Lord John Russell, Lord Grey and Mr Hawes for suppressing documents during the Sugar Duties debate.
Author's collection.

world – a Doyle family trait which became more prominent in his and his sons' works. "The Apparition-The Ghost of Canning, 1829" was an early example, followed by such classical allusions as "The Harpies Attacking the Daughters of Pandarus (after Flaxman)", 1848.

Indeed the quiet, restrained classical style that HB adopted was often borrowed from his famous artist colleagues, like Flaxman. Unlike his un-restrained predecessors Gillray and Rowlandson, the HB formula was founded upon good taste; the figures were carefully drawn, the settings

suggestive, but never overdrawn. His critics called them "wickedly fastidious" in an age when buffoonery was commonplace; his admirers marvelled at his ability to poke fun in the nicest possible way. Those who knew him as John Doyle were equally charmed by his high moral principles and gentlemanly behaviour. Politicians vied for his company, little knowing he might use their dinner table mannerisms in his next political sketch; later it was said he was the dinner guest of the Queen and Prince of Wales, although he was most comfortable with his artist colleagues. "He has an instinct for expression and power of drawing, without academical cant, I never saw before," claimed the painter Benjamin Hayter. And he shared the view with many famous friends and houseguests at Cambridge Terrace, including David Wilkie, Samuel Rogers, Thomas Moore, Wordsworth, and Macauley. "You never hear any laughing at 'HB'; his pictures are a great deal too genteel for that, – exceedingly clever and pretty, and cause one to smile in a quiet, gentlemanly kind of way," wrote another admirer, Thackeray, in *Westminster Review* (June 1840).

But it was only when his popularity died that John Doyle revealed his very personal intentions as HB. Writing in a remarkably frank letter to Robert Peel, he claimed his drawings were "governed by a certain steadiness of moral and political principle. Although commenced in sport, I soon became convinced from the extent of their sale and the importance attached to them in political circles, that I possessed in my hands an agent of some little influence. This influence such as it was, I resolved should not be turned to say unworthy purpose by me, but that scrupulously avoiding all indelicacy, private scandal, and party bitterness, it should – where it was not intended merely to amuse by some harmless jest – be directed to the furtherance of some intelligible public object, and that by such means as would be fair analogy be considered legitimate in public warfare... I never wilfully violated them."[3] Such high principles led even his critics to acknowledge that John Doyle had introduced a new spirit to English satiric art; a spirit perpetuated by his son Richard long after his father's retirement.

Life at Cambridge Terrace was dominated by the strict rules and carefully supervised lessons set out by John Doyle for his children. James, Richard (Dick or Dicky), Henry, Charles, Francis (Frank), Adelaide (Adele) and Annette were obedient and loving children with a devotion to their father, "The Guv'nor", which grew with the years. They were talented, precocious children, each with a special ability which allowed them to excel in music, writing their own plays and histories, and most of all as artists. Their education was insular, originating from a succession of tutors and governesses who came to the house. The boys were tutored in French, history, fencing, and dancing, which prepared them for positions in society, while the girls excelled in needlework, French translation and music. Their progress was carefully watched by their doting father, who insisted each child should record in a weekly illustrated letter the impressions or events which occurred to them. These were to be received by him at the end of each week. To mark the event, he established the "Sunday Show", a weekly display of their talent which sometimes was a play especially created for their father, sometimes the display of their latest painting or drawing, or a joint concert or theatri-

cal based upon their music lessons or favourite readings from their history books. Here young Dick might unveil his latest drawing for a history painting or Annette would play the piano while Dick followed on his violin, James on the cello. They were delightful and impressive displays which pleased their father's extremely high standards of artistic expression, and he occasionally invited his famous friends to witness their performances, breaking his usual reserve to boast about his talented children.

The four-storied house at Cambridge Terrace was large enough for John Doyle to maintain his privacy, while his children worked or prepared their weekly offerings, rehearsing their plays and readings in another part of the house. Their father's success had helped to furnish the rooms in some style. The high-ceilinged rooms were covered in rich panelling, with Chippendale chairs round the large mahogany dining table. It included an upstairs music room, drawing room (where a bust of HB stood sternly in one corner), and balcony overlooking the street. But on the fourth floor – especially in the "Big Room" – was where most of the activity occurred. Here the Doyle children performed their Sunday Show, surrounded by the swords and shields which James had proudly hung to the walls, a large desk and worktable, and the bare floorboards over which they prepared their weekly letters and drawings to their father. It was their domain, invaded once a week by their father to pass his approval on their progress, or to note how their lessons were progressing. Downstairs in the dining room, especially on Sunday evenings after the Show, their father's friends gathered around the mahogany table – men like Walter Scott, young Disraeli, De Quincey, Coleridge, Richard Owen, Wordsworth, and later Rossetti, Thackeray and Dickens. Indeed, the dining table remained a precious family heirloom, a symbol of the Doyle family's new-found status, and on his death John Doyle willed it to his then famous son Dick.

Fortunately young Charles recorded his memory of those inspiring Sundays, writing years later with a vivid clarity of one who was most impressed by the occasion: "On Sunday the day was observed by all the children – Great and Small – Annette, James, Dick, Henry, Frank, Adelaide and myself, going to Mass, celebrated at the French Chapel at 8 o'clock a.m." After breakfast at ten, the sabbath was strictly observed, "in perfect quiet till 8 in the evening when the camphor lamp and the mole candles were lit in the drawing room, and guests began to arrive, often comprizing (sic) the most distinguished literary and artistic men of London and foreigners – Thackeray and [Samuel] Lover – Rothwell and Moor Sculptor amongst others – Most delicious music was discoursed by Annette on the piano and James on the violincello till about 10 when the supper tray was laid – generally just cold meats and salad, followed by punch. We boys all retired when this appeared – but up stairs in bed I have often listened to indications of most delightful conversations till 1 or 2."[5]

Some sense of domestic order in the widowed household was restored with the arrival of their mother's brother Michael Conan and his devoted wife Anne. Uncle Michael was an endearing fellow whom his nieces and nephews quickly learned to love for his Irish wit, his sharp tongue and his habit of always inviting them to the theatre or a concert. As a struggling art, drama and music critic for the *Morning Herald,* his work took him to London's theatres, the opera and ballet, as well as current art exhibitions, and it was through him that young Dick first learned to appreciate music. Uncle Michael could always be relied upon for tickets to the latest operatic or theatrical sensation, and he was willing to take Dick as well as his brother Henry, to sharpen their critical eyes and ears as well as expose them to polite society. Both Dick and Henry's letters to their father began to show strong hints of their outspoken uncle's influence. They questioned and condemned performances, analysed paintings and plays in a manner borrowed from their Uncle Michael. Indeed, Michael Conan was fond of using words for verbal effect alone; for "words were fireworks" to be exploded when necessary. Although a feeble man physically (his wife was always at his side to support his weak legs), his broad face, curly hair and close-cropped grey beard were always a welcomed sight and influence in the Doyle household. In later years Arthur Conan Doyle (who was given his surname) pronounced his famous relative (then Paris correspondent to the *Art Journal*) "a man of distinction, an intellectual Irishman of the type which originally founded the Sinn Fein movement".[6]

* * * * * * * * * * * * *

Young Dick Doyle quickly adapted to life with his brothers and sisters at Cambridge Terrace, where he remained for most of his professional life. Since his birth in September 1824, he had endured the family moves throughout London and developed a personal dedication and self-sufficiency (especially when drawing for his father's approval). He also shared a life-long devotion to his family and their home. He was an imaginative, cheerful and very witty child, who loved words and music, as well as the theatre. But like his father and brothers, drawing was his greatest love. On the other hand, he could be deeply secretive and suffered moods of deep melancholy, especially when a plan to finish a work for his father was thwarted. From the many letters he illustrated and wrote to his father, young Dick emerges as a precocious, highly inventive child, often caught up in his frustrations to please his father's demanding expectations.

These letters formed the core of *Dick Doyle's Journal*, a one hundred and fifty page revision of

Dick Doyle's Journal for 1840.
Title-page, pen and ink, 7¼ x 9½"
British Museum.

one year's letter writing to his father in 1840, at the age of sixteen. Here in fine copperplate his chance impressions and sketches from memory are set out with an expert confidence in the use of a quill pen and chinese ink. It is a remarkably sustained project, which charts his spontaneous humour and boyhood love of adventure – whether walking in the park, watching a military display or listening to a concert – and his delightfully whimsical approach to those subjects he most enjoyed, however serious others thought they should be. Throughout, his flippant, boyish style is maintained in both drawings and text: "Suppose we stop,' says I. 'Lett's,' says Henry, and we did." He began the journal with some trepidation, for he was by then too aware of the threat of failure in his father's eyes: "The first of January, got up late, very bad. Made good resolutions and did not keep them. Went out and got a cold. Did keep it. First thought I would, then thought I would not, was sure I would, was positive I would not, at last was determined I would write a journal...Hope I may be skinned alive by wild cats if I don't go on with it." This first entry is dotted with sketches of his worst fears: two leering gnomes taunt him as spectres

The Doyle children prepare for 'The Show',
from Dick Doyle's Journal.

of failure; a self-portrait figure "skinned alive by wild cats" which leap and torment him with their scratches. Beneath the flippancy then, the journal was a very serious new venture which must not fail; although he concluded, "I am afraid this journal will turn out a hash."

From January until early December, he attempts to fill the journal with his impressions: of life at Cambridge Terrace, in "The Park", the galleries, theatres, concert halls and operas which he visited with his uncle or father, or his favourite pastime – watching and listening to the people in London's streets. He draws the Sunday Show, describes the furious activity preparing for his father's approval, and the processions and street crowds he and his brothers eagerly raced to join. On the whole, Dick's journal entries are far from mere schoolboy doodles. They are carefully composed sketches and comic initials of diminutive characters, with large often grotesque heads inserted as part of the text. There are very few corrections, only the occasional spelling mistake (as is the case with those letters he produced for his father). Meticulous and neatly presented, Dick's letters and journal took him hours of careful work to produce, with never a smudged passage or a rubbed-out word.

This same high standard was applied to all Dick's drawings for his father. John Doyle had taught his children the supreme lesson of

Art lessons for the Doyle children:
a) Dick Doyle examines pictures at the National Gallery, from Dick Doyle's Journal.

b) Henry Doyle to his father, on seeing a bullfinch in Kensington Gardens, 12 March 1842. Pierpont Morgan Library.

c) Charles Doyle to his father, on observing shepherds at work, undated. Pierpont Morgan Library.

seeing: to study first with one's eyes, never a sketch pad, and then to record from memory exactly what one saw without the benefit of sketched notes. It was a lesson he learned from his revered hero, the French history and military painter Horace Vernet, whom Dick came to revere all his life. Vernet had the gift of a photographic memory, whose vast canvases of figures in elaborately composed battle scenes were devised exclusively from watching people, and never from models in his studio. The Doyle children were taught that this was the supreme lesson to learn for any serious artist, and all the drawings in Dick's journal and letters were done entirely from memory, often within hours of the event.

Another mentor was the family friend, William Hilton, now a famous religious and historical painter. Dick's father often took him to study Hilton's canvases in his studio, to make special mental notes of the compositions, or "groupings" as he called them. On other occasions, the Doyle children were sent off to the Royal Academy (then part of Somerset House), for the prestigious annual summer exhibition on 1 May. Dick and his brothers anxiously waited to see the Queen

enter for her private view the previous day. They were often first in the queue for the public opening, eager to see the newest Hiltons, Landseers, Leslies or Wilkies who became their favourite painters. Dick recorded in his journal the frantic crush of spectators, also his own careful scrutiny of each canvas which had to be roped off for safety from the threat of eager spectators who might damage them. He concentrated upon those paintings which immediately struck his eye, then studied the composition and poses of one or two figures and raced home afterwards to make his drawings for his letters to his father, often having to return to the original picture several days running to record the poses accurately. His brothers James, Henry and even little Charles joined him in this very serious game, filling their own letters to John Doyle with versions of their favourite pictures. Such dedication to their father's doctrinaire approach to drawing brought only admiration from his children; they were certain it was the best method of learning to draw, and none of them were allowed to pursue studies in any of London's art schools. In later years Dick Doyle's critics pointed to this weakness in his work; especially his poorly drawn figures done without the benefit of academic training. But Dick remained true to his father's original methods. Once he proudly told

Dick buys supplies at Ackermann's, from Dick Doyle's Journal.

Listening to Liszt and Eliason play a Beethoven duet, from Dick Doyle's Journal.

his engraver employers, the Dalziels, how much he "highly approved of this method and he had derived great benefit from the process himself".[7]

The journal entries also chart Dick's musical interests. His drawings of concerts and opera audiences were intended to show his father how observant he had been. He delighted in witnessing Liszt and Eliason in a Beethoven duet ("the crack piece of the evening"), or Liszt "thundering away at a tarantella", or he listened with rapt attention to a new operatic sensation in concert rooms "crammed to suffocation". He reported his impressions of the family concert, when he and Annette played "spirited fantasies" on the piano and violin, the performance marred only by his violin playing like "the singing of an asthmatic donkey or the conversation of an insane cat". There are descriptions of his boy-

hood reading, the history books in English and French, novels and adventure stories which stirred his imagination and became the subject of journal drawings. His French tutor was a stern taskmaster who set mercilessly long translations from a History of Belgium and France, which put him in "a desperate humour" because they left no time for drawing.

By this time sketching had become very important to him. When his governess suffered some severe disappointment, Dick tried to comfort her with a small sketch of the crucifixion. When he felt the urge to express himself, he searched through the historical novels of Harrison Ainsworth, or Walter Scott for subjects to draw. His favourite Scott hero was Quentin Durward, the chivalric hero of Scott's fifteenth century tale of loyalty and romance. He attempted a large painting of his hero, whose gentlemanly virtues Dick chose to emulate. He was Quentin Durward's disciple, "brave, dashing, honour-able, proud of his birth, pure-minded, gentle to

"The Council of the Gods", from Homer for the Holidays, *c1836.*

women and loyal to his master". Many such knightly virtues appeared in Dick's Sunday drawings. He planned a comic history with favourite knights and their beautiful maidens, but always took a witty, if more irreverent view of history than his tutor explained to him.

It is not surprising that the son of HB should want to have his own work published, and Dick's schoolboy fantasies on historical themes were thought good enough by his father to consider publication. Indeed, this was the enticement John Doyle often used with his talented son: if he liked an idea, he suggested having it printed privately. No doubt even at this early stage, he was aware of Dick's potential as an illustrator. And so Dick began to plan book projects. He turned to his father's revered Flaxman, and his schoolboy love of classical myths, to create his first book of fifteen comic plates in imitation of Flaxman's much acclaimed illustrations to

Homer. He called it *Homer for the Holidays*, a comic reworking of favourite scenes from Homer which, despite the poorly drawn figures and crude faces, contained an endearing element of humour which suggested where this schoolboy of twelve might develop his talent. He even drew himself as the mop-headed Apollo addressing a rapt audience of gods on Mount Olympus. He also started an illustrated *Iliad* which remained unfinished. Moreover, his choice of the classics delighted his father. After long hours in the galleries, Dick decided that here was a rich source of new drawing subjects, long neglected by current British painters. He poured over a copy of John's *Manners and Customs of the Greeks*, fascinated by the classical heroes like Alcibiades, whose physical beauty forced him to hide his head from excited women whenever he went into the street.[8]

Dick developed a sensitivity, especially towards injustice and cruelty, which he often depicted in his drawings. He loved animals; his dog Ruff was a faithful companion on walks in Hyde Park, where he studied the birds, or the more exotic creatures in the nearby Zoological Gardens of Regent's Park. He loved military displays for the horses and the pageantry, once telling his father, "If I were not going to be an artist, I would like best to be an officer in the lifeguards. There is scarcely anything so delicious to me as a review." Horse-racing was a subject his father taught him to admire, and it became the subject of a series of four coloured drawings, "A Steeplechase", 1839 (which are now in the National Gallery of Ireland). They are his impression of the Grand Steeplechase at nearby Notting Hill Hippodrome on 17 June 1839, although Dick soon grew revolted by the excited crowds and displays of cruelty to animals such events usually produced. He and Henry had witnessed a horrific spectacle of human cruelty

at Jackson's steeplechase grounds. Dick returned home sickened by the scene he recorded in his journal. The event was a twenty mile race against the clock by just one horse. The rider beat his animal so hard during the race, and was goaded on by the cries of the ecstatic crowd, that Dick was appalled: "The poor animal was quite done up and being unable to stand was supported home in a miserable state of mind from which I don't expect to recover for a week. I don't ever remember feeling so sick as to think of a poor animal being perhaps killed for the amusement of a crowd of people," he told his journal.[9] And he never forgot the spectacle: years later he attacked the folly of the steeplechase in his "Manners and Customs" series as a ridiculous tumble of horse-flesh and riders.

Just as Dick loved tales of knights and medieval displays of chivalry, his family shared his excitement over its most recent signs of revival during the Eglinton Tournament. John Doyle

Dick's parody of "Ye National Sporte!!! of Steeple Chasynge", from Manners and Customs, *1849.*

had attended this famous national event and brought back delightful stories of the spectacle which Dick and his brothers tempered with their own schoolboy fantasies of what it was like to fight in a tournament. They decided to hold a mock joust in the manner of the tournament, with each young brother astride his older brother's shoulders, the winner to be awarded a reward of valour by Annette, the Queen of the Tournament. Dick drew this delightful Sunday afternoon performance in his journal, spread across three pages. It culminated in the award ceremony; in the best chivalric tradition the reward shared by both brothers, who fought equally well.

The Eglinton Tournament also marked the début of Dick Doyle as a book illustrator, for his first published book was based upon his version of that disastrous spectacle. Staged by the thirteenth Earl of Eglinton at his Scottish castle in August 1839, this romantic recreation of a

medieval tournament was seen not just as an eccentric entertainment among the idle rich, but as a supreme example of the revival of chilvary in nineteenth century Britain. When announced, it aroused anger and delight. Coming in the wake of the Reform Bill, with a need for radical social reform at a time of growing unemployment and trade recession, critics attacked the tournament as a shameful display of extravagance. Others, who had earlier been outraged by plans for the Queen's "Penny Coronation", saw the tournament as a restoration of ancient and revered values of aristocratic virility and national pride. Among the one hundred and fifty knights who attended, it was said some paid at least £200 each for their costumes, while its one hundred thousand spectators, many of whom were prominent aristocrats, arrived at the Ayrshire coast determined to mount the finest display of fashions and wealth seen for many years.

Artists like John Doyle (as HB), Daniel Maclise, Edwin Landseer, the Scottish painters Noel Paton, Octavius Hill and William Allan, eagerly waited, and slowly the long-awaited spectacle turned into a disaster. After a three hour delay the knights finally appeared, just as a

---

*The Doyle Sunday Tournament, two pages
from* Dick Doyle's Journal. *Pen and ink,
7¼ x 9½" each.
British Museum.*

Two scenes from Dick Doyle's The
Tournament [at Eglinton], *1840.*

torrential burst of rain soaked their expensive
suits of armour and sent them scurrying for cover
to prevent rusting. Lances were replaced by
umbrellas, dignity by mudsoaked hilarity.
The spectators too suffered disgrace when the
pavilion collapsed and buckets of cold rain-
water fell down many an elegantly dressed neck.
Chaos gave way to amusement and delight
among the tournament's fiercest critics; one
onlooker compared the surrounding hillside of
umbrellas to an enormous field of mushrooms,
another to the backsides of thousands of elephants. And the rain continued non-stop for the
next three days. After this the tournament was
successfully held, but by then public opinion had
been established against the event, its critics
winning out over the rain-soaked knights, whose
"old world" ardour had been considerably damp-
ened by their experience.

The press delighted in the disaster and the
knight with an open umbrella became a national
symbol of defunct "old world" values, especially
in the satiric Whig and Radical papers. Cleave's
Penny Gazette published a drawing of knights
with umbrellas rocking on hobby-horses as "The
Eglinton Tomfooleryment"; HB offered a more
sober-minded version in his "Practising for the
Tournament, 1838", in which politicians in full
armour prepared to tilt over the Irish question.
Throughout the 1840s the tournament provided
a vast array of opportunities for artists. There
were tournament jig-saws, medals, jugs, plates,
scent bottles with knight's helmets for stoppers,
and souvenir music of the Tournament Quadrilles
performed at the Tournament Ball. A school of
illustrators produced book editions of what they
had seen, or imagined; volumes like Edward
Corbould's first book of *The Tournament* in
1840, or James Nixon's in 1843, (which failed
even to acknowledge the disastrous weather).

The popularity of these books persuaded Dick
to try his hand at an illustrated tournament. He
produced a delightful folio-sized group of seven
drawings on the lithographer's stone, each one
framed by his characteristic whimsical borders
of elfish jesters and lances. Although he borrowed the gothic convention of an archway for his

title-page from his favourite book, Cruikshank's illustrations to Ainsworth's *Tower of London*, his drawings were strikingly original. His knights prepare for the tournament with expressions of haughtiness and boredom. This later changed to strained apprehension as they ride through the mud-soaked crowds, their heads still erect despite the pouring rain. It was clearly the inventive work of a comic artist, whose confident style was praised by many of his father's famous friends.

Little did they know the struggles Dick encountered in producing his first book. His journal entries give some indication of his working methods and how his original enthusiam turned to despair, then elation as he toiled over the demands of drawing his intricate lines upon the unfamiliar lithographer's stone. On one occasion, James brought home the printer's proof of one drawing which was too spoilt by rain to use; another time Dick had to redraw a plate several times, struggling with the thin sheets of transfer paper used to place his original drawing on the stone. But as the prospect of publication neared, his desire to draw for publication increased: "I am meditating a Quentin Durward on a sheet of double elephant [paper] but I must get the Tournament finished before I begin anything else as there is some chance of it being published, if it does, that day will be a very extraordinary one in my life," he told his journal on 9 January. After finishing the drawings three days later, he tried to check his enthusiasm: "Hurra. Don't you be too sure though, perhaps they won't be published at all." And yet he dreamed of having the drawings published, and drew his Tournament in the window of Messrs. Fores, the London printseller, as he stares delighted into the shop. "Now just imagine if I was walking coolly, and suddenly came upon the Tournament in a shop window. Oh crikey it would be enough to turn me inside out."

Eventually John Doyle agreed to order "fifty hot copies" printed by Fores, and when they arrived Dick was elated. "I never knew such fun in my whole life," he told his journal, and ran into his workroom "every half hour" to admire his printed work. These first fifty were quickly sold to family friends, who laughed over his clever drawings during fashionable dinner parties, and helped to spread the news that Dick was a young artist to watch. He had met Count d'Orsay at his printer's and sent along a copy of the finished book to him. The extravagant Count, an artist himself, who had once called Landseer "the finest artist of our day", was delighted by Dick's "extraordinary drawings". Later he wrote to a friend, "They are remarkably clever, and I venture to say that I would be embarrassed to find any old artist capable to enter into the competition with this younger one. He is undoubtedly a genius of the first order and from this moment I will back him against any one –". When Dick heard this, his reaction was typical: "I never knew anything like it in my whole life."[10] But his delight was tempered by financial worry. He was made responsible for sales and repayment of the printer's bill from the start, his father no doubt believing it a valuable lesson in business affairs. To Dick's horror, the printer sent his bill for immediate collection ("the brute"), and after much soul-searching Dick relented and asked to borrow the £4.18s from his father. "There is something pleasant and important in paying a printer's bill but nothing in paying a debt to Papa... But supposing I don't get any more sold, then what will I do?" But such worries were soon overcome and eventually one hundred and fifty copies of the book were printed to meet demands.

John Doyle was delighted with his son's first overwhelming critical success. But then he had always believed in Dick's comic talent, his "most ready pencil, a single original fancy" which he felt was in the sketches and Tournament drawings "the spontaneous productions of [a] boy, not uncultivated certainly, but uncontrolled by education".[11] The Tournament success also brought Dick's first commission, as he explained to his journal: "Here is a glorious piece of work. Fores, a man residing in Piccadilly corner of Sackville Street, keeping a print-shop and being a publisher has sent me an order to do half a dozen envelopes on transfer paper. He has sent some designs which he wishes to have done, namely Courting, Coaching, Hunting and Racing, but I have got myself to design a Dancing and a Musical envelope."

With the promise of certain publication, Dick attacked the envelope drawings "with great vigour" and completed the Coaching subject in one day. He agreed to share the commission with his elder brother James, which gave him more time to pursue those designs of his own

invention. Indeed, the plan was to complete all six envelopes in a week, working as always, under their father's keen supervision. After Dick completed his Musical design, he was relieved to report his father's approval ("Papa says will do."). But the commission brought renewed frustrations, and despair, then elation at the prospect of its completion. "Nothing but work, work, work all day!" he moaned, then despaired when his Dancing envelope had to be redrawn for the third time. "I would a great deal sooner do anything as large as a Tournament than the size of the envelopes on transfer paper."

But the first six envelopes were published just two months after they were commissioned, the first appearing in September 1840. Dick was understandably delighted: "Glorious. Went to Fores's. The envelopes out." They were inventive, if slight line drawings of microscopic figures drawn in his journal style, arranged around the rectangular envelope shape and blank address-space. He used favourite devices like a central figure of a clown or the Lord Mayor, usually astride an animal or object like a plum pudding, in a most undignified pose. It was unkind, perhaps, but the comic strain led to all the envelopes achieving a critical success in a market already flooded by variations on William Mulready's now famous penny postage envelope for Sir Rowland Hill. Fores had in fact produced their own Comic Envelope series, designed first by young John Leech. And the Doyle brothers' envelopes were too original for *The Times* critic to ignore. "As sure as I am living, there was a critique on the envelopes in the 'Times' this morning, and whoever dares to say there was not is a liar. Hurra!" Dick told his journal. And it was a flattering acknowledgement; *The Times* critic (9 September 1840), compared the designs with their numerous rivals and declared them more tasteful, the subjects "all excellently humerous in their respective ways. We recommend those who buy post-office envelopes merely for fun – we suppose few purchase them with any other object – to purchase Mr Fores's envelopes instead. They are better and more amusing, both in design and execution, and are certainly more creditable to the public taste."

Their critical success led to a further four designs commissioned by Fores, which were ready by Christmas. Here was Dick's delightful yuletide clown astride a large plum pudding, with scenes of holiday merriment encircling the page. Again his father was delighted. His son's ideas inspired his own version of the Mulready envelope craze – a figure of Britannia scattering his son's envelopes over both hemispheres of the world in his HB Political Sketch No.654.

* * * * * * * * * * * *

It is significant that Dick's journal should end in early December. The pressures of completing the envelope designs as well as his annual drawing present for his father had then proved too much. But then he greeted the end of the year holiday season with a mixture of dread and elation, for as he confided in one of the last journal entries, "notwithstanding the pleasures of holidays, I must say I feel really happier before they begin, the delicious excitement, as I said before, the immensely hard work, the doubt as to whether Papa will like the things we give him, or not, and the expectation, all combine to place the system in such a ferment, that in comparison with it the holidays are dull." Three days into December he closed his journal and pushed it into a drawer where it remained forgotten until two years after his death, when it was resurrected and published by his family. It seems strange that such a remarkable achievement should never have been shown by Dick to any of his friends. But the lessons he learned by making the journal continued to appear in his weekly illustrated letters to his father.

Over the next three years Dick's letters, and those of his brothers, give a clear picture of his development as an artist. He had now reached sixteen, had two projects published and praised, and set his sights on a career as an artist. He continued his father's lessons, and with his brothers raced out of the house each day to be in Hyde Park by seven in the morning. Dick and his brothers apparently suffered from poor health, which they probably inherited from their mother. Their father was determined to build up his children's health (he would eventually lose two in childhood), and under penalty of a fine of six pence a day for each late day, he challenged his sons to maintain a strict routine of daily visits to the park. They took his challenge very seriously; Henry records in an early letter his monthly account of days missed and money owed to his father as a result. Once in the park, they walked to the spring near the Serpentine to drink at least two tumblers full of precious mineral water

dispensed there by a delightful old crone. On other days they were sent off on energetic walks into the nearby countryside. Once they walked miles out of their way and almost reached Harrow, where Henry chased a rabbit and got lost in a wood, and they eventually trudged home in the pouring rain. On other occasions, they ventured south to find the famous windmill on Wimbledon Common; or they climbed Parliament Hill to join the bank holiday crowds on Hampstead Heath. Once Dick was locked in the high brick walls of Hyde Park. Having been so engrossed in searching for subjects to draw, he forgot the time, and had to scale the high wall aided by his brothers.

Each adventure was dutifully described and sketched in his letters to his father, and sent to him wherever he went, from "somewhere in Acton" to his annual visit to relatives in Black-heath. Dick excelled in his sketches of crowds, the military displays in the park, or chance glimpses of a famous political or royal figure. He always remembered the vast crowds in his neighbourhood "the night the Queen became of age when we all went out to see the illuminations", and how he marvelled at the people, "the most tremendous thing I ever experienced". When the Queen announced her marriage to Prince Albert, Dick followed the wedding arrangements with delight: how the wedding dress cost £300, how the cake was almost ten feet across (this he confirmed after joining the crush in front of the royal confectioner's window where it was displayed). He eagerly noted Prince Albert's engagements and followed him, hoping to catch a brief glimpse before the wedding. Finally the "long-expected day" arrived, and Dick awoke deeply depressed by the pouring rain. Always prey to bouts of hypersensitivity and depression, he wandered the house feeling guilty that he could not even work on his painting, "but I am one of those interesting kind of individuals, who whenever they have once worked themselves up into the idea of seeing any very extraordinary object or animated nature, can not possibly set to work at any kind of business whatsoever; until the said objects of art or animated nature have been duly witnessed, and so it was this day. Despair was in my face at half past eleven, but it passed away at twelve."

Eventually he took Henry ("in the same state as myself") out to join the damp crowds for the royal procession, fighting all the way to get the

The marriage procession of Queen Victoria, from Dick Doyle's Journal.

best view. "I am a boy of about fifteen years of age, measuring something like five feet in height and endowed with such prodigious strength as to be capable of knocking a little man down in a crowd," he playfully boasted. To pass the time, he made mental notes of his fellow spectators, delighted by their conversations: "Well Louisa, never say *you* were not in a crowd after this." He preferred the comic antics of the less pious, Dickensian creatures like "a funny old cobbler, nearly bursting with kindness", or the footman who stood next to him, "a nice specimen of that cheerfulness which is so refreshing to meet in society, his wit and conversation were not to be withstood". When the Queen and Prince Albert passed in the gold coach, Dick and Henry joined in the "tremendous cheers", waved their hats in the air and "screamed with all our might". Afterwards, Dick raced home "very tired" but determined to draw the wedding coach before the memory faded, noting with obvious surprise that the Queen had "looked actually beautiful" as the veiled bride seated alongside her prince.

The seemingly interminable history lessons set by his tutor inspired a new project which had a long and ill-fated history. As early as April 1840, Dick announced his plan to draw "a series

of histories" for which James would supply the text. Their father, "Dear Papa", was excited by the plan, and promised to pay for thirty printed and bound copies. But despite James's text completed in early May, Dick's drawings stretched over several months as his idea of a comic history took shape. He began to doubt the truth of many historical legends; couldn't Richard the Lion-hearted pardoning King John have been so easily invented?" he asked his father in one

a)

Scenes from English History, *1840:*
a) Unpublished ink drawings and comic initials.
b) "Queen Elizabeth and the Earl of Essex in Council".
c) "The Black Prince and the French King entering London".

b)

c)

A Grand Historical Allegorical Classical and
Comical Procession of Remarkable Personages
Ancient Modern and Unknown, *1842:*
a) Michelangelo and the Brothers of Art.

letter. "After all fiction is nothing compared with
reality. The Histories of England and France are
full of the most romantic incidents, and the only
doubt is as to which is the best." After struggling
through two volumes of the *History of France* in
French for his tutor, he surprised his father with
the claim that French history was "the most
fertile, not of course, as to grand historical
subjects, but in those interesting, picturesque
and poetical passages so delightful to meet, such
as Joan of Arc".[12]

Eventually he produced at least twelve designs,
watercolour, comic renderings of favourite English heroes: the Black Prince enters London with
the French king, Queen Elizabeth and the Earl
of Essex "in council" argue violently together.
His figures are recognisable, yet grotesquely
exaggerated and wholly delightful with their
enlarged heads, carefully picked out costume
detail and facial expressions. Here was the
Doyle comic genius which had only flickered
momentarily in select pages of his journal, now
given full expression. Unfortunately, his designs
remained unfinished and the book unpublished
until three years after his death. Perhaps it was
just as well, for the conservative strain in historical illustration at the time marked the fate of

another comic history, Gilbert à Beckett's *Comic
History of England*, 1846. This was attacked
for its shameful liberties with history. "After all,
life has something serious in it. It cannot be all a
Comic History of Humanity," the disgusted
journalist Douglas Jerrold told Charles Dickens.
"Some men would, I believe, write the comic
Sermon on the Mount...surely the world will be
sick of this blasphemy."[13]

Nevertheless poking fun at historical giants
was one of Dick's greatest pleasures, and he
continued to devise clever versions of artistic,
literary, as well as political heroes. These formed
the core of his next published book, *A Grand
Historical Allegorical Classical and Comical
Procession of Remarkable Personages Ancient
Modern and Unknown*, published by McLean
in 1842. Here was a pageant of Dick's boyhood
heroes, headed by an elaborate royal coach and
footmen. The Italians dance and frolic in a
crowd of opera singers; Michelangelo, stern and
broadfaced, is wheeled along hard at work on his
sculpture, saluted by "Brothers of the Art";
Aristotle and Copernicus dance with mythical
politicians and "One of the two gentlemen of
Verona". It was clearly a work more suited to
Dick's comic talents, unfettered by his brother's
historical text. But the project suffered the same
uncertain fate as the Comic History.

The drawings for the procession were done
sporadically from the end of 1840 onward. The
too familiar spectre of failure overshadowed
even his early efforts, for once he had announced

John Smith   Sir Rob.t Harlewood   One of the two gentlemen of Verona   Aristotle   Copernicus.
of Harlewood.

b) John Smith, Sir Robert Harlewood, One *of the two gentlemen of Verona, Aristotle, Copernicus.*

his plan for the book to his father, Dick's greatest fear was to lose his admiration for the idea. "I am in a great state of anxiety to know whether it will be liked (I mean the whole Procession when finished) because without boasting I think I may say I never saw anything like it and that makes the uncertainty so much greater." His original plan for drawings on a long strip of paper to be rolled out "at pleasure", was altered by his father to a book format. Dick was afraid this would not be impressive enough, "for I am tortured with the fear that Papa will think it a little [project] when finished and I know that if I work day and night till Christmas, the volume will still be small". His desire to please his father kept him awake at night, when he was tormented by ideas for the book. He drew the scene in his journal: gnomes and fairies swirling round his bed, a wizard points his wand into the air and fairy-tale characters drop onto the bedclothes, and "crowd into my head every time I think of it. Sometimes after I am in bed at night some idea [comes] to mind more remarkable in point of brilliancy than any preceding it strikes me. I am

Dick Doyle tortured by procession ideas, from Dick Doyle's Journal.

A Book Full of Nonsense:
a) Title-page to one of Doyle's sketchbooks.
Victoria and Albert Museum.

*b) Doyle's nonsense-style monsters, in a letter
to his father, 1843.
Pierpont Morgan Library.*

---

half determined to get up and put it down but
then how am I to get a light, besides dozens of
other ideas equally startling no doubt come
pouring into my head and I begin to seriously
consider, granting that I manufactured a light,
whether I could find time before morning to
place them on paper."

Dick was very aware of his father's expectations and always wished to be taken seriously as
an artist, however comic or whimsical his drawings. His greatest fear for the Procession book
was that John Doyle would dismiss it as "mere
nonsense". The fear hung over many of his quick
sketches and ideas for this and subsequent
books, many of which were first entered in the
sketchbooks he playfully called *Dick Kitcat's
Book of Nonsense* and *More Nonsense*. Among
the pages of intricate, spidery pen doodles were
some remarkably well-composed pages of fairies,
witches, elves and puckish gnomes. There were
also sylph-like dancers of the type familiar to
any opera and ballet enthusiast at the time, or
battle scenes between fairy-tale and historical
heroes. Many pour from openings in the rocks,

Final page from Doyle's Beauty and the Beast,
*c1842.
Pierpont Morgan Library.*

[33]

proceed across the page like a comic frieze of the most grotesque nightmares, the figures or animals grouped for effect, their heads dwarfed by huge hats, or masked with animal faces. The Nonsense books were clearly very important to Dick's development; the sourcebooks of his most fantastic creatures, the place where he considered how clearly he wanted to portray his favourite giants and fairy-tale subjects. Whenever he was at a loss for a subject to draw or paint, he usually turned first to his Nonsense books, "to be going on with".[14]

A favourite fairy-tale was the story of Beauty and the Beast. His sister Adelaide translated a version from the French about this time and Dick agreed to provide the illustrations – the whole project not surprisingly dedicated to their father. It remains one of his most delicate and charming works, despite the fact it was never published in his lifetime. Here the initial letters, gothic tracery and trellise borders were filled with fully developed creatures borrowed from his Nonsense books. Fairies and elves join monkeys, parrots and foxes in climbing over the title-page, while the final page, of the marriage between Beauty and her transformed beast, is a delightful piece of Doyle fantasy. The couple kneel reverently at the castle doorway while a fairy queen waves her magic wand in blessing the marriage to continue "a long time in perfect happiness because it was founded upon virtue".

In complete contrast, Dick worked upon another Nonsense subject, the terrifying giants of Irish, Welsh and Cornish legends which he numbered among his favourite boyhood tales. He was an insatiable collector of such tales, always fascinated by some new piece of folklore or exotic tale told by one of his father's well-travelled friends. On one occasion, a Captain Mayne delighted him with tales of "the natives of South Australia using their feet as much as their hands".[15] He and his brothers spent hours staring at the statues of the most famous giants, Gog and Magog, at the Guildhall, (Dick incorporated them in his Fores envelope design). But the story of *Jack the Giant Killer,* with its chivalric hero, and scenes of brutal mutilation between a series of horrific giants and their unfortunate victims, became the subject of Dick's next book. He delighted in drawing giants with long beards and fierce expressions, two heads and simple-minded grins, while his heroic Jack, in shining armour, set out to capture and torture

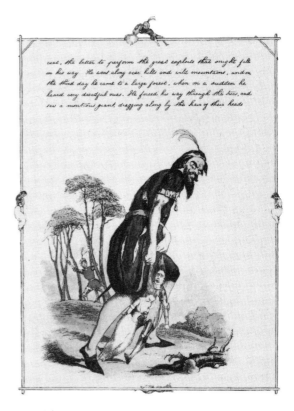

Doyle's boyhood giants, from Jack the Giant Killer, *1842.*

as many of the creatures as he could. He found accounts of the legendary West Country giants, famed for their blood-thirsty habits of eating humans after dragging them to their caves by the hair, or hung to their belts. His Nonsense book contains a sketch of a giant with his victims squirming in a wicker basket slung over his shoulder; others dangle from his belt or hang from the tops of his boots. It was a subject thought too horrific for children and when Dick designed his second giant book, *The Story of Jack and the Giants,* 1850, he changed the victims from humans to cattle, for the drawing of a huge bearded giant stalking the Cornish coast with his club. "It was his custom to come down from the mountains every evening and tie about his waist as many sheep, oxen or pigs, as he could find so that they hung about him like a bundle of candles, and then go back to supper." But even with this alteration the *Athenaeum* critic thought Doyle's story "not the most wholesome food for youth – but Mr Doyle's giants are grand fellows of their class".

Dick's greatest enemy during these early days of book projects was his inability to concentrate upon any one project for too long. He rarely read a book or prepared his lessons for more than an hour without feeling frustrated or leaping up to his drawing table with some new painting idea. In fact these were the most productive years of his entire career. He could jump from plans for a play he called "Don't Care - A Tragedy in 8 Acts", to a juvenile story of "Tommy and the Lion", both childish works with quick ink sketches. Or he'd try more carefully considered watercolour borders and roundels of medieval chivalry to accompany Adelaide's translation of Victor Hugo's "Le Beau Pécopin et la Belle Bauldor," from *Le Rhin*. Here especially, he began to show a talent for meticulous watercolour painting in the densely patterned borders, not unlike illuminated manuscripts, which he chose to fill with ministering angels, devils, dragons, imps, lovers, monks, and knights carousing, dicing or fighting over a beautiful young maiden. These, like his equally elaborate borders to his favourite poem, Byron's "The Corsair", remained unfinished, however, for there always seemed to be some new diversion to prevent their completion. [Colour plate I]

* * * * * * * * * * * *

By the time Dick approached his eighteenth birthday the Doyle family fortunes began to change. His brothers, James, now twenty, Henry, just fourteen, and Charles, now eleven, and Francis, continued to be educated at home, under their father's stern gaze, and on the surface the isolated world of Cambridge Terrace did not seem to change. But then about 1843 Francis ("Frank" his brothers called him) became ill and died, while still in his teens. For one the entire family regarded as the most talented artistically to die so young, his death came as a great blow. Shortly afterwards Adelaide also died, probably of consumption in 1844. Her tragic death brought to an end those book collaborations which Dick had found so inspiring, and like all his family he was shattered by the loss. Moreover, John Doyle began to realise his popularity as an artist was almost over; the genteel pencil of HB now supplanted by the illustrated papers like *Punch*, which featured more spirited cartoonists willing to be controversial.

a) A giant from Dick's Nonsense sketchbook.

b) The tame published version, from The Story of Jack and the Giants, *1850.*

[35]

John Doyle accepted the situation with characteristic stoicism and turned all his attention towards planning for his talented children's futures. Thinking his reputation as HB might help him secure some new employment to help support his family, he wrote a remarkably frank seventeen page letter to the Prime Minister, Robert Peel, appealing for help. He had heard there might be a post open in the public works department of the government, and "without a personal introduction" he wrote to apply, outlining his views on public parks and museums to "establish a just estimate of my character". What made his letter even more remarkable was his decision to confess his identity as HB: "You are the first gentleman connected with public life to whom so such I have ever voluntarily committed my secret," he explained, adding only a "boyhood friend and Liberal peer" shared his secret until now. Although he was aware of recent rumours which linked his name with HB, "still personally, from the seclusion in which I lived, I was unknown".

As HB, John Doyle had often poked mild jabs at Robert Peel, the staunch Tory whose political opinions were so often at variance to his own Whig and even radical views. He first tried to clarify his views, admitted he supported the Whigs and the Reform Bill, although in the end he was "opposed to popular innovation. Throughout however I have preserved my personal independence and it was that I might the better do so, & not from any affectation of secrecy that I maintained to the best of my ability a strict incognito." But he was clearly more concerned to outline his current domestic difficulties than haggle over politics: "I feel now, however, placed in new circumstances and that even this degree of privacy I cannot maintain long. New duties devolve upon me – the duties of a Father to a grown-up daughter and these oblige me to win more with the world than I have done. It would now be very irksome to me to be identified in society with these sketches, but as a thing passed...I may occasionally throw a tiny shot [but] I feel that virtually 'HB's' occupation's gone." He was only pleased that by keeping his identity secret he had not made any enemies. Since "public opinion on the whole has been very kind to me", he considered himself fortunate: "with the pecuniary result – although I might perhaps have occupied some of the best years of my life more profitably and though my publisher

has been much the larger gainer, I am not dissatisfied. They have enabled me to bring up so far respectably – a pretty large family, but no more."

At this point he explained how his family showed great promise, his sons "all showing taste for the arts, and the three eldest evincing the most unequivocal promise, I have reason to look forward with more confidence than fear to the future". He explained how Dick's two recently published books had been highly praised and were signs of a budding artist of great promise. "To foster and direct this native talent will occupy much of my future attention, but being in my 43d year, I still feel young enough to raise up an honourable reputation upon some new foundation." He had hoped to return to oil painting portraits, "which would have suited my taste and my capacity", but was prevented by "an unfortunate defect in my health which incapacitates me from painting much in oil". This led to his application for the government post. To strengthen his case, he briefly outlined plans for the new Nelson Testimonial Column competition, preferring an obelisk shape if a column was chosen, while the best design should be for a colossal bronze group fountain, "with water as an accessory". After discussing Barry's designs for the new National Gallery building, he concluded in a fatherly tone: "It has been my anxious endeavour to impress upon my sons a lesson which I have learnt myself – that it is not to individual patronage but to their own well-directed talents, and the community, that they must look for any solid and permanent prosperity. I ask no favour but such as can be considered to me on public grounds."

Some interest was shown by Robert Peel and by the end of January 1843 John Doyle sent a second, shorter letter, signed "HB". Here he outlined his views on the National Gallery, the decoration of the north Thames embankment, criticized the plantings in Kensington Gardens and proposed a new fountain in Hyde Park, "that species of embellishment in which our metropolis is so singularly destitute". But in the end, John Doyle was passed over for the government post, and Peel was toppled from power four years later. Then, undeterred, John tried yet again, all the while having worked privately among his politician friends to build up his reputation as a critic of the country's parks and public events in the capital.[16]

Doyle border design in a letter to his father,
27 September 1842.
Pierpont Morgan Library.

Nevertheless, there is no evidence of their father's domestic worries in the illustrated letters his sons continued to send him each week. Even plump little Charles was taught to express himself at an early age, once describing the glorious sunrise through the trees in Hyde Park, "speckled with little black devils and on further examination I discovered they were genuine magpies apparently sketching from nature". Charles was the neglected if slightly shunned youngest member of the family, who signed one letter to his father with a round-faced self-portrait and "Your diminutive son Charles, who watcheth". He was not spared the ritual of gallery visits or the drawings from memory. After a trying visit to the Royal Academy, he struggled to remember his favourite picture well enough to draw it in his letter, but "I could remember apparently nothing", he confessed, promising to return as soon as possible for a second look.[17] Charles found in his brother Dick a kindred spirit, even at a young age, and the two were often seen together, Dick dutifully watching over his chubby brother. In later years they shared a talent for drawing from their vivid imaginations to become the most inventive artists of the family.

On the other hand, Henry shared some of his brother James's meticulous, methodical habits. Although a competent draughtsman of crowd scenes, especially when horses were involved, he soon became torn between the sensibilities of the analyst and the artist. His letters are filled with carefully considered observations on favourite paintings or prints; why he liked a Rubens, Raphael, or Leonardo as well as a Landseer or Leslie. He condemned popular prints like Leslie's famous coronation painting of the Queen, because it failed for "want of fervour"; he called the Cousins engraving "a wretched failure". There were hints of his outspoken Uncle Conan's influence in free use of words, like "disgraceful" or "wretched" when paintings failed to meet his rigid standards. But those prints he liked were carefully copied as ink sketches in his letters to his father.[18]

Dick Doyle's critical faculties were also sharpened by his recent experiences in the galleries, concert halls and streets of London, generally with his Uncle as guide. He now listened more attentively at the opera, or found a ballet woefully disappointing, "one step from the sublime to the other thing". But, unlike Henry, Dick's opinions were often too earnest, or when he felt himself becoming too serious, he ridiculed his judgement with a pun or an absurd joke. He was aware of his privileged middle-class upbringing, and while he generally preferred the street urchins and Dickensian faces in the crowds, his class prejudices occasionally crept in with phrases like "so suspiciously Cockneyish", or "human beings of different degrees of respectability" – a favourite phrase. Above all, he was determined to train his eye for a career as an artist, and was constantly building up his knowledge of favourite painters, prints and suitable subjects for his own drawings.

The subjects which attracted him most were the medieval and historical, especially when some bizarre legend might be discovered among them. He was especially taken by an engraving by Horace Vernet which illustrated a strange ghostly ballad by Bürger. He studied Vernet's atmospheric picture, in which the gloomy atmosphere perfectly matched the subject – the arrival of the spirit of a beautiful maiden's dead lover. The spectral knight's face especially haunted Dick, who described it to his father as "One mass of fire, through which you can faintly discern the form of a death head, the eye holes being the brightest part, give it the appearance of the interior of the scull (sic) being in flames". His judgement of painters was often influenced by his growing chauvinism as he, and for that matter the art world as a whole, now searched for distinctly national painters to compete with their continental rivals. The Vernet print, however, had no competition. "Somehow when an English artist attempts a subject of this kind there is almost always something laughable about it," Dick told his father. "What astonishes me most is the immense number of very good artists in France who bring out small lithographs of domestic scenes & c. and whose knowledge of drawing and truth of expression is quite marvellous."[19]

This fervent nationalism in the arts reached its peak with the Westminster Hall cartoon competition, 1843-44. Dick followed every step in the government's plan to decorate the Houses of Parliament with grand, historical frescoes, and read the weighty prospectus for exhibitors before actually visiting the competition several times. The scheme had been originally launched by the Royal Fine Arts Commission, with Prince Albert as chairman, to ostensibly decide upon decorations for Parliament, but the government clearly hoped the plan would help promote public patronage in the arts and go some way towards establishing a new school of "High Art" in England, to rival its foreign (especially German) competition. Dick was among the first to view the entries, and was thrilled by the vast cartoons of heroic medieval figures, like Maclise's "Spirit of Chivalry" which was chosen to decorate the House of Lords. He returned home inspired, as he told his father in a letter filled with sketches of his favourite cartoons: "The cartoons which have called forth a talent in English artists previously unknown to exist, which silenced the scoffers at British art, for a time at least, in the works of Cope, Armitage and Watts – which have attracted and interested the public to an extent quite unparalleled, which have proved that the artists of the country may take their stand beside the best foreign schools, in historical art, and that when a competition is open to all – there may be fine things produced."[20]

He returned twice within one week to study the subjects as well as the style of the drawings. "England will not be beaten in Art no more than she will in Arms."[21] Many cartoons imitated the popular Nazarene style of even firm outlined figures not unlike drawings for ecclesiastical sculpture, and Dick tried his own hand at drawing figures in what one critic later would call his "fresco style". He also studied the crowds, noting on visits during the last days when the public was admitted without charge, "I was very much edified by the attention and good behaviour of the multitude although at least two thirds of it were what would be called 'low' yet for orderly conduct they might set an example to the pit of Her Majesty's Theatre. There were soldiers, sailors, watermelon hawkers, cabmen, orange women, servants and labourers ec. ec. ec. and all – almost all, down to the poorest workman had a catalogue and were reading the name and description of each cartoon, carefully and with the greatest interest as they went on. It made me feel comfortable at the time when I thought the wide difference between a poor man who after [a] day's labour takes a pleasure in looking at such works and goes home in the evening and relates to his family what he has seen and he who spends his earnings in the ale house and returns home late at night intoxicated."[22]

The competition also made him wonder about those capable artists who had been rejected by the judges. It was a typical Doyle response, to take an oblique view of even the most serious subjects. In this instance he planned a new book around the theme of rejected cartoons, and completed some twenty-three drawings parodying the successful winners' styles of Maclise and Pugin. Fifteen of these were eventually published in a large and impressive volume he called *Selections from the Rejected Cartoons*, in 1848, with his own text written in the manner of a disgruntled and rejected artist. Many of his drawings echo his Comic History subjects, with King Alfred caught "sending the Danes into a profound slumber with the sleeping notes of his harp", or a comic King John and his barons signing the Magna Carta. Others, like "The first Knight" in the style of Maclise, parodied the winning chivalric themes, drawn in Doyle's new fresco style of flat, even outlined figures. These led one critic to stare in amazement at the book; "few people with whom the touch of Richard Doyle is perfectly familiar would recognize his hand in these amazing and amusing cartoons".[23]

The cartoons also stirred Dick's ambition to become a successful history painter. This remained his greatest ambition throughout his

"The First Knight", in the style of Maclise, from Selections from the Rejected Cartoons, *1848.*

early manhood, and the source of much despair and embarassment to himself and his family. His long-awaited plan for a large painting from Quentin Durward, on paper stretched over canvas 4′ x 2′, ended in disaster, when, on the appointed day for unveiling it, he unrolled a blank piece of canvas. Moreover, he felt threatened by his equally talented brothers. James was now working on oil paintings, the supreme test of any artist with serious intentions; Frank, when he was alive, had taunted him with superior skills, his History of Scotland drawings Dick found "quite startling" because they were "boldly conceived, beautifully treated and wonderfully executed [it] is truly refreshing to behold – such bursts of true genius are seldom met with". He suffered bouts of debilitating depression at his own inadequacies as a result, especially during that critical end of year rush to finish drawings for his father. "I sometimes get into such a wretched state of hating everything I do, that I feel as if I could not go on with any of them. The only thing to do in such cases is just to wait quietly until I get into a more favourable condition, to go on. Either is better than committing violence on my person or going into solitary situations like 'the cur wot shunned society!' "[24] In the end, he developed what he called his highly developed philosophy of failure, remnants of which plagued him for the remainder of his life. "For my part I think there is as much enjoyment in failing in an object as in accomplishing it, perhaps more, because you expect to succeed and therefore when you don't you get an unexpected pleasure – a surprise, which is always a pleasant thing," he confessed in a letter to his father; although on the next line adding "rather too strong" before he sent the letter.[25]

His depressions usually disappeared after visits to the Royal Academy, "that never ending subject" of which he filled his letters afterwards. On the whole, he preferred the more sedate historical and sylvan landscape subjects of popular painters like Lee, Creswick, Etty and Herbert ("that most German of English artists"). Their genteel canvasses of carefully painted detail came nearest to his own "gentlemanly ideal" for a painter; once he noted with delight Frank Grant's election to ARA status because Grant's paintings "make one fancy that the artist is a thorough gentleman". This was in strict contrast to his uncharacteristic hatred of one particular exhibitor, Joseph Mallord Turner. This rebellious renegade from good taste in art, despite recent claims for his genius by Ruskin, brought out the worst in Doyle: "They say that we must learn to admire it and that it is because Turner is so infinitely above all other painters we cannot comprehend him. Give me an artist who can be understood by the multitude, as Nature is. We have not to learn to admire her." Even John Ruskin's "rather extreme ideas with regards to the artist's merits" failed to win Dick over; they could not "convince me that there is anything fine in it. What a pity it is that a man of his powers should go on year after year painting such ridiculous things," Dick told his father.[26]

Not surprisingly, among those painters Dick admired were the fantasy artists. The most obvious was Richard Dadd, whose fairy visions appeared at the Royal Academy as well as British Institute throughout the 1840s. His famous "Titania Sleeping" 1841, and "Come unto these Yellow Sands" (from *The Tempest*) 1842, with its dance of nude fairies upon a rocky shore, had proved "one of the attractions of the exhibition at the Royal Academy, notwithstanding that it was placed where the mere crowd of gazers would pass it by unnoticed". Dick saw it there, and followed the tragic career of the artist who, the following year, had brutally murdered his father in a fit of insanity and spent the remained unshakable. When he was forbidden Such a terrible crime had special meaning to one so devoted to his father as Dick. So when he wrote to describe the 1843 Academy exhibition to him, he noted (writing the day the Dadd murder was announced), "If however the present year has been so prolific in some respects, its gloomy side is rendered darker by the contrast. Alas! poor Dadd."[27]

John Doyle's influence over his son's progress remained unshakable. When he was forbidden oil paints, Dick surreptitiously borrowed James's colours; afterwards he confessed his guilt, admitting that his father had been right. "I know that it is more difficult to paint in oil colours than in water because you have often said so; but still I feel a terrible inclination to try them – and on something very large. Watercolours are very

TURNER PAINTING ONE OF HIS PICTURES.

Two influences upon Doyle's painting:
a) Turner, a negative influence, drawn by Doyle
for An Almanack of the Month, *1846.*

well adopted for small drawings, and when nicely worked with, produce a clearness, brilliancy and freshness of effect, more pleasing to me than any other kind of painting, but in the absence of that freshness and artistic way of putting on the colours, which I find so difficult to

b) Richard Dadd's "Puck",
exhibited at
Suffolk Street 1841.

get, and which I fancy is only to be acquired by great experience, I prefer the oil colour infinitely, far independently of the much greater richness and depth of tone to be got thereby; there is something so much more substantial in it, less likely to be injured, more likely at least, and in fact better calculated for 'great' works."[28] And in the end, Dick remained a watercolour artist all his life, never attempting to oil paint for the galleries like his brothers James and Henry, who achieved such gratifying successes for their oils there.

Indecision plagued his ambitions to develop as a serious painter. Dick would always prefer a studio full of half-finished work to the limitations of one carefully completed project. So it was by September 1843, while working on the Rejected Cartoons, he flitted from subject to subject, drawing fantasy ink sketches in "that style which cannot be described and is called 'Nonsense' ", while "I would prefer doing something serious next, but whether it be an illustration of the History of England, of France, of the Low Countries, of Lord Byron's Corsair, of any of Sir Walter Scott's novels, of Victor Hugo's Legend of the Rhine, of the Midsummer Night's Dream, The Tempest, the Fairie Queen, or anything else that is interesting, it is all the same to me".[29] Such indecision was only broken by his father, especially when he offered to pay for printing a finished series of drawings. As Dick hinted, following his latest bout of lethargy, "if circumstances will permit of my beginning the 'cartoons' on [lithographic] stone directly, of course I will willingly give up everything else".[30] It is not surprising John Doyle grew worried about his financial state, if he had to entice his son with expensive printing projects before he would settle and complete a work.

There were two sides to Dick's development at this time. He used his whimsical Nonsense books for the fairy fantasies which he developed into a few striking watercolours of sylvan scenes, fairies and elves dancing in the moonlight; others were inspired by Shakespeare's *The Tempest*, set on an exotic island covered in palm trees and strange animals. The second side to his work was when he turned to his reading and memories of street crowds to attempt more realistic subjects.

Fantasy and supernatural elements, which had preoccupied his boyhood, were easily found in Walter Scott's stories. But Dick read for subjects of universal importance. Apart from

"A Daydream", from Doyle's letter to his father, 16 April 1843.
Pierpont Morgan Library.

Byron's poem "The Corsair" ("the most intensely beautiful I ever read of any poet"), he regarded Scott's stories as the most universally appealing of all writers. Scott had "succeeded in every style 'from grave to gay' ", he told his father. His hero's interest in the supernatural only strengthened his own belief in ghosts, legends and superstitions. Scott was "the great wizard of the North", the author of *Demonology and Witchcraft* as well as a favourite tale, *The Monastery*, full of knightly chivalry, a Catholic knight exiled by his religion, and a fairy who revives him following a fatal duel. Here Scott admitted using "the beautiful, though almost forgotten, theory of astral spirits, or creatures of the elements", and Dick was fascinated. "I cannot help thinking that the great wizard of the North, in the days of his youth at least, was a believer in supernatural apparitions. This might have arisen from his great love of ancient tales, ballads and traditions, which (no people more superstitious than the Scotch) must be full of such horrors. He must

[41]

have had a great taste for ghosts and suchlike." To prove his point to his father, Dick chose a Scott tale of a young man plagued by a fleet of green goblins to draw for his father; "the green figurantes whom the patient's depraved imagination has so long associated with these moveables came capering and frisking to accompany them exclaiming with great glee, as if the sufferer should have been rejected to see them. 'Here we are – here we all are!'"[30] Such scenes often filled the margins of Dick's letters, like the startling monster with mouth stretched open to suck in the creatures of his imagination, which was inspired by a new book, *Day Dreams* he had discovered ("I did not read it, it was poetry"). "As I never can recollect my night dreams well enough to illustrate, and as I don't see why I should not have 'day dreams' as well as any one else, let me present you with one."[31]

Fantasy drawings were tempered with study from nature, on walks through London's streets, or by staring at the crowds in its shops. After one particularly successful day collecting impressions of the people in Oxford Street, Dick filled a letter with sketches of himself with two "Society lions" on each arm, and tiny comic profiles of the faces seen there. "Can it be possible that such a thing exists as an artist who is at a loss for a character to draw," he asks his father. "If there does exist a begging (sic) so degenerate only let him just put on his hat and walk out into this lively thoroughfare and watch the figures as they pass and I will undertake to say that in the course of an hour he see's more comical specimens of human nature than he can put down in a year." He loved "the contrast between every face and the one that went before it, no two bearing the least resemblance to each other. What would I give to be able to sketch (as they passed me) one eighth of the intensely comical countenances that passed me bye on that day. What would not I give to be able to recollect even the half of that. Verily I do believe to judge from what I saw that day that nine tenths of the population of London are in essence of fun, and such practical jokers that they dress and make remarkable faces expressly for the amusement and gratification of such wretches as one." Although he admired Cruikshank's comic genius, and would later become his trusted and delightful friend, on this occasion Dick doubted the artist's abilities to capture true comedy. "Cruikshank and other artists in his way, are considered very wonderful

Dick Doyle as a swell walking in Oxford Street, from an illustrated letter to his father, 7 January 1843.
Pierpont Morgan Library.

for inventing comic figures and phays (sic), and yet there are many persons who admiring them, would not feel any amusement in contemplating the 'real originals' in nature, which are a hundred times more racy and delightful than anything Cruikshank and Grandville could do. It is all mighty fine for one to go saying that nature is better than art, just as if it is not known all over the world, but let my excuse be that, I really do imagine that some men are enthusiastic enough to think that they improve a little upon her at times."[32]

Dick's love of animals inevitably led him to study illustrations of that French comic satirist Jean-Ignace-Isidore Grandville, whose anthropomorphized drawings of animals had recently appeared and stirred English audiences. Indeed many of Dick's comic fantasies suggest a clear knowledge of Grandville's work, first borrowed from his devilish attacks on French society in the form of neoclassical line drawings in *Un Autre Monde*, 1844, to the monkeys, dogs and birds dressed as fashionable figures in *Scènes de la vie privée*, 1842. Here curiously on the title-page appeared a composition so similar to Dick's journal title-page of two years earlier, that one wonders who was influencing whom. Grandville must also have been in the back of Dick's mind when he paid his periodic visits to the London

b) Unpublished elephant man sketch by Doyle.

Grandville's influence:
a) Grandville's title-page to Scenes de la vie
privée, *1842.*

zoo. There he compared the animals with a new illustrated *Animated Nature*, while Henry studied the lions for his famous painting of Telemachus, which was later much admired by Prince Albert. Afterwards, Dick recorded how they "actually laughed till we were weak" at Jenny, the orang-utan, "about the most comical creature I ever winked at". She had been trained to drink tea in her cage in an elaborate ritual which began with a lace cap on her head and ended with a look of mild disdain at the grinning spectators as she sipped her tea from a cup and saucer, seated at her tea table stirring the tea with a spoon. Dick drew Jenny for his father, and signed his letter "Dick who is fond of savage animals".[33]

Finally, the family religion offered opportunities for drawings, although suprisingly few religious pictures survive by Doyle. He was more interested, it seems, in the current vogue for temperance meetings, and eagerly accompanied

his uncle to help report these stirring and often massive demonstrations. Dick's last letters to his father in 1843 are full of the descriptions of Father Mathew, "the Apostle of Temperance", who claimed to have converted sixty-eight thousand people in London alone. His meetings were momentous occasions, when crowds rushed the platform to get a closer look at their idol; as Dick recalled, like "a torrent of human beings who pressed wildly on, but it was to no avail, hundreds were pressing from behind, there was one fruitless attempt at order, a brief, terrible struggle, a rush like a waterfall – they are all mixed up in one dense mass". He drew the crush in a remarkably clear crowd scene stretched across two pages of description. He concluded Father Mathew was certainly a living saint; "That he prosper to the end of his days is the earnest wish of your affectionate Dick".[34] He was especially taken by the pathetic scene of a poor Irishman nagged into taking "the pledge" by his wife. "It was a sight worth seeing to watch the countenance of Pat and see what a struggle was going on within him, he wished to do what was right, he knew it would be for his own good, and yet how shocking it was,the idea of never 'drinking another d'hrop o' spirits again' ". Here was a character after Dick's own heart; his description as clear as if he had drawn the unfortunate man "with his tattered remains of a blue coat and brass buttons, his breeches tied at the knee with strings, dark grey stockings, such large shirt collars, such a hairy neck, such a high hat, and such a little brim to it". Eventually to Pat's relief (and Dick's) he "took the pledge".[35]

*Medieval archery, an early unpublished
watercolour by Doyle.*

II

That Demon Mr Punch

1843 - 1850

is ambitions grew when Dick began to think seriously about a career as an artist, by the time he reached his eighteenth birthday. Like his father he believed his work should be signed with an easily recognizable name, and he chose 'Dick Kitcat' – presumeably adopting the term for portraits of smaller than half size – for his surname. For the next few years he produced drawings and etched illustrations for publication as Dick Kitcat, and achieved small but encouraging success.

The first published work by Dick Kitcat was the series of five atmospheric etchings he produced with John Leech from 1842. Leech was highly suitable as Dick's first instructor outside the family home, for although still struggling himself as an illustrator, he had achieved some success with drawings to a *Comic English Grammar* in 1840, and *Jack the Giant Killer* in 1843. He was adept at comic etchings, specializing in the London characters he loved to study on the streets. He had thrown up his medical studies to pursue a self-taught career as an illustrator, encouraged by Flaxman's prediction, "let his genius follow its own bent and he will astonish the world". Most recently he had established himself on the staff of *Bentley's Miscellany* where he contributed over one hundred and forty etchings. When Bentley proposed Leech illustrations to the comic novel, *The Fortunes of Hector O'Halloran and his man Mark Anthony O'Toole*, sometime late in 1842, Leech produced twenty-seven comic etchings in a loose yet subtle style, and agreed to train young Dick Kitcat for the remaining five. It was probably the first time Dick had drawn with the fine etching needle on copper plates, but his own intricate pen work style was easily transformed to the new medium. His most effective plate was a moonlight scene, "Night Attack upon Castle Knocklofty". It remains one of his finest atmospheric drawings: the helmeted attackers are bathed in moonlight, yet the entire scene is filled with deep shadows; the glistening moon on the water a carefully considered contrast to the billowing smoke and flickering torchlight.

Dick's uncle Michael Conan took a careful look at his nephew's comic drawings and saw their comic potential. His friend Mark Lemon had recently established a new comic weekly called *Punch,* which from its start in 1841 promised to be filled with "wit and whim, cuts and caricature", and Michael Conan suggested Dick might draw for the paper. When Dick showed his intricate, whimsical pen drawings to Lemon, the *Punch* editor saw their unique possibilities for his paper (which at that time was dominated by the rather grey wood engravings of John Gilbert, William Harvey and Kenny Meadows). But since Dick had never drawn on wood blocks for the engraver, Mark Lemon suggested the *Punch* engraver Joseph Swain might give him lessons. Dick agreed, little knowing the experience was the beginning of seven exhausting and exhilerating years, working for "the demon Mr Punch".

The engraver Joseph Swain was a rough character whose sharp, critical manner upset Dick from the start. He shuddered at Swain's "somewhat unclassical speech", and grew more nervous with his master's brusque remarks and alarming habit of throwing Dick's drawings about the table, as if they were of little use or promise. On the other hand, Swain later recalled

"Night Attack upon Castle Knocklofty", etched plate by Dick Kitcat for The Fortunes of Hector O'Halloran, *1842-43.*

their strained meetings, how his pupil was so "small and thin in person, greatly agitated in mind and manner, that he persisted in keeping his distance out of simple shyness, and literally dodged around the dining-room table, altogether too excited to lend the slightest attention to the work".[1] Indeed, the task of drawing in fine pencil lines upon hard boxwood blocks was alien to his boyhood experiences – drawing freely on paper whatever emerged from his vivid imagination. He knew nothing about suggestive shading, or firm, even outline which the engraver might follow to cut away the wood around his pencil lines. His first attempt on wood was "a bad, smudgy thing" which Swain immediately rejected. After repeated attempts he succeeded well enough for the engraver, but he felt it necessary to write to the *Punch* publisher, promising his "future drawings would be much smaller to

prevent timewasting by the engraver".[2]

Dick Doyle's first drawings in *Punch* were in fact given prominent treatment by Mark Lemon. They were a series of five full page border designs, in Dick's familiar "Nonsense" style, which he called "Punch's Triumphal Procession". He drew gnomes and sprites throwing flowers or scampering down ladders all around the page; another border framed Thomas Hood's poem, "Song of the Shirt". Then followed tiny drawings for initial letters, composed of Doyle's favourite comic faces or clever reworkings from the articles they introduced. Inevitably, the pressure of producing a large number of drawings and working to a weekly deadline began to take its toll. No longer could Dick start a drawing and leave it unfinished; he was expected to produce work to order. To his delight, he found the challenge stimulating at first, and only when that dreaded pre-Christmas period arrived during his first year on *Punch,* did he begin to have second thoughts. His *Punch* work had left him little time for his father's annual drawing, and he was clearly upset when he wrote, "Whatever will I do?" to his father – his letter headed by a comic sketch of Mr Punch as a juggler, throwing unfinished wood blocks into the air: "Between the [Rejected] Cartoons and Punch and Christmas and goodness knows what else besides, together with the large drawing, I expect that soon I won't have time to eat my dinner or perhaps to go to bed. Don't think, if you please, that I am at all sorry; on the contrary I am very glad, and if I had twice as much more I would not complain but would look upon it as an increase of the joke." Pressures took various forms in his frenzied schedule: "I will seize up a lead pencil, dodge round the easel, arrive at the other side of

---

The trials of working for Mr Punch, from Dick Doyle's letter to his father, 17 December 1843. Pierpont Morgan Library.

the table, and 'fire away' on the blocks of wood for Punch, in the midst of which delightful occupation, my countenance will suddenly express a recollection that no time is to be lost." He then raced to dress for the theatre where he made mental notes of the performance for new *Punch* drawings.[3]

By mid December it became clear his *Punch* work would leave no time to complete his father's Christmas drawing. He sketched an elaborate apology, a self-portrait seated at the easel, "precisely as he appeared at the moment when he gave up all hope on Monday last". Across two pages of description he sketched the creatures of his *Punch* borders who had prevented him from pleasing his father, namely the mischievous gnomes and sprites which spill from his paper cupboard, sliding down a virgin piece of paper intended for his father's drawing. "The

demon Punch perched upon the table, in calculation, points to the 'Procession' *his* 'Christmas Piece'. Harlequin & c., as indicative of Christmas weep over the little quantity of *yours*, a crowd of little urchins, in the foreground by referring to the production of former years, prove what *can* be done, and others in the background are plainly showing that it was not for want of paper." He concluded by anticipating his father's familiar objection – that his time might have been more carefully managed, since "it does not appear that the Punchification has been sufficiently plentiful, of itself, to cause it. Very true!"[4]

The Doyle *Punch* style evolved from early spidery-line fantasies, which usually blurred when engraved, to more confident heavy outlined cartoons and initial letters; also the comic historical figures with exaggerated heads, as well as cut-out "fresco style" cartoons which became his peculiar trademark. The staff quickly warmed to his comic inventions, drawn with the intricate care of one they soon called "Professor of Medieval Design". His whimsical inventions lightened a paper which, throughout the 1840s, grew heavier with articles and political cartoons echoing the impending social evils of the age. He sketched monsters, especially dragons, gargoyles and gnomes, which he suspended from gothic archways or trellis-work over which floated sylph-like fairies, drawn as nudes while others wore diaphanous drapery. He explored more exotic themes like turbaned pashas and belly-dancers, or borrowed arcadian landscapes with eighteenth century shepherdesses. Other times, he became preoccupied with knights on horseback, in pursuit of a dragon or about to save a fair damsel in some distress.

His first substantial drawing accompanied a rhymed version of *Don Pasquale*. This was followed by his first full-page political cartoon (16 March 1844), "The Modern Sisyphus", which depicted Sir Robert Peel as Sisyphus doomed to push the boulder of "Ireland" uphill, while political furies and the Queen watch from the safety of a cloudy sky. The portraits were uncertain, but as Dick's critics pointed out they were drawn very much as the famous HB would have done. His smaller, more inventive initial letters and comic fillers were evidence of the Doyle versatility and fertile imagination. He drew initial letters to accompany such articles as "Mesmerism: its Dangers and Curiosities" (2 March 1844); "A Dream" (9 March 1844),

where a comic long-nosed man endures a battle scene staged on his nose; as well as the Grandville-like songbirds as Italian opera singers in "Migration of the Italian Singing Birds" (24 August 1844); and a goblin chase from Burns's Tam o'Shanter for "The Burns Festival – Repentent Scotland" – which became a favourite subject of his later paintings. But his sprites and gnome borders were most freely used, spread across a double page for "Lord Mayor's Day" (16 November 1844); and sprinkled over the background of his most prestigious and influential design for the *Punch* cover.

Indeed, Dick Doyle was asked by Mark Lemon to re-design the paper's cover within months of his joining the staff. Lemon was dissatisfied with the five previous attempts at cover designs. The most recent by Kenny Meadows showed a rather grey, dark-faced and evil looking Mr Punch astride a trumpeter, surrounded by indistinct frolicking figures in a haze of parallel lines. Dick's first version appeared in January 1844, with a benign Mr Punch at his desk, pen in hand, Toby, his dog perched on volumes of *Punch,* while an unmistakeable Doyle cloud of fairies, goblins, monsters, knights and maidens in distress pour from cornucopias on either side of the page. Much clearer and inventive than previous designs, it was retained for five years, then supplanted in 1849 by a slightly more intricate version of fairy figures, cut into a long classical frieze at the bottom. Here Mr Punch revels with dancing maidens and satyrs in a more acceptable, less ambiguous manner. Indeed some had been outraged by Mr Punch lying back on his mule in the first design: his demonic grin and suggestive pose hinted at Mr Punch in the act of self-abusement. It was as the *Punch* historian M.H.Spielmann tactfully described "more sportive and rollicking, and with less attempt at grace". And when Dick agreed to clarify the pose in his second design, it was retained by the paper for over a hundred years.[5]

The confidence which began to appear in Dick's *Punch* work – the fine lines more sharply drawn, the figures in even, sure outline – was very much the result of his friendship with the *Punch* staff. Under the leadership of Mark Lemon, the writers Tom Taylor, Douglas Jerrold, Percival Leigh, Thackeray, Gilbert à Beckett, and Horace (Pony) Mayhew joined with Dick and Leech each Wednesday evening for the famous *Punch* editorial dinners. These were far from calm editorial meetings, however; each one was prefaced by a large dinner with plenty of wine, port and cigars even before the business of deciding the forthcoming articles and cartoon was discussed. The dinners were held at the *Punch* offices in Fleet Street, while in summer they were transferred to favourite restaurants or hotels at Greenwich, Richmond, Maidenhead, Hampton Court or Dulwich. Here crowds often gathered on the pavement, to catch a glimpse of their comic favourites or to listen "to the voices of the wits within and wait to gape at them as they passed in and out". The staff was easily divided into two categories: the outspoken jokesters like the fiery-tongued Douglas Jerrold, Pony Mayhew, and the witty and warm-hearted Mark Lemon; or "the listeners", like John Leech, Charles Keene and Dick Doyle. Their quiet restraint was in complete contrast to the rollicking jokes and outrageous behaviour of the jokesters; their "silence, however, masked subtle minds that were teeming with droll ideas, and as appreciative of humour as the sprightliest", according to one critic. Here Dick took his place next to Leech, whom he watched at first for signs of the melancholia and occasional stubborn

outbursts which characterized his friend. Although just nineteen when he joined these important meetings, Dick quickly learned to love the unexpected, unabashed performances of his elders, while his father dismissed them as "savage orgies". Indeed, John Doyle first wrote that since his son's health was "not robust" he hoped the *Punch* staff would excuse his son from attending. But this did not last long, and Dick was soon a welcomed and essential member of the dinners. Once he delighted his fellow diners with a dozen mandarin oranges ("to swell the dessert") which a well-travelled family friend had sent from the south Pacific. They were given a place of honour, eclipsing "the magnificent pine-apple, and some grapes of very fine quality" presented by Joseph Paxton, (gardener to the Duke of Devonshire) from plants in his famous glasshouses. "The oranges however snuffed out the pine [apple] altogether, and were admired by everyone and eaten up in an instant," Dick explained with obvious delight.[6]

The discussions during these editorial dinners often became heated over political issues, for these were the "Hungry Forties", and many of

Doyle's first censored Punch *wrapper design, January 1844.*

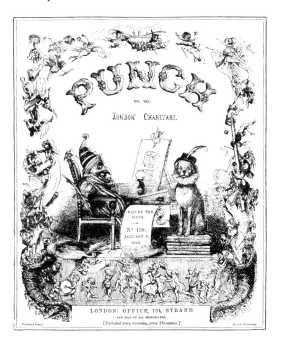

The revised wrapper design, January 1849.

Doyle's famous Great Sea Serpent was re-used in Punch Almanack *for 1849.*

Punch's cartoons and articles echoed the social upheavals and misery. It was a time when seven in a hundred men were registered paupers living under the miserable Poor Law; when cholera, scarlet fever, diptheria and tuberculosis epidemics were common in cities, and the dreaded Corn Laws transformed the countryside into a wasteland of burnt hayricks and wandering labourers. "The distress of the people of Britain this winter I believe excels all that they have ever known before," Thomas Carlyle wrote to his brother in February 1842, from his Chelsea home where even the garden railings had been torn up and stolen for fuel.[7] It was also an age of radical reformers from Chartists to opponents of the Reform Bill, from temperance speakers to religious revivalists. The Irish problem, once a grave problem for Dick's father, now took over as a primary preoccupation of his son. He produced several inspired drawings of Irish fantasies, from a peaceful, idyllic country to the horrors of poverty brought about by the Potato Famine. He also drew portraits of the Catholic Nationalist Daniel O'Connell and the Prime Minister Robert Peel.

Although Dick Doyle was a staunch royalist, who believed in the power of the monarchy, his best known political cartoon was "The Great Sea Serpent of the 1848 Revolution". Here the sea monster "Liberty" rescues the shipwrecked sailors of Europe, while attacking the vessel of the French monarchy surrounded by the misguided and doomed cockleshell boats of the other European monarchs. The drawing proved so effective and popular that it was reproduced as a lantern slide and inevitably appeared as the finale to many chapel reform meetings throughout his lifetime. On the other hand, Punch's readership was primarily the aspiring middle

PUNCH'S DREAM OF PEACE.

Doyle's political cartoon "Punch's Dream of Peace", Punch, *16 June 1849.*

classes, who prided themselves on tasteful yet well presented humour without the cant or forced outrage of the more radical papers. But there were lapses in this cosy, comfortable style of humour, especially when the forceful Douglas Jerrold was given free reign. Jerrold's recent jabs at the monarchy, for example, proved most upsetting to Dick, at a time when the Queen and her new husband were openly adopted as natio-nal symbols of domesticity and the virtues of family life. Indeed, when Jerrold's articles ap-peared, Dick took the uncharacteristic move of threatening to resign from *Punch*. He did not want to be associated with such distasteful attacks, as a later critic explained: "Doyle's influence was always used to prevent any sort of disrespect to the Queen, and in his eyes the shadow of the reverance due to her fell to some

extent over the Prince Consort. He was sadly offended at one or two of the pictures which threw ridicule on the Prince's doings, and protested more than once." There was the unfortunate incident when *Punch* printed an attack on Albert's supposed philistine taste in the arts after he had removed a cartoon by a famous figure painter from Buckingham Palace. Dick was offended and persuaded his friend and fellow *Punch* staff member Thackeray to inspect the picture. Thackeray agreed with the Prince's objections and thereby added credence to Dick's own position.[8]

Such uncharacteristic attacks of pique and anger while working on *Punch* increased with Dick's reputation. Like his father, he firmly believed in preserving his anonymous pseudo-nymn, Dick Kitcat, and when Mark Lemon published his first cover design "by Richard Doyle", he "wrote stiffly to protest". The drawing and all his subsequent *Punch* and later book illustrations were then signed with the familiar "RD" or "dicky-bird" perched over the initials – never as "Richard Doyle".

As early as 1844, Dick was thought competent enough to share the weekly political cartoon with John Leech. Eventually he completed about a third of those published during his seven years on *Punch,* to make over a thousand *Punch* drawings, including small comic initials and insert drawings, for which he was paid a substantial salary (one source gives £800 a year, but it was probably more like £200). His political cartoons were drawn from subjects first chosen by all the staff at the *Punch* dinners, but there was still an opportunity to interpret the chosen theme in his own way. Dick's father had taught him above all else to honour his principles, to be careful and accurate when drawing prominent political figures, and to take the most care when drawing the royal family. But this often proved difficult, when he was pushed by the pressures of a weekly deadline. This meant the idea for the cartoon was presented to him on Wednesday evening to be in the engraver's hands two days later. He also borrowed his father's habit of basing his cartoons upon mythological or theatrical stories familiar to the Doyle household. He drew "Punch as Orpheus" surrounded by animals entranced by his music, the animals symbolic of various European countries, their expressions suited to national stereotypes. "Most prominent of all, the British Lion, with his tongue out and his eyes half shut, lying at Punch's feet," *The Month* critic called "a picture of indolent, good-natured, self-satisfied strength". He drew Disraeli as Gulliver inspected by the Brobdignag statesmen Robert Peel and Sir James Graham, and "Papa Cobden taking Master Robert [Peel] on a Free Trade Walk". His continual visits to the theatre provided subjects like "Recess Recreations, or Rehearsing for a Westminster Play", or another cartoon based upon Shakespeare's *Midsummer Night's Dream.* He could be emotive in his own mild-mannered way. In the double page, "Put Down Your Stakes Gentlemen", which one critic called his best *Punch* cartoon, "his contrast of turmoil everywhere with peace in Old England is very effective. Little groups of massacre and battle hint at the state of surrounding Europe, and in the centre is a pleasant domestic circle of John and Mrs Bull and their young people, all agreeing that 'There is no place like Home'." The theme was repeated in "Punch's Dream of Peace" in 1849, where Europeans embrace one another in a scene of continental contentment.

Doyle was most inventive, however, with his small comic drawings and initials. An early success was the comic initials he provided for the hilarious Mrs Caudle's Curtain Lectures series from January to November 1845. Douglas Jerrold's sharp yet perceptive account of Mr Caudle's nagging wife, who refused to allow the gentle toy and doll merchant to enjoy even the smallest pleasures, was a tremendous success among *Punch* readers and reached a larger public when later published in book form. Mrs Caudle had become a household name, a national institution whose comic exploits Dick tried to suggest in his small comic initials which introduced each new episode. Later, when Jerrold decided to kill off Mrs Caudle, the public clamoured for more news of the Caudle household, and he married the widower to the hopeless but pretty Miss Prettyman, whom Caudle "nagged to death" – thus perpetuating the all too familiar habits of his first wife.

Dick's boyhood preoccupation with historical figures surfaced in "Punch's Historical Portrait Gallery" series in 1846, where he drew the exaggerated faces of Napoleon, Dr Johnson and Richard III among his choice of boyhood heroes. His cut-out fresco style was well-suited to a large sketched proposal for a statue of Cromwell, published as "Should Cromwell have a Statue?". He combined his talent for observation with comic twists during the period when Jenny Lind, "the Swedish Nightingale", took London and the country by storm. Dick and his *Punch* colleagues were devoted disciples of Jenny Lind and avidly followed her concert tours and London performances, although Thackeray was said to long "to get to the end and have a cigar" after his first exposure to her magical voice. To Dick, Jenny Lind embodied all the virtues of beauty and grace he would search for in women throughout his life. Her dark-haired doll-like beauty reappeared in his drawings for *Punch* and elsewhere from now onwards. She became the subject of his cartoons, the centre of a Jenny Lind coin and medallion he designed, as well as political cartoons based upon the infamous "Jenny Lind Crush" at the box office before each of her performances. In fact her popularity reached such astonishing proportions that the House of Commons was kept waiting three times for lack of voting members, most of whom were struggling to get tickets for her concerts. When the Queen attended Jenny Lind's London première the audience scarcely noticed her arrival because they were "so afraid of missing a single gesture" of their heroine. She not only inspired Doyle cartoons but also portraits on the boxes of chocolates or matchbooks, Jenny Lind pocket handkerchiefs, the names of horses, dogs and children. "Now everything is Jenny Lind. That comes out each new day, There's Jenny Lind shawls and bonnets too, For those who cash can pay," went the words of a popular broadsheet song.

Doyle's Irish subjects increased with the news of the terrible Potato Famine. He concentrated upon a drawing of destitute Irish peasants,

a benevolent John Bull ("Here are a few things to go on with, Brother, and I'll soon put you in a way to earn your own living.") and an inspiring Queen after her Irish visit in late 1849. She gazes into an Irish lake in this cartoon, "Ireland, a Dream of the Future", its surface reflecting prosperity and contented workers while on the opposite bank a starving cottier's family stares helplessly by.

Although Dick provided captions to his drawings, he rarely wrote for *Punch*. However some indication of his comic style survives in the one article he did write and illustrate, "High Art and the Royal Academy", 13 May 1848. Adopting the voice of an outraged painter whose two pictures had been rejected by the Royal Academy, he provided drawings of his two masterpieces, calculated to appeal to the current vogue for either "Medieval-Angelico-Pugin-Gothic, or flat style", or the more exuberant "manner of

---

The "Jenny Lind Crush" from Doyle's Manners and Customs, *1849.*

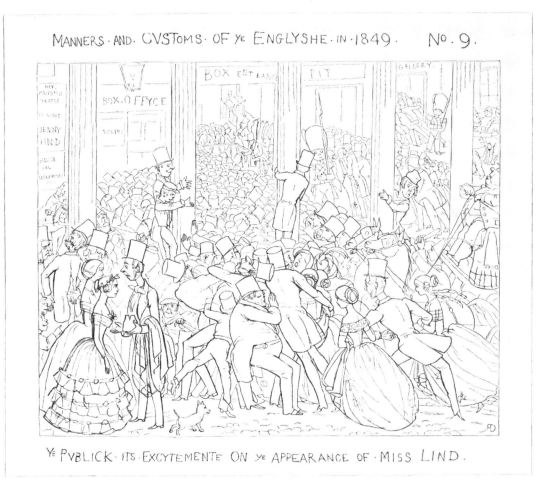

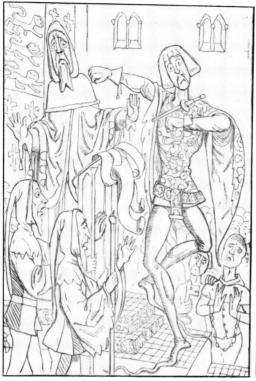

Doyle's comic attack on the Royal Academy, Punch, *10 July 1847.*

the Fuseli-Michael-Angelesque school". Although a comic attack on current fashions for so-called "High Art" (earlier he had drawn Mr Punch on a ladder, struggling over a 30′ long historical picture – "England will never know what High Art really is till it has seen Punch's own historical picture", 10 July 1847), there were shades of Dick's own thwarted ambitions to become a successful gallery painter in his text. He ended in a tone of misery and disillusionment, "how miserably have I been deceived and disappointed!" and signed himself "One of the Nine Hundred Rejected Ones". The article served a double purpose as well, for it heralded the publication of his own *Rejected Cartoons* book which appeared the same year.

Often his *Punch* drawings involved subjects which Dick could only imagine and draw with-

Preliminary pencil drawing for the "Medieval-Angelico-Pugin-Gothic, or flat style".

out the benefit of first-hand knowledge. His comic views of America were surely his finest attempts to bring public misconceptions into clear view. In his bitter cartoon, "The Land of Liberty Recommended to the Consideration of 'Brother Jonathan' " (4 December 1848), he drew a large, sprawling Uncle Sam ("of the spread-eagle type") stretched across a full-page. He smokes a long cigar and blows clouds of evil-smelling smoke (Dick always hated cigar and cigarette smoke) into the ghosts of America's current social evils: black slaves are beaten in one cloud, while lynchings and a threat of Mexican war crowd the opposite sides of the drawing. The entire scene is presided over by a devil, while Uncle Sam rests his boot on a bust of George Washington, in what one critic called a striking "Doylesque phantasmagoria". Other American drawings involved the Gold Rush – a perfect guise for Doyle's comic inventions of greedy prospectors racing to the gold fields, being chased by Indians, or digging in the fields. He introduced Punch's account of Thomas Tyddler, a "Free and Independent" dry goods store owner turned prospector which, according to the title "A Few Days in the Diggins", was far from successful. In "Ye Hygh Seas Showynge ye Vessels Bound for ye Bankes of ye Sacramen-to", he drew a race from England to California, and how on landing the Indians attacked the new arrivals in "A Run upon ye Bankes of Sacramento. Appearance of ye Natyves", which provided its own moral to those foolhardy enough to seek the glitter of gold. Such exploits reappeared in Dick's almanack border, "California. The Latest from the Diggins", of 1850.

Apart from cartoons, comic initials and small drawings, Dick's *Punch* work included an annual *Punch Almanack*, for which he provided comic border designs from 1844. The *Punch Almanack* was an essential annual publication which, from its appearance in 1841, helped to boost the paper's circulation at the end of each year. Dick's first almanack borders were in the "Non-sense" style of whimsical figures racing up and down trellis-work borders; which one contemporary critic praised for they "would elicit laughter from toothache, and render gout oblivious of a reader's toe". He added political overtones to his whimsical creatures by giving them a giant banner marked "Ireland for the Irish" and "The World in a Blaze". He drew the Queen and Prince Albert at court attempting

the newest dance, the polka. He devoted the April 1845 border to the "Art Union and Fine Art Distribution", in which a blinded figure of culture flings money to crowds of scampering artists who either successfully catch coins and notes on one side of the page, or are speared alive by an enormous sharp quill and brushes – presumeably suggestive of self-sacrifice to their work. In other years his almanack designs included portraits of the year's prominent politicians alongside grotesque creatures, parades of elephants and exotic beasts. The Jenny Lind theme reappears in May-June 1848, as she takes her audiences by storm; the Queen appears on the opposite side, drawn not surprisingly as a Jenny Lind double with wide eyes and round face. This almanack featured scenes from the London Season, of Rotten Row swells on horseback, royal balls and society figures in Grandville-like animal disguises and was so popular it was issued in a separate coloured edition. By 1850, the final year of Dick's almanack designs, he had achieved a considerable following for his annual border drawings, proudly telling his brother Charles how "The 'Examiner' praised the Almanack in Sunday's paper very much, and the Times gave it great glorification." While at a children's party for the Dickens children, he also recalled with delight how "Edwin Landseer in the course of the evening spoke to me of the Almanack in very extravagantly complimentary terms which for him is 'something' ".[9]

The Doyle *Punch* drawings soon won a large and enthusiastic following. They were republished in *Punch's Pocketbooks,* and occasional special numbers for the holiday season. And the newest was proudly displayed in the *Punch* office window, where a young wood engraver's apprentice, Walter Crane, spent his lunch hour at the window, studying the Doyle style which would influence his early attempts at illustration. Edwin Landseer apparently introduced his etching and drawing pupils, the Queen and Albert, to Doyle's drawings, for they produced etched copies of his work as early as 1845.[10]

Much of the attention given to Doyle's *Punch* work stemmed from his remarkably successful series of comic views of society, "Manners and Customs of Ye Englyshe". These half-page cut-out style drawings, accompanied by excerpts from Mr Pips's diary by Percival Leigh, appeared throughout 1849, followed by a further ten

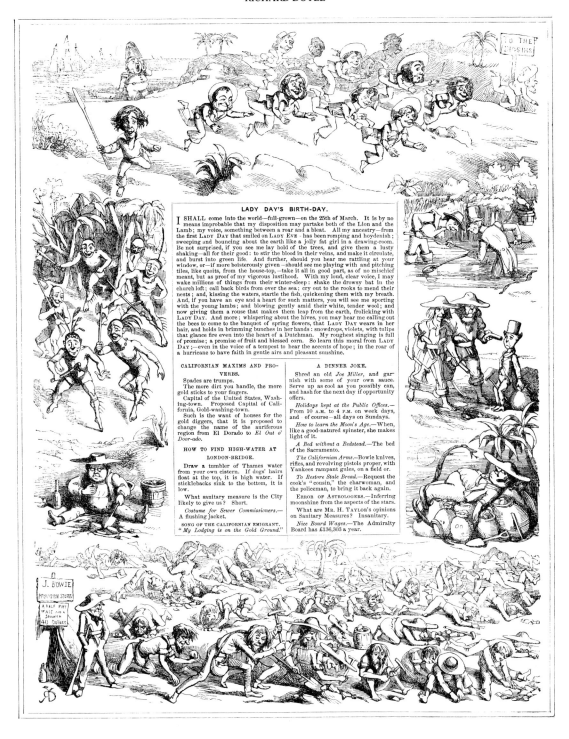

Doyle's American Gold Rush border,
"California. The Latest from the 'Diggins' ",
Punch Almanack *for 1850.*

without text the next year and a subsequent book edition. They were intricate compositions based upon Dick's memory of visits to crowded lecture halls, society "At Homes", balls, concerts and exhibitions, where bored philistines stare into space and well-fed hostesses smile demurely at their young daughters about to be launched into the marriage market. Dick drew his intricate compositions of figures in a new style: an adaptation of his early fresco or cut-out style but with faces now carefully delineated for character, their rotund bodies marked for maximum effect. His round-faced swells and society ladies bulge from their coats and dresses, and young ladies are carefully drawn in the full gowns of fashionable lace and flowers Dick loved so well.

One of the most successful, No.23 – "A Cydere Cellare Duryng a Comyck Songe", was based upon Dick's evening among the rough characters of an infamous London drinking house. It must have upset his father, who

Doyle in Bohemia – the celebrated Cider Cellar where Thackeray took him and which inspired his "Sam Hall" drawing, Manners and Customs, *1849.*

usually disapproved of anything low or coarse, and indeed Dick's account of the evening is tinged with guilt, knowing his father would have been upset to learn he had been "in Bohemia". But the drawing marked the emergence of a new side to Dick's character; that of the curious bachelor, who with his friends Thackeray, Tom Taylor, Eyre Crowe, Dickens and Leech, occasionally escaped the drawing rooms of society, for a trip "into Bohemia". In this instance, Thackeray had lured Dick to the famous drinking house in Maiden Lane, next to the Adelphi Theatre, where the clientale was decidedly mixed. One might find young Disraeli here, or Napoleon III before he became President of France, as well as struggling and famous writers and artists, drinking and smoking the night away. Although not quite as disreputable as the nearby "Coal Hole", this establishment was famous for its impromptu performances from intoxicated guests, and the plaintive street songs of Sam Hall which usually could be heard as the evening ground on into the early hours of the morning. Dick was delighted by the experience as he afterwards explained to his brother: "I committed a terrible piece of dissipation on Saturday, after [the] Punch dinner by going with

[57]

Thackeray and Leech to the Cider Cellar to hear the famous song of 'Sam Hall' and 'damn his eyes' which is not edifying but wonderfully got up as a dramatic performance." Here he had remained until two o'clock in the morning to hear "our Ross, sing the song of Sam Hall, the chimney-sweep, going to be hanged for he had begrimed his muzzle to look unshaven and in dusty black clothes, with a battered old hat on his crown and short pipe in his mouth, did sit upon the platform, leaning over the back of the chair". His audience was by this time drunk and sleepy, or merely bored, so Ross swore at them, "his cursing very horrible, albeit to not a few it seemed a high joke; but I do doubt that they understood the song," Dick recalled the scene, which ended up with a rousing chorus of "Damn your eyes".[11]

Dick delighted in drawing these experiences for the series: his views of Belgravia, Lord's cricket ground, or the Chiswick flower show are countered by the labourers and farmers at Smithfield cattle market. His characters crawl about on their hands at the Royal Academy, to see the lowest hung pictures; they feed the animals at the zoo with their walking sticks, or join the outraged meeting of shareholders or members of a criminal courtroom drama. He catches the smugness of society, the pretence and gluttony of the middle classes striving to better themselves, which oddly appealed to *Punch's* readers, many of whom now lived similar pretences, or at least knew how to recognize polite society when they saw it. He parodied the delights of Society and the London season, many scenes taken from personal experience. Once Dick was invited to a musical "entertainment" by a noted London host who had followed the Manners and Customs series in *Punch* and hoped to be immortalized in a future issue by his special evening of private entertainment. "He said he thought a back view of the piano, with faces of the audience would be new," Dick told Charles of this host's gracious but pointed invitation.[12]

The success of the Manners and Customs series attracted serious artist colleagues as well, men like the newly formed members of the Pre-Raphaelite Brotherhood. William Holman Hunt and Dante Gabriel Rossetti specifically bought *Punch* to study Doyle's curious compositions of figures, grouped not unlike the medieval tapestry designs they so much admired. Dick became

"their idol" – his inventive talent for observation and detail a favoured tenet of the PRBs, as they were known. The lesson was carried on by disciples like Burne-Jones, who remembered being impressed by a Doyle parody hung in the coffee room of the Oxford Union, "Manners and Customs of ye Oxonians in 1856" by Cuthbert Bede, which remained there until the turn of the century.

But it was William Makepeace Thackeray who became Dick's greatest friend and admirer at this time. He was so taken by the archaic titles Dick had given his Manners and Customs series ("Ye Exhybityon at Ye Royal Academy") that he adopted the affectation in his own correspondence. The fashionable subjects Dick chose did however conflict with Thackeray's own articles, like "Mr Brown's Letters to a Young Man about Town", which was originally planned for a *Punch Extra Number*. "This news is very heartbreaking... The Manners & Customs of the English, the great attraction of Punch on the self-same subjects: it appears to me you will cut the throats of those 2 series by your projected Extra number – but I can't commit suicide and slit my own artery: so that you must put the fashionable part into the hands of another writer," Thackeray wrote in disgust to Mark Lemon, who eventually agreed to cancel the Extra Number altogether.[13]

Fortunately the two men shared a talent for ridiculing and parodying the foibles of polite society. Thackeray had a limited talent for comic drawings which endeared him further to Doyle, his obvious superior. In turn, Dick admired his friend's writing skills and had helped Thackeray get journalistic work reviewing books on Irish subjects following his return from Ireland to London. Thackeray would always recall how Dick was "working anxiously in my favour" with his Uncle Michael Conan and through his paper, *The Morning Chronicle,* Thackeray was employed within five days of the proposal.[14] They also shared a common employer in Mr Punch, and Dick was often entertained by Thackeray after the Punch dinner, or on numerous other special occasions at Thackeray's bachelor flat in Jermyn Street. There he was introduced to literary personalities or artists like the famed French cartoonist "Cham". Thackeray loved to send rushed invitations to these impromptu evenings, usually with a hurried sketch like the drunken boy which headed the appeal for "My dear Doyle" and his sister Annette to

Manners and Customs of the English *series:*

a) Smithfield Cattle Market.

b) Exhibition at the Royal Academy.

attend an evening "a drunkin" at his flat: "And will you lend me one or 2 of your books to let the ladies admire?"[15] On these occasions Thackeray adopted a fatherly air to his friend, who was, after all, ten years his junior. And it was a credit to their friendship that after Thackeray's success with *Vanity Fair* in 1847, when many of his old friends abandoned him, Dick remained a trusted and constant companion, whose career Thackeray watched with concern and in search of a chance to repay the kindness Dick had once shown toward him. There is also a hint that Dick's quiet, gentle nature helped to tame the more outrageous and early embittered Thackeray. His *Punch* articles, like "The Fatal Boots" were strong attacks on society which, although Dick may have agreed with them, soon gave way to a more refined style of attack of the type Dick had apparently mastered in his Manners and Customs series. Moreover, Dick was a fellow artist; a breed of men which appealed to Thackeray's bohemian instincts.[16]

By this time Dick was a young man in his mid-twenties, with an artistic reputation and a delightful manner which endeared him to a growing number of famous society hostesses. On this point he and Thackeray shared and compared notes. They were often together at the same dinner party, or at least introduced to the same influential members of Belgravian society, from whom they sought connections and patronage.

Dick was especially successful in his early attempts to cultivate an impressive list of social acquaintances. Lord and Lady Granville took the young artist under their wing and became prominent patrons in later years. When Thackeray heard Dick was admitted to one of Lady Granville's soirées, he wrote to advise Dick: "Lady Granville's swarries (sic) commence *after* the 1 May. But I shall be in the world to night and hear what is the real state of the case."[17] Less grand but still notable were the crowded evenings at the Procter's, arranged by the wife of the literary giant Barry Cornwall, where most of London's artistic and literary figures congregated. On other occasions Dick and Thackeray enjoyed the events of the London season together; one year Dick raced home from a country house weekend to ride his horse with Thackeray to Ascot. There they watched the crowds and the races, unaware of an impending storm, "of that very decided kind known as 'cat and dog' [which] descended indiscriminately

upon the people and upon the 'food of the people' ". They rode on to Windsor when the sun returned and "dried our unfortunate garments, and lit up the beautiful glade of Windsor forest". Afterwards Dick sketched the disastrous rainstorm in a letter to a friend, adding: "Moral: A Sportsman with an umbrella up is a novel and thereupon more interesting sight than a sportsman with no umbrella."[18]

Thackeray was the model for at least six pencil portraits which Doyle drew during these early years. Dick concentrated upon his friend's round face and tiny eyes – usually seen behind wire-rimmed pebble glasses – and depicted Thackeray's many moods, with which over the years he had become quite familiar. He drew him with a sad, forlorn expression, smiling astride a favourite horse, or with his hands in his pockets, dressed for an evening "in society". Sometimes he appeared alongside mutual friends like the hook-nosed Henry Reeve, the *Times* journalist who was reputed to be "one of the best known personalities of his day".[19]

On one of these occasions Dick was invited with Thackeray to meet the mysterious literary sensation Currer Bell, author of the recently published *Jane Eyre* of 1847. Dick was a devoted fan of Jane Eyre's, apparently having read passages carefully enough to remember and quote them to friends or acquaintances who shared his new interest. Once, while travelling on an omnibus to Hampstead, he met the painter Millais and argued that the book was undoubtedly written by a woman. He quoted his favourite passages from memory to make his point, because as another friend and companion recalled "evidently her personality appealed to him strongly".[20] When the mysterious Charlotte Brontë came to London to meet her publisher George Smith, he entertained his new protégée with dinners in her honour. On one such evening Dick was thrilled to join Thackeray – for Miss Brontë had always wanted to meet her idol, the author of *Vanity Fair* (to whom she dedicated the second edition of *Jane Eyre*). Although the meeting between Miss Brontë and Thackeray was far from successful, Dick afterwards recalled the evening in a letter to Charles: "I daresay you heard of Smith & Elder asking me to dinner to meet the author of Jane Eyre, who is a little delicate looking woman about thirty, named Miss Brontë. Thackeray was also asked."[21] And Dick retained his devotion to Charlotte Brontë

W. M. THACKERAY, M. J. HIGGINS, AND HENRY REEVE
From an unpublished pencil sketch by Richard Doyle, in the British Museum

Doyle's pen and ink portraits of Thackeray, M.J.Higgins and Henry Reeve riding.
4⅛ x 6¾"
British Museum.

---

until his death; in later years he made a pilgrimage to Haworth Rectory and Parsonage and painted a rather gloomy tribute to her – a view of the site where she had created his favourite book.

Dick Doyle's admiration for Charles Dickens went back to his own childhood, when he avidly read the latest instalment of *The Old Curiosity Shop* or *Nicholas Nickleby* and was able to quote whole passages from *David Copperfield* to his father. Dickens was a friend of the *Punch* staff during its early days, and Dick soon was included in those bohemian evenings in which Dickens and Thackeray joined forces to explore the less sophisticated haunts of London. As a result, Dick became a welcomed houseguest and friend of the Dickens family, attending parties at Devonshire Terrace for his friend's children; and the delightful evening entertainments where dancing and punch was shared with artist colleagues like Clarkson Stanfield, Daniel Maclise,

David Wilkie, his beloved history painter hero C.R.Leslie, George Cruikshank and Edwin Landseer. More recently his friend John Leech had also been recruited into the Dickens circle, and Dick drew a pencil portrait of Dickens and Leech as firm friends. He also sketched Dickens's closest friend John Forster, and a delightful group of fellow Punchmen Douglas Jerrold and the rotund and jovial Mark Lemon with Dickens.[22]

The friendship with Dickens soon ripened to include all members of the author's family, and in return Dick introduced his famous friend to his father and sister. During the Christmas holiday of 1849 they made up a jolly boating party aboard Captain Morgan's ship bound for Gravesend, stopping for refreshments on arrival, before returning to London. Dick invited his father and Annette along to enjoy the holiday spirit, and they shared the boat with the painters Augustus Egg and Marcus Stone, fellow Punchman Tom Taylor, the Cruikshanks, and Thackeray's "little girls". "It was the first time I have had an opportunity of introducing 'Pa' and Annette to C.Dickens," Dick wrote Charles afterwards. "They got on very well together, did 'Pa' and Boz, and the whole thing was noted successful."[22] On another occasion, Dick bought tickets for a charity evening to hear Dickens's "admirable speech" for the Newsvendors' Benevolent Society dinner, which was Dickens's favourite charity. Afterwards he "went with Dickens to the Rainbow Tavern in Fleet Street and partook of burnt sherry and anchovy toast until a late hour (3 o'clock) the conversation of 'Boz' being very pleasant", Dick told his brother. "In the course of the evening I happened to say that I would like to dine at a *really* rustic Inn in the country, and Dickens on the spot made me promise to go with him some day to Bristol near which he knows one."[23]

Such diversions were now relished as the demands upon Dick's time increased, the *Punch* work and plans for book illustrations preying on his mind. "I have been nearly worked to death," he now told his brother, hinting it was not only *Punch* work but the eleven book illustration commissions he had agreed to complete over the last four years which now tried his reserve of patience.

The first of these book commissions came not surprisingly from Charles Dickens. Each year he produced a moral tale for Christmas, which

---

Doyle's pen and ink portraits of Charles Dickens and John Forster.
2⅜ x 2⅜"
British Museum.

was issued in an illustrated edition with designs by his friends. His most successful to date was the remarkable *A Christmas Carol,* 1843, and the following year he produced *The Chimes,* 1844, *The Cricket on the Hearth,* 1845, and *The Battle of Life,* 1846, each with contributions by his friend Dick Doyle. Dick agreed with the principles behind these contemporary fairy-tales. His friend had once explained how the essential quality in fantasy would help save those struggling under the inhuman demands of the present industrial age: "In an utilitarian age, of all other times it is a matter of grave importance that fairy-tales should be respected." But the more he struggled over the drawings for initial letters, the more demanding he found his friend. Dickens was deeply aware of the power of illustrations when accompanying his work and usually provided a list of subjects he wanted drawn, and where they would be placed in the text. Illustrations must enhance the story, not merely illustrate. Sometimes he rewrote passages to fit especially good illustrations, like those of Maclise to *Master Humphrey's Clock.* For Doyle's first commission, he agreed to four drawings to accompany the Daniel Maclise illustrations to *The Chimes – A Goblin Story of some Bells that Rang out the Old Year and a New Year In.* Dickens intended the story to be "a great blow for the poor", a plea for charity and justice in the world of almshouses, workhouses, and the industrial wastelands of urban Britain. He used his now familiar device of a nightmare to describe the horrors of the future, experienced by the ghost of the main character Trotty Veck's daughter. The old Veck awakens to realise that the horrors Maclise and Dick drew, and Dickens described, were only a dream; and the bells toll in a new year full of promise and change, optimism and love.

Although the tale was written in Geneva, Dickens was convinced he must supervise its production. It had given him "what women call a real good cry", and he raced back to London to try it out on his friends, reading each chapter to them in his customary way for their opinions. He secured a Maclise illustration for the striking frontispiece, in which a tolling bell heralds the arrival of a foetal new year and the departure of a shrouded old one; and two drawings by Clarkson Stanfield, five by his new friend John Leech and four from Doyle. These last two newcomers gave him problems, however, and he arranged a breakfast meeting with them at his favourite Covent Garden coffee house to discuss their rather weak drawings. He dismissed two as "quite unsuitable", but was sufficiently tactful to get their promises to try again; afterwards telling his wife "with that winning manner which you know of, I got them with the highest good humour to do both afresh".[24]

Dick's four drawings were essentially elaborate initial letters, surrounded by vignette scenes from the story Dickens had chosen for illustrations. The best of these accompanies the "Third Quarter", in which the familiar Doyle goblins and fairy nymphs of his Nonsense books spill from the tolling bells to unleash Dickens's nightmarish future: "Black are the brooding clouds and troubled deep waters, when the Sea of Thought, first heaving from a calm, gives up its Dead. Monsters uncouth and wild, arise in premature imperfect resurrection; the several parts and shapes of different things are joined and miced by chance; and when, and how, and by what wonderful degrees, each separates from each, and every sense and object of the mind resumes its usual form and lives again..." The Doyle sprites tumble down upon a despairing Trotty Veck, the bells releasing a cloud "swarming with dwarf phantoms, spirits, elfin creatures of the Bells. He saw them leaping, flying, dropping, pouring from the Bells without pause... He saw them ugly, handsome, crippled, exquisitely formed. He saw them young, he saw them old, he saw them kind, he saw them cruel, he saw them merry, he saw them grim, he saw them dance, and he saw them sing, he saw them tear their hair, and he heard them howl. He saw the air thick with them." The result of Dick's attempts to please his friend were, however, quite gratifying. Dickens declared *The Chimes* "a sweeping success", despite the story's mixed critical reception. The illustrated book sold well, enough to earn its author a £1,400 profit on the first twenty thousand copies alone, and as usual Dickens' friends Mark Lemon and Gilbert à Beckett worked hard on the dramatized version of the story, performed for Christmas holiday audiences in London.

After his struggles over *The Chimes,* the two subsequent Dickens Christmas book commissions were less of a challenge for Doyle. In fact he provided just three drawings for *The Cricket on the Hearth,* 1845, of which the most impressive introduced a tragic domestic scene, "Chirp

the Third". The *Art Journal* critic praised his uncharacteristic sympathy in this "extremely impressive" drawing: "The Carrier and his wife sit in real misery about each other. To look at the honest man's face is to understand that there is some sorrow of which one may die if it endure very long." The troubled man is in fact a portrait of Dick's father, whose own domestic worries at the time certainly inspired Dick's sympathetic rendering of the bearded figure seated at a table, his hand spread over his forehead in despair.

Dickens was not consulted when his publishers invited Doyle to illustrate his next Christmas book, *The Battle of Life,* 1846. Dick provided

Doyle's haunting nightmare vision for Dickens's The Chimes, *1844-45.*

CHIRP THE THIRD

THE Dutch clock in the corner
struck Ten, when the Carrier
sat down by his fireside. So
troubled and grief-worn, that
he seemed to scare the Cuckoo,
who, having
cut his ten

Doyle's poignant domestic scene with portrait of his father, for Dickens's The Cricket on the Hearth. *1845-46.*

just three drawings, however, which appeared with drawings by Stanfield and Maclise (who was extremely upset by the poor quality engraving and printing). But Dickens was again pleased with the result, and although the critics were far from enthusiastic, dismissing the story as maudlin and self-indulgent, the book sold as well as any of the previous Christmas books, and was again dramatized, at the London Lyceum.

* * * * * * * * * * * *

Most of the book illustrations Doyle produced between 1846 - 1849 could be divided into two categories. There were renderings of scenes from fairy-tales and favourite legends based upon his boyhood love of fantasy. Secondly, he

developed a classical style of illustration inspired by his early studies of Flaxman and classical myths and legends, which he drew under the influence of his father's restrained sense of line.

The fairy subjects came from two sources: Dick's love of Shakespearean plays like *A Midsummer Night's Dream* or *The Tempest,* where the mysterious creatures "creep into acorn cups" at the sign of trouble, inhabit sylvan woodlands or palm covered islands; or the recent vogue for fairy-tales by the Brothers Grimm. The Shakespearean subjects proved perfect for elaborate drawings and watercolours of the kind admired in the galleries, painted by artists like Maclise and Landseer and which were much praised and purchased by the Queen. *A Midsummer Night's Dream* had inspired new music by Mendelssohn, as well as paintings and ballets which helped to establish a vogue for fairy pictures and illustrations throughout the 1840s and 1850s. Dick included his version of the story in his *Rejected Cartoons* volume, in which a sleeping knight in full armour lies beneath a tree in the full moonlight, while fairies and elves dance happily around him: it was truly a "Midsummer Knight's (sic) Dream".

The Tempest story had always fascinated Dick as a child, when he planned to do a large painting of his version for his father. He produced "The Enchanted Tree", a fantasy based on *The Tempest* in 1845, a large watercolour beach scene with figures scattered across the sand drawn in Doyle's Nonsense style. He concentrated upon the scene where Prospero releases fairy spirits from the palm trees with his magic wand; the whole painting a subtle mixture of pale pastel colours, indigo, ochre and green, marred only by the rather smudged brown of Caliban crouching in the foreground.

The appearance in English of fairy-tales by the Brothers Grimm, illustrated by Dick's friend Cruikshank, heralded a revival of interest in foreign tales and legends. Cruikshank's illustrations had set the style for fairy illustrators; according to Thackeray in 1840: "Cruikshank is the only designer fairyland has had. Mr

"A Midsummer Knight's Dream", from the Rejected Cartoons, *1848:*
a) Preliminary pencil and ink drawing.
Huntington Art Gallery.
b) Published lithograph.

a)

b)

Cruikshank has a true insight into the character of the 'little people'. They are something like men and women, and yet not flesh and blood; they are laughing and mischievous, but why, we know not."[26] However, when Dick illustrated a new collection of Grimm's tales, *The Fairy Ring,* translated by John Edward Taylor in 1846, Thackeray graciously altered his opinion to declare Doyle the new master of fairyland. Here in clear, confident outline and an etched line style, he surrounded each story title with elaborate vignettes and intricate illuminated letters. He developed his love of dwarfs and giants in introducing "Bruin and the Dwarf" and "The Dwarf in the Bottle". He drew a group

"The Enchanted Tree", fantasy based upon "The Tempest".
Watercolour 32 x 23"
Private collection.

———————

of knights in search of dragons which culminated in "The Dragon and his Grandmother", a delightful domestic scene with a typical whimsical Doyle dragon about to serve dinner to his grandmother, a withered old witch, while a knight anxiously peeks through the trap door in the floor. Monsters appear in several guises, like the seven-headed flying creature in "The Two Brothers". Altogether it was an impressive achievement which combined many of Dick's

———————

Doyle's praised drawings to the Brothers Grimm tales in The Fairy Ring, *1846:*
a) The knight intrudes on the dining witch and dragon.

b) Doyle's skill at animal drawing was used to fine effect.

talents for whimsy, accurate yet expressive animal drawing, and a knowledge of book design.

Thackeray was delighted with the book from the moment it appeared, asking Dick to send him a copy to entertain some of his more important evening guests. As a journalist and book reviewer on *The Morning Chronicle,* he also felt it his duty to review it for the paper, in words which helped to establish Dick Doyle as a new and impressive artist of the fairy-tale: "We read every now and then in these legends of certain princes and princesses who are carried off by the little people for awhile, and kept in fairy land. This must have been surely Mr Doyle's case, and he must have had the advantage of pencils and paper during his banishment. If any man knows the people and country, he does... He has such an intimate acquaintance with dwarfs, ogres and dragons, that it can only be from nature that he had designed them: his fairy princesses are the most slender and delicate; his princes the most brilliant and noble; his bears, lions and foxes have exactly that mysterious intelligence with which they are endowed in the fairy legends." His only criticism was based upon personal knowledge of his friend's well-bred manner: "His only fault is that a natural gallantry towards the opposite sex, and gentleness of disposition as we take it, prevent him from making the old hags, hunch-backed sorceresses and hideous step-mothers, in which all the stories of the 'Mother Bunch' kind delight, horrid and ugly enough." He went on to praise the translation, which retained what he called the 'Old Style' in tales untainted by excessive sentimentality or updated by contemporary slang. They were in fact enchanting tales of the type Dick had loved and collected throughout his childhood, full of the chivalric virtues and high-minded morals, yet told without fear of frightening children by the terrible monsters and wicked creatures: "Little Hop-o-my-thumbs go on their travels and overreach giants by their cunning: wicked stepmothers prefer one-eyed children who spit snakes and toads to those who expectorate guineas: king's children are spirited away and restored: hapless damsels are shut up in steel towers, subject to the odious addresses of the landlord, who is an ogre: and even, when it seems their need is at the sorest, a prince in armour bright comes riding through the forest; and vice is punished, and humble beauty and virtue rescued."[27]

The success of this book led to further fairy-tale commissions. Dick drew twenty four illustrations to Anthony Montalba's translations of *Fairy Tales of all Nations* of 1849, for example. Here, his drawings of knights and dragon for "The Russian Tale" followed the famous first English translation of the Norwegian classic "Eastward of the Sun and Westward of the Moon", illustrated with an enchanting princess riding a polar bear. There were macabre stories as well, like "Snow-white and Rosy-red", a tale of an evil mother who banished her daughter's children to play in a snake pit, which Dick drew in a rather stilted fashion. Although they are not among the best Doyle drawings, they were successful enough to be republished in a second edition of 1872, and in *The Doyle Fairy Book* of 1890.

More successful and impressive as fairy illustrations were the twelve elaborate floral borders to Mrs Hervey's *Juvenile Calendar and Zodiac of Flowers,* 1849. Here the fairy themes which had long preoccupied Dick surrounded the March page, "Titania and the Violets". He drew a fairy ring, impish pixies torturing insects and birds, and a romantic embrace between fairy prince and princess. It was the type of drawing which the public soon began to associate with Doyle the fairy illustrator, and reviewers praised his inventions in "a very elegant work, most beautifully illustrated... with a decidedly poetical feeling and a good moral tendency" (*The Ladies' Companion,* 29 December 1849); or that they would appeal to children: "The dream-loving child will discover, without teaching, how beautiful is the actual world" (*The Art Journal,* 1 February 1850).

Dick's love of folklore and legends led to an interest in street songs and those romantic ballads which were collected together in the extremely popular *The Book of Ballads* of Bon Gaultier. Here Spanish, American and Continental verses were combined with illustrations originally by Crowquill. Doyle was asked to draw small yet exotic headpiece drawings for several new ballads in the 1849 edition, where his work appeared alongside designs by *Punch* colleagues John Leech and Kenny Meadows. His most effective was a wide-eyed Jenny Lind like exotic beauty as "The Cadi's Daughter – A Legend of the Bosphorus", dressed in a full gown and jewelled turban. His drawings continued

Doyle's sylvan fairy style in the Juvenile Calendar and Zodiac of Flowers, *1849:*
a) The first appearance of Doyle's fairyland creatures he re-used throughout his life.

b) Children, birds and flowers were part of Doyle's gentle style.

to be used in the numerous editions which appeared well into the turn of the century.

The vogue for fairy-tales prompted Dick's more talented friends to try writing their own stories. Mark Lemon was a witty, jovial man with a childish sense of humour which made him a popular playwright as well as *Punch* editor. He wrote *The Enchanted Doll,* a tale about a poor doll maker Jacob Prout, whose workshop is invaded by kind fairies. Lemon originally intended it to entertain Dickens' children, to whom the story was dedicated; but it proved so popular a book was planned and Dick agreed to illustrate the tale. He provided a striking frontispiece of fairy antics in the workshop, a rustic lettered title-page in which the bemused workman is presented to the fairy world, as well as twenty one smaller initials and drawings throughout the book. It appeared in time to compete with the annual Dickens Christmas book, with which many reviewers compared it. *The Athenaeum,* for example, called it a lesson "into charity and

contentment" which "would hardly have been imagined had Mr Dickens's Scrooge never existed". But the Doyle illustrations were praised as triumphs of the fairy world, although the same critic thought they "very nearly rise to the state and dignity of pictures", *The Ladies' Companion* was convinced they secured Doyle's importance as an illustrator for children, "to be appointed the artist in ordinary to the nursery".

At the same time, Dick perfected his classical style illustrations in the arcadian landscape vignettes and initial letters to Leigh Hunt's anthology, *A Jar of Honey from Mount Hybla,* 1847. The book was essentially a collection of Hunt's favourite poetry from Greece and Italy, to which Doyle added his vague idea of these ancient lands. He drew a smoking Mount Etna, satyrs dancing to the music of a giant's pan-pipes, and sheep grazing under the care of a classical shepherdess among the broken temple ruins. They are atmospheric rather than precise drawings, originally drawn in pencil on wood blocks, and were praised for their "graceful fancy" in a book of "genuine sweetness" by the

Frontispiece and title-page to The Enchanted Doll, *1849.*

ASTORAL poetry is supposed to have originated in Sicily, at one and the same time with comedy. At all events, it was perfected there. Comedy is understood to have been suggested by the licence with which it was the custom for peasants to rail at passengers, and at one another, during the jollity of the vintage ; and pastoral poetry was at first nothing but the more rustical part of comedy. Its great master, Theocritus, arose during a period

Doyle's classical style: initial to "Theocritus" in A Jar of Honey from Mount Hybla, *1847.*

Athenaeum critic (25 December 1847).

Similarly Dick attempted a study of Oliver Goldsmith as a Roman statue in his illustration to John Forster's *The Life and Times of Oliver Goldsmith,* 1848. He drew Goldsmith in a roman toga clutching a scroll, with scenes from his life encircled by thorns. It was an impressive composition, the stern face and crowned head "rises out of the thorns of the world, stands serene, with laurels arching its noble head – laurels and sunlight", according to one critic. Doyle also agreed to contribute one drawing to the Art Union of London's large illustrated edition of Milton's poem, *L'Allegro and Il Penseroso,* sharing the task with Kenny Meadows, John Tenniel, John Gilbert, Edward Courbould and Phiz. He chose a scene from "L'Allegro", in which a sylvan revel is acted out for a classical goddess seated in the foreground. It was virtually a variation on the Doyle fairy scenes; unfortunately it was poorly engraved to make Doyle's soft pencil lines hard and facial expressions all but ridiculous.

By the end of 1849, as the demands upon Dick's time continued, he began to wonder whether he might refuse some commissions which he considered unsuitable to his growing reputation as a comic and fairy illustrator. One of these came from his society friend, the redoubtable literary wife of the famous botanist, Mrs Loudan, who was now editing her own magazine, *The Ladies' Companion.* Since she had published enthusiastic reviews of Dick's books in the first issues of her paper, he felt somewhat bound to provide her with a title design, and a few further drawings of what Dick dismissed as "women's subjects". But he was far from happy by the obligation, telling Charles how his heading and two small cuts appeared in the first number: "They are bringing it out with spirit, but I doubt its being successful, as Ladies don't like things being exclusively for themselves, they like to read the same things that men read, and if anything is to be got up purposely for them alone, they think it is written 'down' to them." Indeed, Dick's preliminary sketches for the magazine heading suggest his mood: beneath the classical figures of art and music, he sketched profiles of a wicked-looking dowager, a demure

Doyle's view of women in society below a preliminary ink design for The Ladies' Companion, *1849.*
Christie's.

Preliminary pencil sketch for Milton's L'Allegro, *1848, before the engraver ruined Doyle's delicate line.*
Christie's.

aging spinster, and a wide-eyed young beauty – his views of womanhood according to his experience of society drawing rooms.

Over the next few years Dick continued to study those women he saw in the drawing rooms and concert halls of the capital. He was now a highly eligible young bachelor of twenty-five, noted for his wit and charm, his gentlemanly manner and sensitivity towards members of the opposite sex. He frequently discussed his desires to know young women in his letters to his brother Charles, but he always returned home in the evenings, to his childhood rooms, where his family awaited him. For, however earnest were his desires to establish his independence, Dick would never really leave his childhood home. There he had spent the most productive and exciting time of his life. And he refused to forget his obligations to his father, his artist brothers – who were now struggling with their own futures – and his loving and devoted sister. Indeed, together they produced drawings for a suitably titled book, *The Lover's Stratagem,* 1849, Dick joining forces with his brothers James and Henry illustrating this elaborate gift book, engraved by the enterprising W.J.Linton. It was a sign that the Doyle family could work successfully together, as they had done throughout those early childhood years. And during the next few years they would need that reassurance.

James Doyle's chapter heading to
The Lover's Stratagem, *1849.*

III

Brown, Jones and Robinson

1850 - 1851

ure of romance and acts of medieval chivalry preoccupied Dick Doyle throughout the close of 1849. These boyhood loves formed the basis for his first collaboration with Thackeray, illustrating his Christmas book, *Rebecca and Rowena – A Romance upon Romance*, which appeared late in 1849. In it, Thackeray offered a comic sequel to Dick's favourite childhood hero, Ivanhoe, who was now married to the domineering Lady Rowena, and from whom he eventually escapes to fight with Richard the Confessor in France. There he is left for dead on the battlefield where Richard is killed, and when Lady Rowena learns the news she remarries, the congenial Athelstone, who in turn is killed during the bloody seige of the castle by an irate and resurrected Ivanhoe (Dick planned this scene in an exhuberant ink sketch, with furious soldiers battering and hacking away at the castle door). When his wife eventually dies, Ivanhoe feels free enough to remarry Rebecca, the devoted Jewess now turned Christian with whom he happily spends the remainder of his life.

In a sense Thackeray's comic twist to the fate of a popular if not national hero was compatible with Dick's own attempts to turn history into fantasy. The story was also a satiric, if carefully disguised look at the fashionable tenets of medieval chivalry and romance revived by Walter Scott and a succession of more recent writers and artists. Dick's illustrations clearly indicate how fully he believed in the vogue, for he filled the book with intricate initial letter designs depicting knights on horseback, beautiful damsels about to be rescued, or scenes of courtly love, as well as the violent battles and

vicious torture scenes which Thackeray had written into his text. In one, King Richard brutally attacks a child with an axe: "the brute nature of Richard was aroused: his fiendish appetite for blood rose to madness, and grinding his teeth, and with a curse too horrible to mention, the flashing axe of the royal butcher fell down on the blond ringlets of the child, and the children of Chalus were no more". In another, Dick drew a knight about to torture an unfortunate Jew with a red hot iron. In contrast, Dick drew scenes of courtly love and revelry, like the delightful serenade by King Richard, a wild and woolly looking character in thick beard, confidently strumming a lute for the enjoyment of his courtiers (who look far from

Preliminary pen sketch for the brutal battle and seige of Chalus's castle in Thackeray's Rebecca and Rowena, *1849 - 50.*

*Doyle's preoccupation with medieval chivalry
inspired some of his most carefully observed drawings.*

happy) while a pair of puzzled pug dogs rest at
his feet. The dogs remained a Doyle trademark he drew into the corner of many illustrations from now onwards, to soften a particularly
unpleasant scene. Thackeray's daughter was
especially delighted by them, and after her
father redrew their round faces in a letter to her,
she demanded to be taken to Doyle's home to
search for the original models.

Dick provided eight such plates to the book,
but each one met with Thackeray's intense
critical comments, for he had originally planned
to illustrate the book himself, prevented only by
illness from doing so. It was a difficult collaboration from the start, plagued by unreasonable
demands from the publisher, who told Thackeray
to cut down his hundred-page manuscript by
two lines per page. When he heard this, Dick
quickly wrote to console his friend, "in great
indignation [and] sorrow about the cuts". But
eventually he too suffered the cuts, when two
clever tailpiece designs – a group of vine-
encircled figures, and a man rescuing a beautiful
girl from her angry mother – had to be dropped.[1]
And in the end, Thackeray was grateful for the
attention Dick had given the commission, which
after all had to be shared with his demanding
Punch work. In the preface Thackeray explained
why he had not illustrated the story: "It need
scarcely be said, that the humble artist who
usually illustrates my works fell ill at the same
time with myself, and on trial his hand shook so
that it was found impossible he could work for
the present volume. But this circumstance no
one but the Author (who disapproves of odious
comparisons) will regret, as it has called in the
aid of my friend MR RICHARD DOYLE to
illustrate the tale." And on the whole critics
were generous. *The Athenaeum* (29 December

King Richard serenades his court, from Rebecca and
Rowena, *1849 - 50.*

1849) called it "a capital Christmas book",
noting in the King Richard serenade drawing
"Mr R.Doyle has never been happier". However, Thackeray's friends were less enthusiastic.
Macaulay doubted the "very pretty and clever
piece of fooling" would attract the general
public to "taste the humour as I do". He was in
fact correct, for sales of the book were poor, and
as a result its publishers refused to agree to
publish Thackeray's next book.

Dick Doyle's *Punch* work was more gratifying
at this time. His "Manners and Customs" series
appeared in book form in time for Christmas
sales, and he agreed to begin a new series of ten

drawings in the new year. These were without the comic text by Percival Leigh; presumeably by this time Doyle's drawings spoke for themselves. Indeed, by the end of 1849 Dick wrote in a weary tone to his brother Charles how he was "expected to begin another series at once, equally successful", but he had refused until after the Christmas holidays. "I intend to take a rest first."[2] As the result of the series, *Punch's* circulation had rocketted, while in the 2 February 1850 issue a special comic tribute was paid to Doyle. This was in the form of a parody, "A Note from Elysium", in which Oliver Goldsmith attacks *Punch's* ill-treatment of "peasants and royalty", then adds a "P.S.Reynolds and Flaxman, with a crowd of painters and sculptors, have been looking and wondering all the afternoon at Doyle's book of Manners and Customs of ye Englyshe, which even Reynolds pronounces 'miraculous!' "

The ten subjects Dick chose for the new series depicted the amusements of London society: skating on the frozen Serpentine, joining the crowds at Astley's for a circus performance, at Ascot or the Derby, or at the pleasure gardens of Vauxhall. He included memories of recent experiences, like a children's party not unlike those Dickens staged for his children, or a smoke-filled room at his own club, The Stafford, where the well-fed members doze contentedly through teatime. Again he used his familiar cut-out style for the figures, with clever details to exaggerate the characters of his subjects. But each drawing lacked a focal point; a narrative thread on which the diverse sequence of events staged within each individual drawing could be hung. As a result, Dick planned a new series which would concentrate upon three distinct individuals as they explored the social world of London. Thus his famous Brown, Jones and Robinson were born.

The trio – which would quickly become a national institution and household name – was cleverly devised from familiar characters in Dick's own life. Brown was the small, sensitive artistic young man with an endearing innocence not unlike Dick's own personality: he was clearly modelled after Dick himself. Jones was the tall, fiery-tempered yet compassionate character, who sheltered his friend Brown from unexpected upsets, although he usually dragged his friends into his own scrapes and dangerous trials, precipitated by his uncontrollable temper.

Although Jones was modelled after Dick's *Punch* colleague Tom Taylor, the journalist and future *Punch* editor, there must surely have been some characteristics he borrowed from his elder brother James – an equally tall and responsible figure who watched over Dick as the fictitious Jones did Brown. Robinson was the most endearing of the trio; a portly, check-trousered character with amusing wide shoulders and self-indulgent manners, who usually bore the brunt of some comic disaster or unfortunate accident. Dick found his inspiration for him in the young painter Watts Phillips, who had recently turned comic illustrator for *Punch*. Phillips was just a year Dick's junior, had once been a pupil of Cruikshank, and possessed a robust if at times rude manner which Dick first found objectionable. He called him "the portrait painter and coxcomb", but the more he studied this outspoken colleague, "on acquaintance I like him better", he told his brother; and by 1850 the two artists had "become thick".

The intrepid trio made their *Punch* debut in the 6 July 1850 issue, with a series of comic preparations for the Derby. Dick drew it like a cartoon strip spread across a full-page, extending the story into two weekly parts: first they ride on horseback to Epsom, their heavy Fortnum's hamper of food spilling onto the road behind them. They transfer to a coach, but Robinson is forced to sit on top with the hampers and promptly gets slapped in the face by a low tree branch and topples into a stream. The series in fact succeeded on such slap-stick humour. But as its readers began to know the trio, and to expect the inevitable disaster, they warmed to Doyle's subtle characterisations of each one. When the police chase Robinson off the racecourse ("Robinson will cross the course"), they sympathize with him and the ecstatic crowd, which jeers his capture. When the three lose their bets and Robinson despairs and wanders lost in the countryside, a sad silhouette in the moonlight, here too readers shared in his new predicament. In another sequence the three visit the zoo and attempt to ride the animals. Here Dick's talent for drawing animals – camels, elephants and lions – is tested when Jones attempts to ride a camel, seated between its two humps, and all three perch precariously upon an elephant's back. They marvel at the zoo's "hit of the season", the young hippopotamus with an angelic expression on its face which attracted

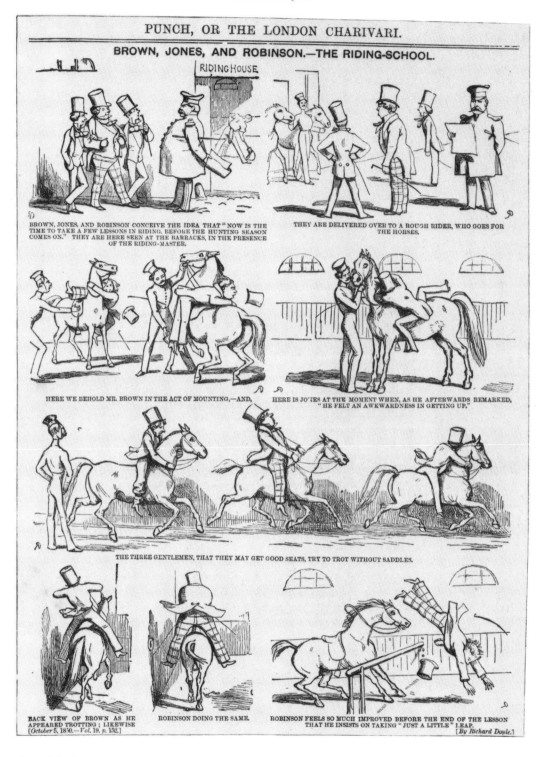

One of the first appearances of Brown, Jones and Robinson, Punch, *5 October 1850.*

tremendous crowds to the zoo that year.

But it was when the three attempt an onslaught on the London "Season", that the Doyle comic genius comes into its own. It was a subject on which Dick was becoming an expert, his invitations to society balls and "At Homes" having increased with his artistic reputation. And so when the trio receive their own invitations to a society ball, much of the frantic preparations – the dancing lessons to learn the latest steps (in this case the polka), the visit to the barber, and finally the disastrous evening full of *faux pas* and insults – echo Dick's own early experiences in polite society. They are announced at the ball and a young woman takes offense and strikes one whom she thought had insulted her ("Unfortunate event!"). This sets the tone for the series of disasters which follow: Jones falls in love with "a heavy dragoon's girl", who is spirited away by her lover, leaving him boiling with anger. "He hates the world from that moment, and ends up in a fight with his competition." This leads to a duel on Wimbledon Common, where Jones's opponent misfires his gun but Jones faints from fear. They are all "seized by the police", whom a terrified Brown had bribed a boy to fetch, and arrested by "the arm of the law".

In other sequences the trio combine comic exploits with a genuine wish to be accepted by polite society. Doyle's inventions are never crude, and always tied up with the social conventions familiar to his middle class audience. Their fears and fantasies about rising in Society are echoed in the antics of three easily recognizable and endearing characters. And as a result the Brown, Jones and Robinson series attracted an even greater audience than Manners and Customs. The public, according to contemporary critics and book reviewers, were tired "of lean jest and caricature"; they wanted realism and subtlety, without crude violence or unpleasant mishaps. Dick's inventions influenced a number of writers to try their own hand at imitating his winning formula, and the trio became national favourites. Indeed, within months of their first appearance, *The Woman's Companion* used them in the anonymous serial, "The Hunnybuns at the Seaside" (26 October 1850), in which a trio of tourists appear at Scarborough beach ridiculously dressed in hunting clothes, "the identical Brown, Jones and Robinson of *Punch*. There they were, all arrayed in shooting-jackets

and shot-belts, and armed with double-barrelled guns." More flagrant attempts to borrow Dick's characters surfaced in *The Cornhill*, then under Thackeray's editorship when George Robinson's "The Struggles of Brown, Jones and Robinson", a serial of the haberdashery business, was published in August 1861. By then the vogue for the three comic tourists had secured a place for Doyle among the most influential comic illustrators of the day, not only in Britain, but on the Continent and in America.

During the early days of the series, Dick decided a travelogue of his heroes' visit to the Continent might give him a chance to see and travel abroad, as well as subjects for future drawings in the series he planned as "The Pleasure Trips of Brown, Jones and Robinson". He joined with Tom Taylor and Watts Phillips early in 1850 and spent several months on a long and arduous journey from London to Belgium, Germany, Switzerland, Italy and back. The trip was used in just two *Punch* drawings, which eventually appeared in November of that year, but the sketches Dick collected throughout the journey were used in his enchanting illustrated journal, *The Foreign Tour of Messrs Brown, Jones and Robinson*. Being the History of What They Saw and Did in Belgium, Germany, Switzerland and Italy, published in 1854.

This book consisted of eighty comic illustrations and his own comic captions describing the antics and amusing observations of the trio. It was based upon Dick's own perceptive descriptions of the journey in letters he sent home to his sister. In fact the three month journey was one of the highlights of his life. Curiously, it was also the only time Dick left his native Britain, despite the overwhelming impression travel and studying his favourite art treasures and landscapes undoubtedly had on him. The journey was a variation on the long established Grand Tour, which took the three to Dover, across the channel to Bruges, Ghent, Bonn, down the Rhine, with a stop at Frankfurt, Baden and Basel. In Italy they clambered over the Alps on mules, explored the streets of Milan, Verona, and spent long hours in the galleries of Venice, before crossing to Trieste. They went north to Vienna for the opera, to Prague, and lastly returned up the Rhine and home again via Belgium.

"I was not sick in crossing the water, but probably would have been had the voyage been a couple of hours longer," Dick wrote home at the beginning of the journey, after crossing the channel. When they reached Ghent he had recovered enough to describe how "the place was alive with little soldiers, women with fruit-baskets on their arms, priests with broad-brimmed hats looking thin, long, amiable, black and with slender umbrellas under one arm and a book under the other". With his sketchbook as constant companion he searched for subjects, but was disappointed by the country: "The fields are as flat as chessboards and marked out in squares almost regularly... The landscape is varied by long avenues of poplars, as straight as regiments of soldiers, and forcibly reminding the spectator of pictures by Hobbema." When they reached the Prussian border "a long-bearded man poked his fierce head into the railway carriage window, and demanded passports in a language 'unknownst' to me, and in tone of voice not 'civil', perhaps because it was military". They approached Cologne in "an enormous omnibus, with trunks, portmanteaus, bags, piled upon the top to an enormous height". (Dick later drew this in his *Foreign Tour* with Brown, Jones and Robinson perched precariously among the bags, always fearful of toppling to the ground with a thud when they stopped. "The height of the Omnibuses is quite disgusting," Robinson was fond of saying, after he fell off the top at Basel.) The city of Cologne greatly impressed Dick, with its tall houses and shop-lined streets, courtyards for carriages and horses "which seemed to have gone to bed" when they arrived. "No pavement anywhere, rough stones everywhere, stunted sentinels with helmets and lances, and striped sentry boxes, and fortifications, and bad smells, and interesting antiquities, and churches, and peasantry, all the women have white handkerchiefs tied round their heads, and all the men smoking, these things all strike the eye," Dick wrote home to Annette.

Dick was especially moved by the atmosphere of reverence in foreign cathedrals. The "rather Byzantine in style" church at Coblenz had beckoned him with organ music which he heard through the mist and rain early one evening. "It looked very fine, black dark, except the altar candles and the white vestments of the priest, which shone through the gloom. Everyone seemed to join in the singing, and the solemn effect was greatly increased by the kneeling mass of people being scarcely perceptible in the dim religious light, while the deep tones of the organ, which

there was no indication of, seemed like the singing of the church walls," he told his pious sister. He carried on and entered another nearby church, "equally dark, and where about twenty people were praying, there being no service going on, and in the middle, a little infant scarcely of an age to be able to walk, toddled up the middle with a dog in her arms, which had a pretty and almost ludicrous effect amid the grandeur of the architecture and the darkness".[3]

Such was his personal view of the journey so far. But the version he published in the *Foreign Tour* was spiced with disasters, mishaps and those familiar opportunities for Brown, Jones and Robinson to show off the weakness in their characters. They become the archetypal British tourists, calm and demure until forced into outrage by bureaucracy or discomfort. Brown is, like Dick, prey to over-excitement; he had torn his room apart, stuffed all his clothes into a tiny bag, and at Ostend discovered "I've left the key to my bag at home!" Dick drew him "surrounded, a little bewildered, by the natives who overwhelm them with attentions" in the Ostend Customs Hall. Brown is a passionate observer, with his sketchbook always under his arm. He draws in all weathers, undeterred by pouring rain, tourists' curiosity or ridicule. We see him quickly recording the peculiar sights which flashed by his railway carriage window – a dog cart pulled by a poor muzzled animal, the crowds of pipe-smoking Germans he grew to admire. His companions share some of his passion for sight-seeing. When they reach Cologne they "do" the cathedral, guide-book in hand, stepping among the pious local worshippers to stare high into the vaulted ceiling. It remains one of the most enchanting drawings in the *Foreign Tour,* and echoed Dick's own excited reactions when he wrote to Annette, "The cathedral is certainly noble and when on Saturday morning we were greatly impressed with the wonderful grandeur of the whole business." But Cologne was a city of contrasts. Here, despite its fame as the source of eau de cologne, Dick discovered narrow streets filled with disgusting smells, and drew Brown, Jones and Robinson stumbling through the darkness with fingers pinched over their noses, surprised by "The Real Eau de Cologne".

Like Dick, Brown was fascinated by people, and the *Foreign Tour* is filled with sharp vignettes and perceptive comments on his fellow tourists.

There was "The Great Briton" he met on the steamer puffing down the Rhine through breathtaking scenery, a castle on each mountain. This provoked the man's need for domination: he told Dick how it "might be a good thing" to own one of these fairy-tale castles, although he wondered about the practicality of making it rise to English standards of domestic comfort. Or there was "the English grumbler", a thoroughly unpleasant creature, "big, burly and as if in danger of choking from the tightness of his cravat". Best of all was the archetypal bored English tourist, the "English Milord", who Dick drew safely protected from the crush of a railway station crowd in his carriage, with copies of *The Times* and *Quarterly Review* sheltering his view of the common German natives: "How happy he looks! He dislikes the hum of men."

Brown's sketching habit led to some unusual encounters and provided numerous opportunities for comic sketches. He refused to be deterred by the rain on board the Rhine steamer, even when a gust of wind blew his drawings away, and the

---

The Foreign Tour of Brown, Jones and Robinson:
a) "They 'Do' Cologne Cathedral".

THEY "DO" COLOGNE CATHEDRAL.

fog like "London November" and "Scotch" mist marred his view of the scenery. But there was always the chance of a brief glimpse at what Dick described to Annette as "wonderfully picturesque" views with "a perfect glut of ruins" on misty mountainsides. He was amused by the ubiquitous American tourists, one assuring him "This here Rhine ain't much by the side of our Mississippi". But then such displays of insular devotion were to be expected from a man who thought "Old Europe is 'tarnally chawed up".

Robinson continued to suffer from mishaps and unfortunate accidents which inflamed his self-centred opinions against anything "foreign". At Frankfurt he arrived in the pouring rain, soaked to the skin after his bag had burst open on the journey into the city. At the hotel he was appalled by the meagre sanitary facilities and threatened to write home to *The Times* about it. To quell his anger, Brown and Jones took him on a tour of the city's Jewish quarter. (This Dick described to his sister as "a wonderful sight, picturesque enough to put you in fits, and fall, at the windows, the doors, and on the rough stoned road, of the children of Israel, but to speak truth, not of a very malignant species, as to the proboscis and other Mosaic features, but rather gypsy-like, particularly the women, some being

---

b) "The Real Eau de Cologne", and its effects upon the noses of three illustrious individuals.

THE REAL EAU DE COLOGNE, AND ITS EFFECT UPON THE NOSES OF THREE ILLUSTRIOUS INDIVIDUALS.

HOW THEY VISITED A "QUARTER" OF THE CITY OF FRANKFORT, AND WHAT THEY SAW THERE!

Brown, Jones and Robinson in the Frankfurt Jewish Quarter.

---

very handsome". The resulting drawing was based on this unfortunate Jewish stereotype – which demanded long, hooked-nose faces hanging out of every window in the quarter – drawn from memory after his two hour walk through the district. Dick declared Frankfurt "the handsomest town I have yet seen on the Continent", and his drawings certainly suggest his delight at exploring the narrow streets. There too they met their dreaded fellow tourist, "The Bore", who always seemed to appear when they least expected him. He was the classic lonely tourist, who fastens himself to any unsuspecting person and unleashes large portions of his life story in a boring and time-consuming confession. The Bore is one of the most delightful running jokes in the *Foreign Tour.* Brown, Jones and Robinson successfully managed to avoid him in Frankfurt by hiding in a dark doorway as he passes, but in Heidelberg "suddenly, to our horror there appeared upon the Terrace The Bore!", and this time they were trapped and forced to listen to a long letter he had received from someone none of them knew. But there were elements of self-indulgence in Robinson as well. He was the one member of the trio who loved to souvenir hunt: he buys a huge German carved pipe "to encourage the native industry", and accepts his companions' dare to buy a large fur coat in Vienna, so he can wear it down Pall Mall when he returns home.

The intrepid trio are the objects of misunderstandings and hilarious incidents of mistaken identities. At Heidelberg the local paper reports their arrival in time for a military review as "Count Robinson, Sir Brown and the Reverand Jones", and they accept these impressive new positions, and the royal treatment they receive during the procession. Robinson, however, fails to live up to his title and disgraces himself by falling off his horse ("the disgusting brute"), in full view of the crowds: "Robinson at that moment desired that the earth might open and swallow him." At Baden they are forced to leave the city immediately after Jones is arrested for fighting with a cruel soldier who attacks a small dog. But when they reach the Alps tensions ease momentarily and Brown and Jones are left "spell-bound" by the scenery. Dick devotes a large section to views of the alpine scenery and lakes along the Swiss border, having written to his sister: "This is a sight! The Lake of Lucerne!! I am sitting in a bedroom writing, and looking out of the window alternatively at one of the most beautiful views that can be conceived. We are on the very edge of the lake, and are surrounded by mountains, the moon is shining on the water, picturesque towers and churches rise here and there, the celebrated Rei is over the way immediately, and an awful mountain of singularly wild and rugged appearance – Mount Pilata, where Pontius Pilate is said to have drowned himself in a lake at the summit – rises on the right-hand side. The beauty of this whole business overwhelms me with feelings of joy and wonder, and I feel as if I must sit down here and defy Nature (or any other person) to bring or produce any landscape or view that could put the nose of this landscape or view out of joint. Hurra! I have not lived in vain."[4]

They take a steamer across the lake, and a terrifying coach ride down St Gothard, the coach racing to the bottom, almost out of control. Their guide, however, reassures them by travelling this way "they can better enjoy the grandeur of the scenery". Their sense of adventure and appetite for exploring the mountains whetted, they agree to ride mules along a precarious pass toward the Italian lakes. Dick drew the scene which seemed to typify the gullibility of his three heroes, each one stretched across the backs of sturdy yet woefully small mules, Brown clutching his large sketch pad under his arm, Jones' long legs extended out over the rocky precipice, and Robinson squarely perched on the back of his mule, while their guide walks safely behind them. To add to the comedy which Dick labelled "Pleasant", the three stare in disbelief at the fat man and shocked woman who approach them from the

opposite direction on the narrow, single-track road. The inevitable disaster occurs, and the following drawing shows Robinson tumbling head over heels down the mountain, his companions rushing down the slope to help him.

But the ordeal was well worth the effort, for Brown and Jones at least declared the magnificent Italian lakes beyond their expectations; they had "fully realised all their imaginings of Italy". Robinson was equally enthusiastic until he noticed a small lizard crawling up a stone wall, and "from that moment he was more subdued". The three climb above the lakes so that Brown can sketch in various lights, and he draws Lake Maggiore in the dusky sunlight, while Robinson goes off exploring on his own. He discovers "no end" of grapes growing along the roadside, and decides they must be picked, taking as many as he can carry back to the hotel. There young Brown falls in love with the romantic, dark-haired chambermaid, which if the young woman really existed, certainly echoed Dick's own preference for dark-haired and wide-eyed classical beauty – an Italian version of Jenny Lind. In fact he drew her in a sequence of frustrated love scenes which the unfortunate Brown suffers like a true gentleman: "Oh! Marie of the Lago d'Orta, Maid of the Inn, and most beautiful of waitresses, how well do I remember thee! How graceful were all thy movements; what natural ease, together with what a dignified reserve; – how a lady were't thou: " When he sees Marie bullied by "that wicked old landlady", who shakes her fist and scolds his love, Brown is sent into fits of uncharacteristic anger: "Brown was not naturally of a savage temperament, but at that moment he felt that he could have – but it is best not to say what he could have done – it was too terrible for publication in these pages."

Italy was the land of art and artists, which Dick had longed to visit for its galleries and museums, its medieval cities and churches – the seat, after all, of his family's religion, although he curiously did not visit Rome. He avidly explored the famous cathedrals, horrified by the irreverent English tourists in Milan Cathedral, who carved their initials in its roof ("Enlightening behaviour in a foreign church"). In Verona he walked the streets of Romeo and Juliet, then climbed into the hills outside the city to sketch the view. There the soldiers watched him suspiciously and inspired Dick's comic sequence in which Brown is arrested for sketching military installations ("They think he is taking the fortifications"), and has his camp stool confiscated as "a political weapon". Jones threatens violence by this new outrage, and the three are arrested, only to be released by Brown's "distant near relation" Field Marshall Lieutenant Count Brown, who sends them safely on their way to Venice.

In Venice Brown devotes all his time to sketching in the galleries like the Accademia, and the churches. He spends a tortured night fighting Venetian mosquitoes with his pillow ("Madness"), turning his room into a shambles

which left him with barely enough energy to return to the galleries in the morning. He hoped to have a quiet day sketching his beloved "John Bellino" in the Accademia: "It is difficult to say which is the greatest pleasure... copying these splendid pictures, or painting from nature, those beautiful blue skies and crumbling palaces outside." But his solitude is soon interrupted by an English tourist and his family, a true philistine who peers over his shoulder and asks, "Very good – V-E-R-Y good... Now, I wonder what one could make a year by that kind of thing." His children crawl over Brown's sketches, and argue over which one their father should buy for them: Brown promptly settles the argument in a biblical fashion, and tears the precious sketch

A 'delightful' ride to the Italian Lakes.

PLEASANT!

into two pieces to settle this annoying interruption.

The trio eventually turn back, travel north to Prague and Vienna. There they are horrified by the audience at the Viennese opera they had longed to visit, where the Viennese yawn and slouch inattentively in their seats, seemingly bored with the privilege of hearing some of the best opera in the world. This made the three English members of the audience proud to be members of a country where audiences knew how to behave at the opera. Surging with pride, they returned home through Cologne, Belgium, reaching "Old England" with a sigh of relief – especially since the Channel crossing this time was decidely rough. Dick drew Brown and Jones on deck as two pale, fragile figures; beneath them he attached the label "Sic(k) Transit". But the *Foreign Tour* ended with a jubilant toast among the unpacked bags at Brown's home: "Gloria Mundi!"

The *Foreign Tour* appeared in 1854, almost four years after the journey had been made. Dick had worked hard on its witty captions and drawings taken from his travel sketches and letters sent home to his family. The large volume, bound to look like an artist's portfolio with wide margins around the one hundred and seventy-four drawings was arranged like an elaborate scrap book or album account of their destinations. Its publication brought enthusiastic reviews and secured his position as a major comic artist. The *Art Journal* (1 April 1854) suggested, in a long and gratifying review: "Mr Doyle is the Rowlandson of our Time, equally skilful as an artist, and with far more refinement in his delineation of character; in his hands wit and satire do not degenerate into coarseness and vulgarity; the most sensitive and delicate mind may turn over his pages in this portfolio in the full assurance that nothing unseemly will be

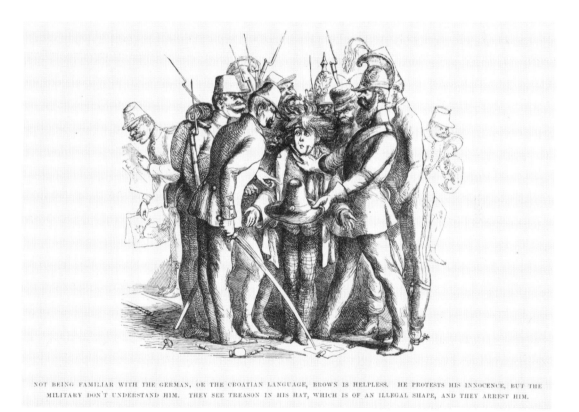

NOT BEING FAMILIAR WITH THE GERMAN, OR THE CROATIAN LANGUAGE, BROWN IS HELPLESS. HE PROTESTS HIS INNOCENCE, BUT THE MILITARY DON'T UNDERSTAND HIM. THEY SEE TREASON IN HIS HAT, WHICH IS OF AN ILLEGAL SHAPE, AND THEY ARREST HIM.

The arrest of Brown near Verona: "He protests his innocence, but the military don't understand him. They see treason, in his hat, which is of an illegal shape, and they arrest him."

MISERY.

NOTE.—If the Musquitoes appear rather large in this and the following scenes, let it be remembered that in the "heroic" it was a principle of many of the great painters to exaggerate the "parts."

Brown's miserable mosquito-filled night in Venice.

found therein." Dick's characterizations were praised for their restraint and good taste; "neither travellers nor people are vulgarized; they are treated humorously and satirically". Brown, Jones and Robinson earned the epithet "the glorious triad": they were well-cast and thoroughly recognizable tourists of the type that "behave themselves before folks" and are a credit to their mother country: "... in short if not gentlemen in the proper acceptance of the term, still less are they to be classed among those to whom that title somewhat abbreviated is generally applied. We could laugh, were we fellow travellers together, but are satisfied they would never annoy us by their officious impertinence, by unwelcome familiarity, nor by rudeness to the people among them whom they may happen to sojourn for a time." The reviewer found "so much of true and real character in these sketches", that the book was recommended to "any continental tourist" as well as "for any day, and for any time of the day; one to increase the laughter of the merry, and to arouse the desponding into an hour or two of cheerfulness".

When William Michael Rossetti, brother of the painter Dante Gabriel, reviewed Brown, Jones and Robinson in *The Spectator,* he praised the book as "the most humorous and amusing" of the Christmas season. He admired Doyle's "exhaustless fertility" and childish invention: "His fancy and his pencil enjoy perpetual adolescence. His powers are always ready, and depend upon themselves entirely, needing no extrinsic aid for dull development." He was also the first to delineate the three distinct personalities of Dick's glorious triad in an attempt to ask why they received such enthusiastic support: "Brown is a good-looking likeable kind of little fellow, of artistic propensities and enthusiasm; Jones, a lanky maypole, the most thoroughly English of the three in character, with a taste for decorum, and yet for free-and-easiness, and with a spice of pugnacity in his nature; Robinson, verging towards middle-age, is the most comfort-loving, vain and pliable." Indeed, these three indomitable travellers became the archetypal British tourists to American readers of the book, where it was pirated in numerous editions "with nearly 200 most thrilling comic engravings" throughout the 1870s. It was parodied as *The American Tour of Messrs Brown, Jones and*

Robinson, by Toby, as an account of their exploits in America, Canada and Cuba. For over twenty years the three delighted British and American readers, and as late as the 1880s an anonymous English parody of their travels to Biarritz and the Pyrennes proved that the British public continued to love the comic antics of their "glorious triad". Even the novelist Anthony Trollope attempted a rather heavy-handed and ultimately unsuccessful version as "The Struggles of Brown, Jones and Robinson", which was rejected by several publishers before it appeared as a serial in *The Cornhill* in 1861.

* * * * * * * * * * * *

When the real Brown, Jones and Robinson returned from the continent, they were warmly greeted by their friends. Dick was sent a cheerful letter from Dickens, who playfully suggested he had been away too long: "My dear Doyle, Welcome to your native land! You will find us all a good deal changed since you went away on that long voyage. I am very rheumatic and Leech (you recollect him?) uses a tin trumpet, but we are still good for a bowl of broth, or a social glass of punch." At first Dick tried to plunge back into his *Punch* work, but he noticed his family had grown more unsettled during his absence. His brothers now struggled to find their footing as artists: James was constantly away in search of painting commissions, while Henry had befriended Dr Wiseman and joined him as a houseguest in numerous Catholic country houses for extended stays and promises of portrait commissions by their wealthy owners. Dick worked hard on his drawings adopted from the journey and eventually produced two full-page comic versions of Brown, Jones and Robinson "Up the Rhine" for the November *Punch.* He also struggled on weekly comic initials, and to his dismay was told to illustrate a new *Punch Extra Number,* "called Punch's Holidays, a sort of midsummer almanack, only it concerns nothing but places of amusement about London," he explained in a weary letter to Charles. But by far his greatest worry now was his father.

The last Political Sketch of HB appeared at this time, and John Doyle was clearly resigned to his forced early retirement. He invited his friends, like Thomas Cubbitt, to visit his studio "to look over the trifles which I have to show you", in the hopes of selling some work.[5] He was worried about the growing debts he had incurred to support his family, and while his sons were away in search of painting commissions, he preferred to remain home with his daughter, to wait for news. In the end only Dick found regular employment, with his *Punch* position, until many years later, when Henry became a museum director. As a result it is safe to assume that Dick alone helped to support his family during his period on *Punch.* His father refused to accept a lowering standard in the home, despite his loss of income, and it was only with great reluctance he accepted the decision to allow Annette the running of the house when there was no longer enough money to pay a servant. John Doyle slowly became a recluse, taking only the occasional horseback ride in Hyde Park, visits to the galleries with his sons, or staying for brief periods with his prosperous and influential Catholic friends. He turned further inward for comfort, to his religion and his obsessive desire to maintain his family's ancestral ties to the Catholic Church. He insisted all his children must continue to attend mass, and none of them failed him, remaining devout Catholics all their lives. Moreover, they remained devoted to their father for the most of their adult lives, only leaving the family home for brief periods, and these generally in search of some new painting commission or valuable patron.

Despite his retirement it is not difficult to see why John Doyle still commanded and received respect from his children. He was a dignified and handsome man, "recognized by his tall, graceful figure, and by a noble cast of features. The prestige of his repute ever insured a welcome, which he was sure to justify. His intelligence commanded every prominent topic of the day, and his manner, whether grave or gay, was unfailingly pre-possessing. An innate amiability of the most winning kind was united in him with an unaffected self-respect, on which no levity could trespass," explained one friend. "He was one whom to know, even but a little, was insensibly to esteem; to know much, to love much. In a word, he was from the hands of nature a rare gentleman."[6] Moreover, he refused to be beaten by circumstances. It had been seven years since he first wrote to the Prime Minister to apply for a government post, and now, in June 1850, he tried again. He wrote a thirty-two page "direct appeal to your lordship", the new Prime Minister, Lord John Russell, in which he outlined his views on London's parks and why he preferred the new National Gallery in Trafalgar Square not Kensington Gardens. He concluded why he thought private patronage of the arts must never be ignored : "No longer is the patronage of art confined to the aristocracy: a new collector had appeared, in the wealthy trader and manufacturer; and for the first time, perhaps, in the history of art, it has been discovered that the purchase of modern pictures – especially by commission to the artist – is 'a good investment' –" He was speaking from his own, and more recently his sons' experience here. But in the end the post for which he applied failed to be awarded to him, and it was to be another four years before he tried his luck with the government yet again.[7]

Another worrying member of the family was Dick's youngest brother Charles, who in time would become the most troubled. Born when his mother was herself ill, young Charles grew up prey to emotional disturbances, a deep melancholia and, despite his considerable talent as an imaginative artist, with a sense of inferiority, always under the shadow of his older artist brothers – not to forget the domineering presence of his father. In 1849, at the age of seventeen, he was, for some unknown reason, sent off to Edinburgh, exiled from the family he loved to seek his fortune. He grudgingly accepted the move and started work as an assistant to the surveyor in the Scottish Office of Works, a position of some responsibility which allowed him to use his considerable skills as a meticulous draughtsman to copy and later help design various public monuments in the city. He was in fact the second of three assistants to Robert Matheson, the Chief Surveyor for Scotland, whose work included designs for Holyrood Palace fountain, a commission Matheson regarded "more in the class of a work of Art than ordinary building work", but which Charles dismissed, hating the palace design itself which reminded him more of a prison or a madhouse than a royal palace.

Originally Charles had accepted the post because he believed it would allow him enough spare time to pursue his real interest, drawing and painting. But the job proved a tedious disappointment which taxed his patience and left him in little mental state to pursue his drawing. Those designs he produced for Matheson were presented in the end under his superior's

signature; thus the hours of patient work he hoped would gain him some recognition were always hopelessly forgotten. For this self-sacrifice Charles was paid £220 a year, which never rose above £250, despite his twenty-seven years of service in the department. As a result, Charles grew melancholic; he worried his family, and longed for news of them. He especially depended upon Dick's letters, for since childhood they had shared a common bond, drawing and inventing exclusively from their vivid imaginations. In fact Dick soon became the most important influence in Charles's struggles to become a part-time illustrator, as well as a mental solace during periods of depression. His fairly regular flow of letters to Charles, his "old fellow", were intended to cheer him up, to poke fun at his exile in "The Land of Lakes". He loved to maintain the age-old pretence that the Scots were savages, descendants from Sawney Bean who still ate cannibal meat in caves, and he often asked, "How do you fare among the Sawneys?" Although unintentional, his tone was sometimes condescending, as he generally wrote his letters from his club, often pausing in between some new social conquest, brilliant literary evening, or on the way to the Houses of Parliament, where he watched the progress of the debates and made valuable contacts with politician friends in the Commons as well as House of Lords. His letters are filled with impressive names, guest lists of parties or country house weekends where he now spent a great deal of time. To Charles, who was never socially gregarious, such reports must have only fanned the flames of his depressions and homesickness.

From the moment he arrived in Edinburgh, Charles had found adjusting to the city and people almost impossible. He wrote longing letters home to his family – a habit which continued over the next twenty years. His only solace was wandering in the old part of the city with its famous hill-top castle "a sort of paradise to lovers of the picturesque if they had no noses". True to his upbringing, he embarked upon a series of social calls on the prominent Catholic families, but this was a short-lived experience since he found the curious Scottish sense of humour and character of the people alien to his more romanticised view of the country, with his boyhood love of Walter Scott's land-of-heather adventures quickly fading. He hated the drunks, the New Years' Eve revellers, and failed to understand the local humour: later from his asylum room he would write, "I believe I am branded Mad solely from the narrow Scotch misconception of jokes." The only consolation came after six months, when he met his landlady's daughter, Mary Foley, a good high-spirited Irish Catholic whom he married in 1855.

Dick viewed his brother's despondent letters and obvious unhappiness with growing concern. Always optimistic, he encouraged and praised Charles' achievements, like the time he discovered his brother had played a vital role in welcoming the Queen to Edinburgh. It was towards the end of his first year in the city, when he was given the honour of hoisting the flag on the palace to announce the Queen's arrival, after having made preparations for her comfort

---

Charles Doyle's architectural fantasies.
Ink and watercolour drawings from a sketchbook,
7 x 9⅞"
Huntington Art Gallery.

in the royal apartment. Dick wrote how delighted he was to hear the news, although the London papers failed to mention his brother in their long accounts of the preparations: "WHO!! it was *who* superintended, *who* assisted in the arrangement of, *who* watched over, *who* devoted his time, his taste, his talents, and his labours, to that apartment!! *But I know.*" He tried to imagine his brother "showing her (HM) to her chamber, walking backwards with a wax candle in either hand... enthusiastic shouts of an overjoyed, an excitable, a loyal, but at the same time a 'canny' People. 'God save the Queen' Hurra!"[8]

More important, Dick offered valuable advice to steer his brother carefully away from the pitfalls of an artist's life, and tried to boost his brother's confidence. When Charles thought he might enter the competition for stained glass window designs in Glasgow Cathedral, Dick wrote in September 1849: "My advice, after turning the business over in my mind, is, go in and win, make play with your 'left' with a pen in it, while with your 'right', with a pencil in it, 'you pitch into 'em unmercifully'. Knock their blue

bonnets over their eyes and take titty bits of fur off their Highland noodles." Charles eventually entered, but sent home his designs first for his family's approval, his father being "especially delighted" with his progress. When Charles began toying with the idea of illustrations for magazines and books, again Dick offered valuable professional advice: " 'Keeps up your spirits' is my advice – and above all while the summer lasts give all your spare time in the mornings and evenings to drawings, for I am certain you can make money in that way. I think you will be an artist yet, but of course it would not be wise to give up the office. The 'thing' is to carry on both. Try your hand at one or two popular subjects from Scott's novels, or Scotch ballads, and send to next year's Edinburgh exhibition. I am certain you have it in you to succeed."

Dick's comic view of a Scottish Highlander.

Sadly, although Charles took his brother's advice, and produced several striking magazine and book illustration commissions, as well as numerous watercolours, all were tinged with his inner struggles to escape into a fantasy world of his own. While the real world – which in time would include a wife and ten children to support – continued to torment him.

* * * * * * * * * * * *

Apart from his family worries, Dick's own career began to turn sour; and his lackadaisical manner and high-minded principles eventually brought him to crisis point. Shortly before his continental trip he had agreed to produce a series of book illustrations for the Dalziel brothers, for a new series of nursery tales which the wood engravers were initiating to sell to publishers for distribution. Dick had already provided them with *The Story of Jack and the Giants,* the first in the series which appeared in 1850. He agreed to the second title, *Sleeping Beauty,* and took its preliminary drawings with him on the continent, presumeably to sketch in fairy-tale castles and alpine landscapes for backgrounds. The Dalziels planned an Easter 1850 publication for *Sleeping Beauty,* but since Dick prolonged his journey and did not return home until April, the Dalziels grew worried. Moreover, he returned home with some of the book's drawings badly smudged and damaged, while others were totally ruined. He promised to "doctor" them and redraw the final plates "in time to be out for Easter", but failed to honour his promise. Despite a plea for more money, "half the sum agreed upon for the illustrations (30 pounds)", which the Dalziels agreed to provide, the drawings were left unfinished and it was not until fifteen years later that the book was published by Routledge as *An Old Fairy Tale Told Anew* in 1865.[9]

Part of the difficulty lay with Mr Punch. In 1850 alone he demanded Doyle drawings which totalled some one hundred and seventy-seven small comic fillers and initial letters, twenty-two full-page political cartoons, the *Punch Extra Holiday Number,* as well as twelve annual almanack borders. He had in fact become somewhat disillusioned by the devious and seemingly ungentlemanly ways of Mr Punch and his publishers. The *Punch* office archives contain several letters of Dick's, asking for advances or payment for work. This unpleasant task upset Doyle, who maintained a rather naïve view of publishers throughout his free-lance career. He was especially offended when his Manners and Customs series was re-issued in book form, for which he was paid "a small sum" but no subsequent royalties. Then a compilation volume of his *Punch* drawings was planned, after he was "urged that it would be a source of profit to myself"; but again no mention was made of royalty terms. Finally Dick put his foot down and wrote to his publisher F.M.(Pater) Evans: "I cannot allow that you have a right as a publisher to make any use you please, when and how you please, of drawings done by me for a specific purpose – namely Punch. If it is not a question of right it is one of common fairness it seems to me – and that I think constitutes some claim."[10]

Furthermore Dick began to feel uneasy about the paper's religious stance. Since the late 1840s its cartoons and articles concerning the so-called "papal aggression" had increased in number, their firm stand on the Protestant side of the issue offending Dick's belief in neutrality, or at least equal treatment for both sides of this heated issue. The *Punch* articles especially upset his father's personal crusade to preserve the sanctity of the Catholic religion within his family, while pressure mounted at home and among influential Catholic friends for Dick's association with *Punch* to come to an end. By 1850 the *Punch* stance became intolerable, its cartoons of papal fashions, tasteless attacks on the Catholic Church with the Pope a favourite target, deeply upset all the Doyle family. And so on the 27 November 1850 Dick submitted his resignation from *Punch,* and despite pleas from his colleagues and friends, he refused to reconsider his position.

The subject of Dick's *Punch* resignation is crucial to his life and later career. It marked the end of a fairly brief period of untroubled popularity and promise as a comic illustrator. The work he created during his *Punch* association, most of it firmly based in his childhood style, was for many critics the finest he would ever produce. Thereafter his struggles and sporadic free-lance book illustrations and later fairy paintings for the galleries only varied those early successes; while his search for a new and saleable style never really ended.

The religious basis of his decision to leave *Punch* has been over-emphasized, however. Unlike his father and brothers, and especially his pious sister Annette, Dick found it best to keep his Catholic beliefs modestly in the background. It was more a tactical move, which allowed him to include major figures in the Protestant Church among his friends. And yet to those who knew him, Dick displayed an unshakeable faith in the Catholic Church and its doctrines. A friend once asked him, "Why are you a Catholic?" to which Dick replied, "Because I possess but little religion, so that what I have must be of the very best possible quality". He had grown up to believe that his religion was

closely linked with principles of medieval chivalry, at a time when that chivalric classic Digby's *The Broad Stone of Honour* had been revised to encompass the author's own conversion to the Catholic Church. He attended weekly mass with fellow members of the expatriot Irish community, and from early childhood had been taught to suffer the unpopularity of his religion: in one of his journal entries he recalled his disgust at a November 5 guy dressed as the Pope on a donkey ("The sarcasm here conveyed was so biting that I quitted the ground instantly"). Although devout, young Dick experienced some doubts about his religion, like the time he and his brothers were stopped by "an inspired divine" on their way to the Guildhall. This fearful religious fanatic would always fascinate Dick, who recalled how he "dashed his hat upon the pavement and taking a little volume from his pocket began to preach with a most awful severity of countenance". But fascination turned to fear when the man turned against them, attacked their affluence as members of "the wicked rich, who robbed the poor and did all sorts of things 'also' ".[11] More to the point, Dick was taken to Exeter Hall to hear the foot-stomping diatribes of "a Christian man denouncing the Pope", which he recently drew into his Manners and Customs series. It remains one of his most startling drawings, presumeably drawn from his memory of a crowd of stern-faced matrons listening to the ranting, arm-waving speaker denounce the evil Catholic infiltration of the country in a flurry of flying coat-tails and waved fists, while a rather worried chairman sits in quiet toleration of the proceedings. Indeed it was this drawing which Dick's *Punch* colleagues cited as an example of *Punch* allowing an alternative point of view – here a ridicule of Protestant fanatics – in its pages; but Dick refused to concede the point.

Such violent displays of emotion were against the "papal aggression" – the decision by Pope Pius IX to create an archbishopric and twelve bishops in England for the first time since Henry VIII's Act of Supremacy. Both public and the press greeted this as a provocative act of aggression by a foreign power. Tempers flared and street processions led to violence, with scores of broken windows and looted Catholic churches as well as bitter attacks by the press in comic books and cartoons on the "No Popery" theme. Moreover, the Pope chose Henry's close friend

MANNERS · AND · CVSTOMS · OF · yͤ · ENGLYSHE · IN · 1849 · No 10.

A PROSPECT · OF · EXETER · HALL · SHOWYNGE · A CHRISTIAN · GENTLEMAN · DENOVNCYNGE · yͤ POPE ·

Doyle's satiric look at Protestants "denouncing the Pope".

Nicholas Wiseman, to head the Catholic Church in England, and many believed this was at the core of Dick's resignation. Dr Wiseman was a much respected Irish Catholic and firm personal friend of the Doyle family; a figure Dick admired for "his social qualities, his bon-homie, as well as his piety, learning, and literary reputation" which "caused him to be liked amongst all parties, as well as his own".[12]

The public outcry was firmly acknowledged in the *Punch* cartoons and articles written especially by the fiery-tongued Douglas Jerrold. John Leech consented to cartoons on the papist theme, and drew the Pope in numerous clown-like disguises; as a saboteur "Preparing to Blow Up England", and breaking into Westminster Abbey. The public feeling took numerous forms,

from embittered religious cartoons to a page of "Fashions for 1850", drawn like a fashion plate of cowls, mitres and habits. But the cartoon which most deeply affected Dick and caused his resignation, was "The Puseyite Moth and Roman Candle." – "Fly away *Silly* Moth", which accompanied the deeply offensive article by Douglas Jerrold in 16 November 1850. Jerrold suggested the Pope should be tried for treason for his aggression on the country, while his followers "shall be better fed with the old Vatican wafers". He conceded the Pope and his band of sheep-like followers should be spared the ultimate penalty of High Treason, and mercifully banished "to the antipodes rather than be publically hanged".

For Dick this cartoon proved the last straw, and eleven days after it appeared he resigned from *Punch*. His reasons were clear to him, although his colleagues were confused. When they pointed out his Manners and Customs cartoon of Exeter Hall he admitted he had been guilty of attacking Protestants, just as *Punch* now seemed to attack Catholics. But this was not enough. When Thackeray, Mark Lemon and even the offending Douglas Jerrold argued for his return to *Punch,* Dick refused to reconsider. *Punch* was "The Republic", as he termed it, and the principles of equality he had once enjoyed on the paper he felt had been seriously eroded. "I don't mind, as long as you keep to the political and personal side of the matter," he argued, "but *doctrines* you must not attack." When they argued that Catholic members of *The Times* had not resigned over its recent violent articles attacking the papal aggression, Dick explained, "That is very well for *The Times,* but not in *Punch.* For *The Times* is a Monarchy, whereas *Punch* is a Republic."

It was a mark of his reputation as an artist that the press gave generous coverage to his resignation. By December, within a month of his announcement, newspaper editorials declared their positions and thrust Dick into the niche of national hero – or foolish young man with misplaced allegiances. The *Daily Telegraph* took the former view: "He made a wise and prudent choice. The loss was ours, not his; and apart from the claims of his genius to admiration, such conduct at the critical moment of a career will never cease to command respect... It is deeply regretted, that the deplorable spirit of sectarian hostility should have driven such a man from the proper arena of his worth and fame." Later the Catholic magazine *The Month* explained why his was such an admirable position: "At least he could show that Catholic belief was no empty superstition, no set of mere traditional observances, which sat lightly on the man of culture, even if in his heart he accepted them at all." On the other hand, critics attacked his resignation as a futile and ultimately disastrous decision. "English fanaticism and English prejudice persisted in regarding him as a supporter of the 'papal aggression' and he permanently lost from that moment the ground which his talent and his reputation had so honourably won for him."[13] There was a rumour, started by the publisher John Murray, that Dick was under threat of excommunication unless he resigned, and although this was untrue, it points out the strength of public feeling which surrounded Dick at this time. Even the Catholic papers upset him, if only because they misrepresented his case to his

friends. "My attention has today been called to a paragraph in the 'Tablet' newspaper, published in Dublin, concerning my separation from Punch," Doyle wrote to "Mr dear Lemon", his former employer Mark Lemon, "and as there is more than one mis-statement in it I hasten to let you know that it was done altogether without my sanction or knowledge and has given me great annoyance." He urged his old *Punch* editor to be understanding: "You must acquit me of *all* connections directly or indirectly with any gossip that may appear". And he promised to "drop a line to the 'Tablet' to set him right in the matter".[14]

Despite Dick's efforts, sadly it did not take long for Mr Punch to turn nasty as well. Perhaps from pique or strain of over-work, Dick had neglected his annual *Punch* almanack drawings the year he resigned, and when Mark Lemon discovered this, he and some of his staff turned against him. It was probably inexcuseable, for Doyle had left Lemon in a terrible dilemma, with the drawings long over-due. Eventually this was solved by turning over the almanack designs to John Tenniel, who quickly took over Dick's *Punch* cartoonist position. But the damage had been done. As the *Punch* historian, M.H.Spielmann explained, "But for once in his career Doyle was guilty of behaviour which, if not excusable in the circumstances, was certainly indefensible. He left the paper in the lurch."[15] And while Mark Lemon continued to use old stocks of Doyle drawings for several years, he agreed to publish the following veiled yet bitter attack on Dick's folly, under the title "Very Ridiculous" (4 January 1851):

"We frequently hear of men gaining the confidence, and the hearts, and the money, of unsuspecting people from the cleverness with which they carry out 'a false front of hypocrisy'. Now this has always appeared to us most supremely ridiculous, for we never could understand the possibility of any one gaining the slightest credit, from the fact of his wearing a *Dickey* – which we take to be the 'false front' alluded to – and which, though strongly marked with 'hypocrisy', is more likely, we should imagine, to excite suspicion than confidence, or at all events, not sufficient to induce you to press the man who wears it to your bosom. There are many mysteries in society, and this 'false front' is one of them!"

To counter such attacks, Dick received numerous letters of support from his Catholic friends, as well as messages "of regret and sympathy, of congratulation" from Catholics as well as Protestants. His close friend Thackeray was shaken by his decision, and anxiously watched over Dick's future to make sure he had enough illustration work and continued to enjoy his social life. In fact Thackeray also resigned from *Punch* some four years later, upset by the paper's continued attacks on the royal family. And while he was not a Catholic himself, once noting "It is hard even to sympathize with persons who receive them as genuine", and he disliked Cardinal Wiseman ("a tawdry Italian quack"), whom he thought "as great a hypocrite as ever lived", Thackeray respected Dick's decision. As he later wrote, *Punch* had lost "the valuable services, the graceful pencil, the harmless wit, the charming fancy of Mr Doyle".[16] And during the following difficult months, when Dick tried to find his footing as a free-lance illustrator, Thackeray was always there to offer needed relief: "Let us meet as much as we possibly can in this world, mon ami, and as for the next who knows," he pleaded in one invitation to dinner, tactfully neglecting to mention his guests included prominent Protestants and Catholics.[17]

The greatest sacrifice in resigning from *Punch* was the loss of his annual salary on which to support his family. His wealthy friends quickly offered assistance to help put him on his feet financially, and Dick was overwhelmed by their generosity. Lord and Lady Ashburton, for example, were admirers of Doyle's gentle wit and brought some of his later paintings. Lord Ashburton in fact proposed a generous business arrangement at this time. Dick proudly explained this to Charles, how he "so kindly put a 100 pounds at my disposal at his banker's on condition that at my leisure I do something for him! the original of something that I 'may be publishing' as he puts it". Others offered moral support, like Lord Maidstone, who attacked *Punch* for giving up its prize artist by writing in the *Morning Herald,* "Where's Doyle, your great adjunct – And Thackeray – defunct!" And yet Dick remained steadfast to his position and carefully weighed up each new offer of employment. He refused to illustrate for a new weekly magazine because he did not agree with the paper's principles, "or want of them". He refused Disraeli's offer of work

drawing for a new political journal ("at the rate of 800 'puns' a year"). Instead he carefully watched the press attacks on his fellow Catholics, was outraged by the Duke of Norfolk's Protestant sympathies ("the disreputable old curly-wigged old 'wagabone' "), and finished off his obligations to the Dalziel brothers.

At this time these prominent wood engravers were a welcomed source of work and confidence in his comic abilities. They had long championed the Doyle style, securing work for him on almanacks for the *Illustrated London News* in 1847, and insisting that Dick "stood out" until the paper paid the proper amount for his drawings. And now, despite the *Sleeping Beauty* fiasco, they agreed to provide him with new work. When a paper asked for illustrations they got as far as sending Dick the blocks before he changed his mind: "Circumstances to which it is unnecessary here to enter, have induced me to withdraw altogether from the new paper... I hope however to furnish you with plenty of 'work' of other kinds, if you can undertake it during the next few months."[18] And in the end, the Dalziels remained devoted to Doyle; they quoted his infuriating letters filled with excuses for not meeting deadlines yet affectionately wrote of him in their autobiography.

By the end of 1850, the Dalziels finished engraving Dick's *The Story of Jack and the Giants.* Fortunately the correspondence between Dick and his engravers survives to give some indication of his working methods at this time. For example, he began the project with an agreement between Edward Dalziel, "My dear sir", and himself for a series of drawings illustrating "Jack's History", for which he was to receive £60. He sent the first drawing, "which has occupied me almost all the week and you will see that there is plenty of work in it". It was based upon the lines, "He delighted in reading stories about Wizards, Giants and Fairies and listened eagerly whenever anybody related the brave deeds of the knights of the round table." His drawings were intricate pen sketches which he transferred in pencil onto the wood blocks for the Dalziels to cut around with their gravers. "I have never yet had that 'etching' style of drawing engraved perfectly to my satisfaction," he warned them. "Perhaps that is impossible but at all events there is plenty of time. I shall expect in this case a *chef d'oeuvre* of wood-engraving as I certainly have expended more than ordinary

Doyle's brutal giant murder for his Dalziel commission The Story of Jack and the Giants, *1850.*

care in the drawing." There was some uncertainty at first about the exact number of illustrations required; Dick preferred to leave the decision to him and promised "as many as you can give me time to do". Eventually he provided twenty-seven small drawings and seven large plates, drawn in a dense "etched" line style, and skilfully engraved by the Dalziels. But work was interrupted by his trip to the continent, followed by a demand for half his payment of £30 (despite less than half the drawings completed), and eventually news of the Sleeping Beauty disaster on his return. It was then that the Dalziels decided to stop further work on Jack, and publish what Dick had so far produced, fearing the book might go the way of its planned sequel. They suggested just £40 total payment, instead of the agreed £60, and Dick objected, eventually suggesting a compromise of £50 and a promise to have all the drawings "in your hands by Saturday night next". He even abandoned his concern over the engraving and

suggested "if you will send me a large block or two – each composed of three pieces of wood joined – it would facilitate the engraving as several engravers might be at work on one drawing at once."[20]

The book was published by Cundall & Addey in a plain and coloured version in time for the Christmas market. The Dalziels had done well with interpreting Dick's drawings into engraved line, although Dick had to wait some days after publication to see the results. "Are you aware that no copy of 'Jack' has yet been sent to me, although the Book has been out several days?" he wrote to Edward Dalziel, asking for "a few copies this evening".[21] Nevertheless reviews of the book were quite encouraging, especially at this difficult time in his career, with the *Punch* affair still simmering in the public's mind. *The Athenaeum* (28 December 1850) thought his choice of story, with gruesome scenes of giants slain by Jack, was "not the most wholesome food for youth", but the Doyle giants were "grand fellows of their class. The wonder of Jack's exploits certainly grows as we look at them. The 'Giant sitting on a huge Rock' is the very genius of gianthood." The *Art Journal* (1 March 1851) agreed: "Mr Doyle's pencil has been so frequently appreciated, that it needs little commendation from us to ensure its popularity." The book was "an admirable present for children, who cannot fail to imbibe a taste for correct drawing from the illustrations".

The Dalziels also engraved one of Doyle's most famous book commissions at this time: Dick's rustic style drawings of alpine scenery (borrowed from sketches made on his recent visit to Switzerland and Germany) to John Ruskin's fairy-tale, *The King of the Golden River*. The drawings alone are generally recognized as some of his best post-*Punch* work, especially his delightful frontispiece creation, the South-West Wind, Esq., knocking at the evil brothers' cottage door. Although the creature's nose was originally conceived as a trumpet, in subsequent editions Dick altered it to a cherry-like conventional nose. Nevertheless he retained the cape flowing in the breeze, the long plumes and tall hat of this delightfully gnarled, gnome-like creature, and he filled the book with other, delightful inventions. The story involved two evil brothers and the innocent third, Gluck, who lived in Treasure Valley and were forced by circumstances to become goldsmiths. They search

Original version of South-West Wind, Esquire, frontispiece to Ruskin's The King of the Golden River, *1850.*

Doyle's international homage to the Great Exhibition, from An Overland Journey to the Great Exhibition, *1851, (coloured edition).*
a) The Italians.

for gold nuggets in the mountains, and try in vain to turn the water of the Golden River into gold. Ruskin had written it as a moral fable for Effie Gray in 1841, and after ten years agreed to publication, although his reactions when the book apeared were mixed. The publishers, Smith & Elder, were anxious that the addition of Doyle's drawings would help sell the story by such a famous author; illustrations they claimed "embody the Author's ideas with characteristic spirit". It took seven wood engravers including the Dalziel brothers, to get Doyle's intricate line inventions right, and the book went into numerous editions and served as the standard school prize book throughout the 1890s. And yet by this time Ruskin had dismissed the story at least, writing in his autobiography it was "a fairly good imitation of Grimm and Dickens mixed with a little true Alpine feeling of my own... But it is totally valueless, for all that. I can no more write a story than compose a picture."[22] Nevertheless Dick's illustrations helped to boost his career; they were admired by his colleagues and in the case of young Edward Burne-Jones influenced his early attempts at fairy-tale illustration.

Meanwhile the Dalziel brothers were constantly looking for new commercial ventures to maintain their large workshop and keep their apprentices in work. With the approach of the Great Exhibition in the middle of 1851, they, like numerous artists, publishers and souvenir manufacturers, saw the potential for this lucrative new marketplace. Indeed, a plethora of commemorative volumes, comic booklets, china as well as printed memorabilia flooded the shops of the capital throughout the year. They marked what was billed as the greatest display

of ideas and national achievements in industry and the arts ever assembled. "The Great Exhibition of the Works of All Nations" was to include an international display of products as well, to carry out the greater theme of harmony, friendship and cooperation between Britain and the nations of the world.

It was this international theme which appealed to Dick when the Dalziels approached him for designs for their contribution to the event. He proposed a comic procession composed of foreign figures from each country bearing national emblems, dressed in native costumes, not unlike his early *Grand Historical Procession.* The Dalziels willingly agreed to the idea, and Dick dismissed other offers for similar projects, like a proposal from D.Bogue which he told the Dalziels, "if I see my way in anything about the realities of the exhibition, I feel bound to do it for you".[23] He began with eight groups of figures drawn in his early processional style, but work went slowly and the all important deadline, which would insure the book could be sold at the exhibition opening, passed before he finished work. Curiously only the Dalziels were upset by this; Dick calmly paid several visits to the Great Exhibition, making mental notes for the book and studying the numerous rival publications. Once he went with Thackeray to select favourite items among the one hundred thousand exhibits, which included such bizarre items as a collapsible piano for gentleman's yacht, a knife with three hundred blades, and a selection of bronze furniture in the gothic style. They were most impressed by the machinery, "the great calm

leviathan steam-engines and machines lying alongside like a great line of battle ships". They agreed, however, that the paintings and sculptures were most impressive; "our painters, artificers, makers of busts and statues do deserve to compare with the best foreign".[24] On other occasions Dick agreed to take the young children of his wealthy friends, delighting in their more childish reactions to the spectacle.

Eventually he wrote to the Dalziels about the ill-fated book project, adopting a lackadaisical, rather off-hand tone: "I would like to have your opinion as to whether, now the 'Glass House' being open and the public so much seriously occupied with the Exhibition, my drawings will be relished. I don't express any decided opinion myself, but I put it to you." He had seen the other processional books now, and suggested "I greatly think that mine will be thought stale, however original I can make it. It is, in fact, next to impossible to represent any of the countries by other types than those already done in publications already out." Finally, he admitted he was at fault for delaying so long, "perhaps the drawings of the 'procession' might be engrafted upon something else, of which it might form a part. I would rather sacrifice it as lost time than bring out a failure."[25] But the Dalziels persisted, determined to produce the book however late or derivative it might be. It proved a long wait, however, for Dick did not finish the last drawing until the final day of the Exhibition. They engraved these in sixteen sections which folded out, and published them in plain or coloured editions as *An Overland Journey to the Great Exhibition,* showing a few extra articles and visitors. Dick's drawings are grouped around familiar objects: the Italians sing opera and

---

b) The Germans.

surround a violin, the Germans carry a carved pipe of the type Robinson had bought in Germany. This was one of the most successful drawings, echoing Dick's delight when he discovered how in Germany, "beyond a tender age, a German takes to a tobacco pipe, which engenders a laziness that utterly incapacitates him for active duties". However, he liked the Germans, as his drawings indicate; they were "a very cheerful, honest, good-humoured, kindly race, whether some of the 'elders' who have spectacles, hairy whiskers, and beards and pipes in their mouths, are equally praiseworthy members of society, I can't say yet, but they don't look it".[26]

Despite the delays, when the *Overland Journey* was announced for publication, Dick grew excited. He wrote to Charles: "My slow but 'unsartain'

Overland Procession to the Great Exhibition which has been so long 'coming', and which has excited so much interest amongst those who were much interested about the matter, broke out upon the unsuspecting people of England (and I may even say of Scotland and Ireland) last week. The 'Morning Chronicle' of this day gives it a very favourable notice but at the end of the article "puts it seriously to me whether it is well to go on only doing 'big heads' ". The critic means well, but he does not succeed in carrying out his meaning."[27] And yet despite good reviews the Dalziels recalled the book was "a dead failure". Attempts to revive it in a new format a year later also failed. But it remains one of Dick's most successful comic inventions, even if the public and critics had begun to grow weary of his "big heads".

Despite their curious customs, Doyle liked the German people: "The inspection of luggage at Cologne" – Jones's portmanteau undergoing the ordeal "by touch", from The Foreign Tour of Brown, Jones and Robinson.

IV

"The workings of my innermost soul"

1851 - 1855

o one regretted Dick's *Punch* resignation more than Thackeray. He was alarmed by his friend's stubborn refusal to reconsider his position, and even more worried about his future as an artist, now that the press seemed determined to condemn him as frivolous and irresponsible. Moreover, Thackeray worried that since Dick was prone to bouts of depression and lethargy, which had clouded their collaboration on *Rebecca and Rowena,* he might slip silently from prominence and go the way of his many old forgotten friends. He therefore made sure to include Dick in as many social events as he could; if only to keep a careful eye upon his despondent young friend.

Part of this plan included Thackeray's new lecture series. He made certain Dick was invited to the inaugural performance of the "The English Humorists of the Eighteenth Century" in May 1851, expecting Doyle to take a prominent place in the crowded hall to give him essential moral support. For Thackeray was terrified to face his audience: "Oh Lord... I'm sick at my stomach with fright." He sent the following letter just before the dreaded day, and hinted that Dick was indispensible to him at this particularly trying time:

"My Dear D---

I hope you will come to the tight-rope exhibition to-morrow, and send you a card. You and your friend will please to sit in distant parts of the room. When you see me put my hand to my watch-chain, you will say, 'God bless my soul, how beautiful!' When I touch my neckcloth, clap with all your might. When I use my pocket-handkerchief, burst into tears. When I

pause say Brav-ah-ah-ah-ro through the pause. You had best bring with you a very noisy umbrella: to be used at proper intervals; and if you can't cry at the pathetic parts, please blow your nose very hard. And now, everything

Thackeray by Doyle.
Pencil sketch, 9½ x 6¼"
British Museum.

The young eligible bachelor Dick Doyle, a self-portrait at about age twenty.

Doyle's design for a fairy-tale romance.

having been done to insure success that mortal can do, the issue is left to the immortal Gods. God Save the Queen. No money returned... Babies in arms NOT admitted."

Dick agreed to attend, but his instructions were unnecessary, for the lecture and subsequent five performances were a tremendous success. But Thackeray persisted with his invitations and Dick was seen half-way through the series, as Thackeray's doorman this time, "to let stray sheep into the fold".[1]

It is intriguing to speculate how Thackeray's lectures, filled with romantic scenes and humorous stories, affected Dick at the time. He was certainly enchanted by Thackeray's characters, and the romantic threads he wove so expertly into his tales. He often argued the fate of some new Thackeray hero with his hostesses, and at the time was especially interested in the *History*

of Pendennis, with its poignant tale of romance between Laura, who tragically loved "a man of so much higher a nature" and the fate of the inferior Arthur Pendennis, whom she marries. One prominent hostess remembered Dick was "much excited" by the idea; how he discussed and speculated freely upon the romantic principles involved in marrying for love. He preferred the chivalric virtues of romantic love, on the whole, which Thackeray had dismissed in his lecture: "I suppose as long as novels last, and authors aim at interesting their public, there must always be in the story a virtuous and gallant hero, a wicked monster, his opposite, and a pretty girl who finds a champion: bravery and virtue conquer beauty, and vice, after seeming to triumph through certain number of pages, is sure to be discomfited in the last volume."

However Dick continued his fairy-tale view of love throughout his life, drawing and painting the theme on numerous occasions. His early *Sleeping Beauty* and *Beauty and the Beast* illustrations were strongly influenced by the idea. In *Punch* his initials frequently depicted knights rescuing maidens, while others introduced marital articles: he drew an initial "O" around a single unfortunate man being pulled apart by over-zealous women to introduce the lines "Oh, never get married". He drew an old man on bended knees before a young beauty, making the initial "W" to introduce the article "Marriages in Middle Life". He even included his own self-portrait as a bushy-haired young suitor seated next to a wide-eyed young woman, in the letter "R" of "The Gotobed Letters" series. These drawings were coloured by Dick's limited experience of romance at the time; especially his infatuation with Jenny Lind and the lovely Italian chambermaid Maria – paragons of a dark haired, wide-eyed, unattainable beauty.

Indeed, Dick shared with his friend Dickens the belief that a woman represented an ideal, while the man was her protector and shield against the world. "I wish I had been born in the days of Ogres and Dragon-guarded Castles," Dickens once wrote of his ill-fated love for Ellen Ternan, forbidden to him by his marriage. "I wish an Ogre with seven heads had taken the Princess whom I adore... to his stronghold on the top of a high series of mountains, and there tied her up by the hair. Nothing would suit me half so well this day, as climbing after her, sword in hand, and either winning her or being killed...".[2] For most of his life Dick was content to just watch and admire beautiful women, and in turn those he delighted with his wit and humour regarded him as a mere diversion from the boredom of the drawing room, and little else. Nevertheless, Dick's letters to his brother Charles during this period are filled with allusions to young women. He watched a group of rather unattractive neighbourhood ladies gathered outside a public house, staring into the sky at a display of fireworks, and told Charles afterward, "And if they (the ladies) were not exactly 'fire' works, let us hope at least, that their hearts were as warm, and their eyes as bright, and their wits as blazing, as that renowned element. After this burst of emotion I must change the subject or my feelings may become too many, or too much for me." He preferred the highly-strung, uninhibited young ladies like Mrs Bristed, the wealthy wife of John Jacob Astor's nephew. Together they went for long carriage rides and freely laughed at convention. Dick described her to Charles as "very young, very fascinating, smokes two cigars after dinner with relish, is very likely in her 'Manners and Customs' and in short I like her very much". He might have added she was "very married" as well. Moreover, he was not above a slight mercenary streak, at least when it came to match-making for his brother Henry: at

mass one Sunday he watched the "rather nice looking Miss Talbot" nod and smile at Henry, and Dick considered her highly eligible because "Her money how nice it is!"[3]

Meanwhile Dick was introduced to the woman who would capture his heart and break it so completely that he would never contemplate romance seriously again. Her name was Blanche Stanley and she was the beautiful, flirtatious daughter of Edward Stanley, a recently created baronet, and Lady Henrietta Maria Stanley, herself the daughter of the 13th Viscount Dillon. Blanche lived with her eight brothers and sisters at Alderley Park in Cheshire, the family seat, but she seldom enjoyed the country life and longed for London society. When she reached twenty-one in 1850, she was the acknowledged beauty of the family; a head-strong, moody, snobbish and spoilt woman, who also possessed that unmistakeable quality of youthful, spirited charm which Dick loved. Her mother wearily agreed Blanche had "the poorest manners" of all her children, but she was "a romantick girl" and allowances must be made. And when Blanche was presented at court, launched into a world of society balls and dinner parties she had long dreamed to experience, she delighted and conquered. With her innocent yet deceptive flirting, her wide-eyed classical beauty, she became the talk of London society. "Poor Blanche, the life you lead is murder," her grandmother wrote to her in May 1850. "I am so tired of seeing your name in the newspaper lists, knowing how many hot crowded rooms you haunt. It is well *you* hold out so stoutly as you do." And a year later, while she was still very much in society, her grandmother warned of being constantly "surrounded by *clever* men – it is setting up for a character which seldom ends well for matrimony –"[4]

It was in one of these "hot crowded drawing rooms" that Dick Doyle probably met and fell in love with Blanche Stanley. He was delighted by her beauty as much as her flirtatious attentions toward him, but as the daughter of a wealthy aristocrat, there was no question, on her side, of a romance with a mere artist. Moreover, despite her religiously tolerant family, she was not a Catholic, and this would never do for a daughter-in-law in John Doyle's eyes. And yet Blanche flirted with Dick whenever they were together in the homes of mutual friends, and he was delighted and flattered by her attentions.

Among her many admirers, apart from Dick, was his friend Thackeray, who was an occasional houseguest at Alderley Park. There he watched her, fascinated by the impending romance between the mercurial Blanche and the shy, mild-mannered twenty-five year old Lord Airlie, a wealthy young Scottish aristocrat and highly eligible bachelor. After a stormy and frustrating romance for the young lord, they announced their engagement. Lord Airlie was, according to some, "completely mesmerized" by Blanche's beauty and high spirits, and as a result he either ignored or dismissed her "capricious and changeable manner". A visit by Thomas Carlyle, who arrived to give his approval of the match, preceded the marriage; and on the 23 September 1851, Blanche became the Countess of Airlie.

The news that his beloved Blanche was married and to live in distant Scotland came as a bitter blow to Dick, and in many ways he refused to believe his misfortune. He continued to search her out whenever they were in society, if only for a brief glimpse and a smile. His patrons Lord and Lady Ashburton usually obliged him with invitations to their newly acquired estate at The Grange, near Southhampton. Dick became a frequent visitor to "the hospitable mansion", as he called it, especially over the Christmas holidays, when he hoped "that SHE will be there. I mean the late Miss St----y". His letters to Charles now become plaintive cries for help, filled with the frank outpourings of a young man who had lost his love. He recalled during the first Christmas of Blanche's marriage how she and Lord Airlie had appeared at The Grange and spent long periods talking with him. He explained this to Charles, first listing the impressive guests, then saving the best until last: "above all there was the Countess of Airlie – my beloved BLANCHE, and her 'usband the Earl of A. They have invited me never to go to Scotland without visiting them, so that whenever I go to see you I will make a triumphant progress through the nobility and gentry's seats."

Although Dick was at first delighted by this unexpected and gracious invitation from his rival, he decided it was mere courtesy and forgot about it; until he received a letter from Blanche herself three week's later. She stressed it had been a sincere invitation, not mere politeness, and that she now needed him to help make up a house party in Scotland. Although her intentions were probably innocent, the letter was expressed in the manner of a woman determined to establish herself as a competent hostess among new

Blanche, Countess of Airlie.
Detail from an oil painting by
Henry Weigall, Jnr., exhibited
RA 1860. 82½ x 51"
Cortachy Castle.

friends. This threw Dick into a mixed state of elation and depression. He explained his feelings in the following remarkably frank letter to Charles, filled with the frustrations of his unrequited love for Blanche which would follow him for years afterwards:

"O! Charles, oh my friend! You little know what I have been going and undergoing lately. A very acute incident has befallen 'yours very sincerely'. His most superior feelings have in a manner been rent and torn, and what looked at one time like the 'merry sunshine' has become undoubtedly the winter of his discontent. As this bit of introduction seems in danger of becoming 'wordy', and perhaps is already a little 'misty', you may be mentally grunting 'Don't be a fool, you fool, but come to the point'? If so, I would ask you 'not to be in a devil* (*This strong word is used in return for your calling me a fool in the foregoing sentence.) of a hurry, and my reason for proposing this is, that were I to precipitately plunge into the subject, without calmly leading up to it, it might be dangerous, as calculated to throw me into a sudden fit of grief.

"Lady Airlie, better known (to me) as B-----e St----y, wrote to me about 3 weeks ago from Cartouchy [Cortachy] Castle, Forfarshire reminding me of having made a promise, if ever I went to Scotland to pay her a visit. This is strictly fact. I did make the promise when at The Grange. I had forgotten it. But when the note came, and I saw HER handwriting, I was thrown into a 'state', and within an inch of a fit." He explained how with great regret he wrote to Blanche, refusing her invitation. He was forced to remain in London, where three of four weeks of work pressed, "but that after that time 'I might perhaps' ". He clearly longed to help her make up what she called "a pleasant party", despite the hardships it would cause him. But in the end, as he told Charles, "I wished much to go because I would have looked in on you on my way going and coming. But it cannot be this year unless something very unexpected turns up, which is not likely. I ask you, however, as a man and a brother, to survey the whole case. Ask yourself if it be not a hard one, and if I am not a miserable VICTIM!"⁶

Nevertheless Dick continued to spend his Christmases at The Grange in the vain hope of seeing Blanche. Indeed, three years after her marriage he was still preoccupied with her,

writing to Charles of his disappointment that "B---che, now unfortunately Lady Airlie, was invited but could not come, being so far north in Scotland. 'When I tell you' to use the words of a celebrated brazen image you 'wot of', that Lady Stanley told me that her daughter Lady Airlie would be 'so sorry she had not been there when she heard I was there'. When Lady Stanley made use of these words 'I thought I should have bust'. I however controlled my feelings and countenance by a powerful effort, and succeeded in looking as if nothing was the matter. But little did that imperious woman, and mother know the workings of my innermost soul!"⁷ And on this occasion Dick had to content himself only with an invitation to Blanche's childhood home from her mother. He passed the time learning to play billiards with Blanche's sister Alice, and walked the grounds of The Grange hardly noticing the house which he had once called "the most beautiful place imaginable".

Over the next few years Dick continued to think about his beloved Blanche. She dominates his drawings, replacing the wide-eyed Jenny Lind and Maria with her classical beauty and haunting, dark eyes. A favourite subject for paintings was a Blanche figure trapped in a tree as "The Eagle's Bride", her regal-looking husband sternly guarding her movements while a knight approaches to rescue her. It was a poignant and, to Dick at least, deeply significant subject, now that his beloved Blanche had been spirited away to a distant castle by an equally imposing Lord Airlie. In another poignant watercolour called "The Stolen Kiss", he painted a Blanche-like figure lying asleep on a couch in a dimly lit room. A young boy with Dick's features creeps silently out of the darkness and gently places a kiss upon his beloved's forehead. It was a gesture both reticent and haunting: a perfect expression of Dick's forbidden affection for his beloved Blanche.

But generally Dick slipped back into the familiar bouts of lethargy and dreamy fantasies which Thackeray found worrying. Moreover, Dick seemed to relish his unhappiness and when he occasionally attended a friend's dinner, he sat silently musing on the edge of the room, no longer the witty guest with a host of stories to entertain his fellow diners. At this time Thackeray left for a lecture tour of America. Since Dick lost his most concerned and devoted friend, he

Doyle's love for Blanche inspired "The Eagle's Bride".
Watercolour, 14 x 9¾"
Sotheby's Belgravia.

Jones & Robinson]. It would be capital, it would suit him wonderfully." But Dick could not agree, and he never left his native country again.[9]

Part of his reluctance to leave England was worry over his father's future. John Doyle continued to dominate the family home, despite his retirement from duty as HB. Occasionally he left home to visit friends, like the time he called upon the famous geologist Richard Owen at his home near Oxford. But even that brief visit ended in disappointment, when an obstinate nightingale refused to sing in the Owen garden and he left his umbrella behind. Afterwards he wrote to thank the Owens for their kindness, to apologize for his absent-mindness, and to explain how much he had enjoyed the escape from home, "the silence of the nightingales notwithstanding".[10] The most pressing problem was money – or lack of it. His sons brought in very little from their paintings, although James's recent engraving after his painting, "A Literary Party at Joshua Reynolds'" had been successful enough to reprint, and was followed by plans for other prints in larger editions. He also had a series of designs after Sir Walter Scott selected by the Queen and Prince Albert for the walls of the Royal Summer House at Buckingham Palace. Henry had begun to illustrate magazines like *Punch,* when Dick was on the staff, and later humorous books, signing his work "Fusbos" with a hen insignia. But all of these projects brought in little regular income on which to run the family.

Moreover, all the Doyles were agreed that Dick had done the right thing by resigning his lucrative *Punch* position. Two years after he left, they stood behind his decision to reject a renewed offer of a staff position on *Punch,* despite the very real need for the money such work would bring in. Instead Dick preferred to wait and sift through the occasional offers of work which came his way.

* * * * * * * * * * * *

began to shun society, like his father, and refused to work. Mrs Procter invited him to one of her famous dinner parties while Thackeray was away, and afterward she reported to Thackeray: "Your friends are all well – Richard Doyle cheers up when your name is mentioned – I say 'cheers up' because he looks sad and is doing nothing – and this is a great pity."[8] Significantly Thackeray was at the time also in love with a married woman, Jane Brookfield, wife of an old Oxford friend, and chose to escape his torment by touring America. By then familiar with the cause of Dick's moods, he urged the same course of action for him, as he explained to another friend: "I wish Doyle would come out and make a pictorial tour of the States for *Punch,* like Br J & Robinson [Brown,

By September 1853, Thackeray had returned from America with a proposal which Dick could not refuse. Having half-heartedly put the finishing touches on the book edition of Brown, Jones and Robinson, and helped his friend, the painter George Frederick Watts, with costume designs for a pantomime of Christopher Columbus, he

COLOUR PLATE I

Dick Doyle's unpublished title-page design for "Le Beau Pécopin et la Belle Bauldor," 1842,
from Victor Hugo's Le Rhin.   *Private collection.*

COLOUR PLATE II Dick Doyle's "The Knight and the Spectre". Watercolour, 5⅞ x 13¾".

British Museum.

COLOUR PLATE III Dick Doyle's "The Goat Legend", 1870. Watercolour, 13½ x 19½".   Private Collection.

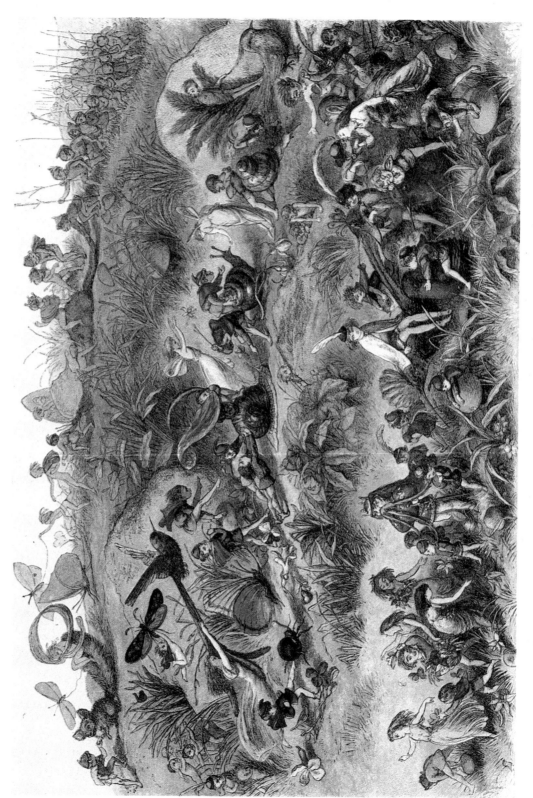

COLOUR PLATE IV Dick Doyle's "The Triumphal March of the Elf-King", from In Fairyland, 1870.

COLOUR PLATE V Dick Doyle's "Elves in a Rabbit Warren", 1873. Watercolour, 13½ x 19½".

E.Joseph.

COLOUR PLATE VI A page from Charles Doyle's sketchbook, 9 October 1888. Watercolour, 7 x 9½".

E.Joseph.

was free to consider Thackeray's offer, knowing he had little else to occupy the remainder of the year. The offer involved Thackeray's latest novel, *The Newcomes,* which he had begun in July and planned as usual to illustrate himself. But illness and his uncertain movements travelling on the Continent while he was writing each instalment of the serial made him give up the idea; and so he asked Dick if he would like to illustrate the story. Dick agreed to the challenge and received the first instalments of what would become the most difficult and disturbing commission of his career.

The Newcomes: Memoirs of a most Respected Family, was published in twenty-four instalments from September 1853-August 1855, and thus occupied almost two tortured years of Dick's working life. Told through Thackeray's familiar voice, Arthur Pendennis, the story involved elements of chivalric virtue, disgust at the injustices toward women in Victorian society,

---

Doyle's evocative illustrations to Thackeray's The Newcomes, *1854:*

a) Ethel Newcome and her ill-fated lover Clive Newcome.

as well as the lure of wealth, ancestral honour and respectability. All these themes Dick and Thackeray had often discussed and agreed upon. Moreover, as the story unfolded, Dick began to realise many of the characters were clearly modelled upon persons painfully near to his own experience, and it was this which soon caused the unfortunate rift between author and illustrator. The story centred around the career of young Clive Newcome, a generous, sympathetic son to Colonel Thomas Newcome, officer in the Indian army and a true gentleman guided only by principles of duty and honour. Clive falls in love with his cousin, Ethel Newcome, daughter of the wealthy banker Sir Brian Newcome, but the romance is thwarted by her scheming grandmother, the Countess of Kew, (a model of worldly cynicism), and her selfish relatives. Among the opponents is the mean, thoroughly evil and snobbish Barnes Newcome, Ethel's brother and the villain in the story. Ethel obediently agrees to her fate, and becomes engaged to her family's choice of suitors, her cousin Lord Kew, then the worthless Scottish Lord Farintosh, but she breaks each of these engagements off. Meanwhile Clive escapes to the Continent with his painter friend J.J.Ridley. He returns despairing over his doomed love for Ethel, and he marries the pretty though ineffectual Rosey Mackenzie, daughter of a scheming widow. But soon Colonel Newcome loses his fortune, and Clive's household is plunged into poverty. The good and virtuous Colonel is eventually driven to take refuge from his son's nagging mother-in-law by moving to the Greyfriars almshouses, where he dies a noble death. Rosey eventually dies as well, and we are left to assume Clive is eventually united with his beloved Ethel.

Dick received only individual chapters of this poignant story, and it was not until the last instalment that he, like Thackeray's readers, knew the outcome of Clive and Ethel's romance. But these two characters in particular, as well as the fairy painter J.J.Ridley, were creations which Thackeray had borrowed from real experience. Moreover, Dick's eventual drawings, especially of Ethel and her Scottish suitor Lord Farintosh, as well as J.J.Ridley, are too closely taken from his own experience to be ignored: Ethel is drawn with the wide-eyed dark-haired beauty of Dick's beloved Blanche; Lord Farintosh, her unfortuanate suitor, is made to look ridiculous in his kilt and sporran suggestive of Blanche's Scottish husband, Lord Airlie; and the inventive young fantasy artist J.J.Ridley is given many of Dick's own features.

It is tempting to think Thackeray knew his story of romance among such familiar characters might upset his artist friend; and that this was the reason he was originally reluctant to commission Doyle's illustrations. He had told Mrs Carmichael-Smyth shortly after his decision, "I have arranged with R.Doyle to do the pictures for my new book: and now that is agreed on I feel almost sorry I am not to do them myself." But the first drawings and the writing went well enough to dismiss doubts: "I can go where I like now there are no pictures to do," Thackeray wrote to another friend from the Continent, adding cryptically, "and there was more than good reason for giving Doyle that job. But the chief reason was – well if you can serve your friend and yourself too, aren't you lucky?"[11]

Thackeray's characterizations of J.J.Ridley and Ethel Newcome were the most strikingly familiar to Doyle. J.J.Ridley, painter of fantasy and fairy subjects was well suited to appear in *The Newcomes*, however, for Thackeray acknowledged the story was his attempt at writing a new fairy-tale; and he borrowed themes from the popularity of animal and fairy stories by Hans Andersen and the brothers Grimm – just as Dick borrowed fairy-tale characters for his initial drawings. Moreover, the dreamy young J.J.Ridley was an opponent to the established conventional occupations of the other characters; he was an artist of romantic, other-wordly temperament, who could be sent into flights of fancy by a piece of fine music – as Dick Doyle could – and had only one weakness, a love of "fine company" (which he shared with his counterpart, Dick Doyle). "One day I am determined he shall dine at Lord Todmorden's table, and he shall get the prize at the Royal Academy, and be famous, sir – famous!" Thackeray made J.J.'s piano teacher say of her pupil's ambitions. He added how much J.J.'s talent for drawing his daydreams meant to his teacher, and Dick drew the scene as "J.J. in Dreamland". He hinted at his own boyhood and more recent *Punch* fantasies, with the young J.J. seated in a trance, while the music of the piano coloured his dreams. J.J. shared Dick's talent for drawing "knights in armour, with plumes, and shield, and battleaxe; and splendid

b) "J.J. in Dreamland".

young noblemen with flowing ringlets, and bounteous plumes of feathers, and rapiers, and russet boots... wasp-waisted peasant girls, and young countesses with oh, such cherry lips! – all these splendid forms of war and beauty crowd to the young draughtsman's pencil, and cover letterbacks, copybooks, without end." And Thackeray's admiration for Dick Doyle's invention is echoed in J.J.'s friend, Clive Newcome: "I can't think where that chap gets his ideas from... Somehow he seems to see things we don't, don't you know?" Sadly this is the only large Doyle fantasy illustration in *The Newcomes*.

Apart from the obvious artist associations between J.J.Ridley and Dick Doyle, Thackeray's descriptions of J.J.'s character echo his knowledge of Dick's own personality. Thackeray carefully kept J.J. in the shadows; he is a mysterious figure who drifts in and out of the action, delivering the inspired remarks of an outsider; a representative of the noble, classless profession of artist. "Out of that bright light looked his pale, thoughtful face, and long locks and eager brown eyes. The palette on his arm was a great shield painted in many colours... With these he achieves conquests, wherein none are wounded save the environs: with that he shelters him against how much idleness, ambition, temptation! Occupied over that consoling work, idle thoughts cannot gain the mastery over him: selfish wishes or desires are kept at bay." J.J. is also deeply religious, and when he and Clive attend a Catholic mass in Rome, J.J. "is immensely touched by these ceremonies. They seem to answer some spiritual want of his nature, and he comes away satisfied as from a feast." Finally, just as Thackeray admired the gentle "modesty and quiet amiability" of Dick Doyle, he described J.J.Ridley as a model of inner peace and artistic dedication: "Study was his chief amusement. Self-denial came easily to him. Pleasure or what is generally called so, had little charm for him. His ordinary companions were pure and sweet thoughts; his outdoor enjoyment the contemplation of natural beauty; for recreation the hundred pleasant dexterities and manipulations of his craft were ceaselessly interesting to him: he would draw every knot in an oak panel, or every leaf in an orange-tree, smiling and taking a gay delight over the simple feats of skill: whenever you found him he seemed watchful and serene, his modest virgin-lamp always lighted and trim. No gusts of passion extinguished it; no hopeless wandering in the darkness afterwards led him astray. Wayfarers through the world, we meet now and again with such purity; and salute it, and hush whilst it passes on." Although Thackeray's daughter Anne Ritchie dismissed the claims that J.J. was modelled after Doyle, she wrote to Doyle's first biographer, "I never thought of it before:– his beautiful fanciful art was certainly akin to J.J.'s, but his personality was so homogenous, his genteel confidence was so sympathetic that it never occurred to me to think of him as anybody but himself, – charming, exceptional, dignified and gentle."[12]

The fascinating character of J.J.Ridley was virtually written out of the story later, much to the chagrin of Thackeray's readers. J.J. experiences a brief moment of fame and fulfills his piano-teacher's dream by exhibiting the successful fairy painting "Oberon and Titania" at the Royal Academy; then he disappears from the story. As a result, Thackeray was deluged with letters from irate readers, until he was forced to

explain his decision in a cryptic confession: "Again, why did Pendennis introduce J.J. with such a flourish, giving us, as it were, an overture, and no piece to follow it? J.J.'s history, let me confidentially state, has been revealed to me too, and may be told in some of these fine summer months, or Christmas evenings, when the kind reader has leisure to hear." Was Thackeray referring to Doyle's uncertain future here, one wonders?

In Ethel Newcome, Thackeray created a character who echoed his experience of Blanche Stanley, for Ethel was strong-willed, flirtatious, conscious of her obligations to her family yet high-spirited enough to throw them over at the last moment. Thackeray shared Dick's awe of this type of young woman, with her magnetic powers of beauty and charm; just as he had explained to Blanche's mother shortly before her daughter's marriage: "You see there's something affecting in looking at a pretty young thing just embarked upon that career to where all pretty young things are destined with good and evil fortune God knows." From the first he delighted in Blanche's unabashed behaviour in society; her consciously thwarting conventions whenever she felt like it. During one dinner party he recalled how Blanche had openly refused to leave the room with the other ladies to let the gentlemen alone with their port and cigars. Instead, she waited in the dining room for the men to follow her, then chose the least boring for conversation. Such behaviour fascinated yet grated on Thackeray's nerves: Blanche became "Lady Giveyourself Air-lie" and usually lived up to the title by "putting on airs" in boring company.

In addition, Thackeray's romantic story of Ethel Newcome was recognized by his friends to be modelled after Blanche Stanley's own marriage for convenience and position to Lord Airlie. Blanche had been a victim of the "marriage marketplace", when young women are sacrificed by their families for wealth and future position, just as Thackeray intended Ethel Newcome to do when she became engaged to the Scottish Lord Farintosh. "He had ample opportunity to observe the workings of the marriage mart in London and elsewhere," one Thackeray friend explained about the author's plan in *The Newcomes*. "The thought that such favourites of his as Blanche Airlie and Sally Baxter, who both served as models for Ethel Newcome, might be sacrificed themselves to Mammon had long moved him to indignant remonstrance."[14] Was it any wonder Dick Doyle found the task of illustrating scenes describing his beloved Blanche such a terrible strain?

As Dick had discovered while working on *Rebecca and Rowena,* Thackeray was a demanding and highly critical judge of his illustrators. Although he had generously praised Dick's fairy illustrations, from the start he doubted whether his friend would succeed with the more realistic interiors and precise characterizations he demanded in *The Newcomes.* He admired Cruikshank's "ideal personages" in his illustrations to Dickens: "Once seen, these figures remain impressed on the memory, which otherwise would have no hold upon them, and the heroes and heroines of Boz become personal acquaintances with each of us." But he hated "prettiness", like those weak designs in popular annuals full of "eternal fancy portraits of ladies in voluptuous attitudes and various stages of deshabillé, to awaken the dormant sensibilities of misses in their teens, or tickle the worn-out palettes of rakes and roués". However, from the first numbers which Dick received from Thackeray, it became clear *The Newcomes* would not be an easy collaboration. Thackeray did not mark his manuscript as to where and which subjects he wanted illustrated. He relied instead upon his character descriptions on which to judge Doyle's accuracy. This upset and eventually blocked Dick's powers of invention: "Thackeray scarcely ever describes a character as Dickens does, all at once – he leaves them to work themselves out by degrees, so that after reading the MS of a couple of Numbers one really knows scarcely anything about the story," Dick moaned to Charles when he started work. And when he asked for clarification of a character, Thackeray supplied only vague descriptions, unless Dick had completely missed the point in his first attempts: "If you do Lord Kew make him smart handsome & like a young swell – a square faced brisk blue-eyed bushy whiskered fellow is the gentleman I have in mind. Belsize does not look buck enough, and his beard is too long: but that's a trifle." If Dick invented scenes, however, he was prey to Thackeray's often unreasonable outrages; like the time he drew the boys of Greyfriars (modelled after Charterhouse, Thackeray's old school) playing marbles, which "they would as soon have thought of cutting off

their heads as play," Thackeray fumed in a fit of old school pride.

In the end, the first number did not augur well for the future. Thackeray had grown impatient with Doyle's delays and threatened to take over the drawings himself. He knew the frontispiece was the most important drawing in the series, since it introduced a new story to his public, and he finally agreed upon the "J.J. in Dreamland" drawing. This was etched, as were all the full-page plates, while the initials were wood engraved. But Dick was far from satisfied with the results, as he told Charles: "The first No. of 'Newcomes' is out. You must not judge of the next by it. It was done in great hurry (sic), in fact Thackeray sent sketches for some of them which he had already done intending to illustrate it himself, and I adopted them considerably for safety not knowing anything about the characters, or what he intended."

The first appearance of Ethel Newcome as a convincing beauty was indisputably essential to the story, and Thackeray made this quite clear to his illustrator. In the text that precedes Doyle's drawing he described the pressure

Doyle's ill-fated drawing of Ethel Newcome as a beauty.

Doyle faced: "I have turned away one artist: the poor creature was utterly incompetent to depict the sublime, graceful, and pathetic personages and events with which this history will most assuredly abound, and I doubt even the designer in his place [Doyle] can make such a portrait of Miss Ethel Newcome as shall satisfy her friends and her own sense of justice." In this tactless

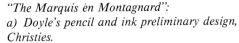

"The Marquis èn Montagnard":
a) Doyle's pencil and ink preliminary design,
Christies.

b) Published etching, shades of Blanche's unfortunate
husband Lord Airlie appear in Lord Farintosh,
Scottish suitor to Ethel Newcome.

remark it is tempting to believe Thackeray then knew the impossibility of his demand. He was certainly upset by Doyle's resulting illustration: a small quarter-page insert. In it Ethel bows to Colonel Newcome (himself a portrait of the aging John Doyle): the viewer's attention immediately focuses on the wide, expressive Blanche-inspired eyes and firm classical profile now so familiar in Dick's memory. However, from the figure's neck downward the drawing fails miserably, with a ridiculous wasp-waist, rubbery arms and hastily shaded dress. Even Thackeray's limited anatomical draughtsmanship would have been better, as he suggested in his accompanying text: "As our artist cannot come up to this task, the reader will be pleased to let his fancy paint for itself."

Doyle had failed his first test, and did no

better with subsequent scenes from the book. Though he bravely chose the painfully evocative meeting between Ethel and her Scottish fiancé, his personal feelings again took control of his pencil. Lord Farintosh (e.g. Lord Airlie in Doyle's mind) appears as a parody of pomposity, dressed in kilt and lace, his well-bred manner exaggerated by throwing his nose in the air, his eyes almost closed to the beauty of his partner. On the other hand, Dick was unable to imagine Ethel's reaction and safely turns her back to the viewer. Was he taking Thackeray's advice and letting the reader's "fancy paint for itself"? Or perhaps he found the scene too familiar to his own experience of watching Blanche and Lord Airlie together? Whatever his motives the illustrations continued to disappoint both author and public alike. Each new instalment brought renewed attacks by the critics who inevitably centred their comments on one point: "The figure of Ethel is decidedly inadequate. One has so much of Ethel in the book that a failure with her means that the whole is rather a failure too."[15]

Dick's failure to give Thackeray what he wanted, however vague his instructions, was the cause of an inevitable row and cooling in their relationship. Thackeray was disappointed that his original reservations in giving Doyle the commission had been well-founded; Doyle was tortured by the ceaseless demands of his friend and his own inadequacies. The minute Thackeray saw Doyle slip he tightened his grip and forced all future illustrations from his reluctant hand. Tempers flared and courtesies were forgotten in the heat of the moment. It became a battle of wills and Thackeray had the upper hand. He had given his friend complete freedom of judgement at first: the original *Newcomes* manuscript lacks the familiar blocked areas that indicate where Thackeray wanted illustrations. He had clearly believed in Doyle's skill and only offered brief hints or suggestions, such as two drawings of Colonel Newcome.

Then in 1854, with *The Newcomes* nearly half finished, Thackeray was forced to take a stronger stand with Doyle. The work was just not getting done, and he became frantic. Threats appeared at Doyle's door, warnings that if deadlines were ignored "I shall take them in hand and do them henceforth myself!" These Doyle usually ignored or countered with infuriating, feeble excuses: "Eh – er – the fact is, I had not got any pencils."[16] In the end, the strong-arm tactics worked for Doyle was frightened into complying, and he usually sent the required drawings, despite their messy, half-finished appearance. He had no other choice: for although Thackeray's violent temper offended his sensitive nature, he needed the work.

Dogged by Thackeray's bully tactics, Doyle easily slipped back into the dazed, lethargic mood that had ironically been the original reason for taking on *The Newcomes*. It affected his judgement and turned the final stages of the book into a nightmare. His life-long friend William Holman Hunt recalled this difficult period and afterwards suggested the hoplessness Dicky was forced to endure. Prey to indecision he "would begin amending something which had suddenly struck him, at the last moment, and then of course, having once begun to amend

one part, one goes on amending another part, – finally one does the whole thing over again."[17] His work and life had become one indistinguishable muddle, and for once he could not escape.

The Newcomes illustrations did little to enhance author's or illustrator's reputation. Thackeray felt persecuted by their failure, upset at the loss of his popularity. One day, while leaving the Travellers' Club he was stopped by Frederick Locker and quizzed about the *Newcomes* drawings. Locker was a shrewd judge of book illustration, having befriended Cruikshank and later played a vital patron's role to Randolph Caldecott and Kate Greenaway. But now he was considerably disturbed by Doyle's illustrations. In a typical jest he suggested Thackeray's readers might think he had done the poor drawings, and Doyle the text. Thackeray stared in horror at this idea then turned without further words and stormed off. Equally disappointed was the influential art critic John Ruskin, who had read instalments of *The Newcomes* with great interest. He was intrigued by the matrimonial theme, with its "pieces of wonderful truth" no doubt shedding light on his present marital difficulties with his young wife Effie, whom he was soon to divorce. However, he pronounced the presentation "more disgusting in the illustration than usual", alluding to Thackeray's previous habit of illustrating his own books. But he also suggested how far Doyle had fallen in his estimation since the time he had illustrated his own *The King of the Golden River*, two years earlier.[18]

But there were unmistakeable signs of invention to make present-day critics consider Doyle's Newcome drawings some of the best illustrations he ever did. In particular the marvellously suggestive initial letters with themes to enhance the story, are some of his finest: the sinewy dragon attacking Rosey, Clive and Colonel Newcome to signify the evil which befalls the family; the withered alligator in the graveyard, dressed in widow's weeds, to signify the death of the ogre Lady Kew. Or there were significant and now familiar scenes of knights attacking the dragon of evil, or rescuing distressed maidens, for example in "Lady Clara's rescue by Lord Highgate" as the letter "T". Here Dick excelled, his racing horse fleeing with a Blanche -like maiden and a gallant knight in armour – all drawn within less than a third of the page. Some of these were drawn from Dick's own sense of

a)

Doyle's Newcome initials held secrets of his own chivalric view of the world. (a, b,).

b)

loss: a grief-struck knight mourns the loss of his lady-love attended by his faithful squire, to signify Clive's loss of his beloved Ethel. A later critic said that there was "much mute eloquence in this simple study... Doyle is not often so tragic in fantasy". The poignant drawing, "The Old Love Again", which depicts the sad meeting between Ethel and Clive after fate has separated them, Doyle's biographer called "the best drawing of this set", although he suggested its inspiration went deeper: "It hardly conveys the idea of a chance meeting between two persons, once lovers, separated by social destiny, who now, with outward calm and inward agitation, desire that if they can be friends, at least each shall think well of the other."[19]

As *The Newcomes* appeared, the critics greeted it with substantial reviews. The *Art Journal* (1 November 1853) reviewed the story after the first month, and concluded while Thackeray was "the most difficult of all modern writers to anticipate or to calculate upon, his results are often terribly painful and unsatisfactory... if his nature is too stern for sympathy, it has much of stoic dignity in its nude truth, and the sketch of Colonel Newcome is at once elevated and more genial than any development of character we have met for a long time. That Colonel is a court card, and we know it will be well played." *The*

"Lady Clara's rescue by Lord Highgate" to Chapter 20 of The Newcomes.

Athenaeum waited until all the story was revealed, then devoted an entire page to retell it (5 August 1855). Little was said, however, about Doyle's illustrations, although "Mrs Mackenzie, the tremendous mother-in-law, might have been invented, not for Mr R.Doyle to illustrate, but Mr Leech". Later critics pointed out Doyle's weakness for perspective drawing ("the floor of the room, if judged by aerial perspecive only, is as broad as the Lake of Lucerne"), but acknowledged the "all but inestimable dramatic value" of the *Newcomes* illustrations. The young Burne-Jones devoted over ten pages to "An Essay on the Newcomes" written for the *Oxford and Cambridge Magazine* in 1856. He wrote it six months after the story was completed, in effusive praise of the "wonderfully faithful picture of the great world as it passes daily before us". Thackeray's genius was "very near a consummation", and as expected Doyle's illustrations were worthy of praise. However, even at this early period in Burne-Jones's career, he was a shrewd judge of illustrations for he added his reservations: "Many of the scenes chosen perhaps do not really afford a subject for illustration, and we have no right to be disappointed, or our disappointment may be accidental, arising from our preconceived mental pictures not being coincident with the author's arrangement... The main illustrations, however, seem to me far less successful than the rest, not striking or great in conception, nor, if faithfully interpreted in the engraving, always well executed: but in the symbolic drawings, which form round the initial letters of chapters, it is very different; here he is wonderfully successful, and, as an artist should ever be, no faint echo of the other men's thoughts, but a voice concurrent or prophetical, full of meaning; they are little sketches apt to be passed over in carelessness, but on examination found to be full of real art and poetical comprehension."[20]

Although the praise for *The Newcomes* was heartening, the repercussions Dick experienced by illustrating the story, especially attacks from irate Catholics, were among the most disturbing upsets of his career. Indeed, part of the reason he had been unable to complete the drawings on time was that his conscience was under continual attack in the press and among his influential Catholic friends. Many saw his agreement to provide illustrations to Thackeray's story as a deliberate reversal of his *Punch* position: Thackeray was well-known for his distrust of Catholic dogmas and its Church, and by associating himself with such a critic, Dick openly compromised his own position. He was working for the opposition, and this could not be tolerated. The Catholic papers persecuted him in their columns, and Thackeray was outraged. "I hear the Sneaks in the Catholic papers have been attacking Doyle for illustrating – The Cowards!"

he wrote from Rome. "But persecution is Religion's handmaid – you must persecute to be consistent... I thought of writing to Mr Punch once or twice but stopped for love of poor Dicky Doyle. *Bon Dieu* what can the people mean by crediting this Heathenism?"[21] But the attacks continued and severely curtailed Dick's plans for the future. It was not until a year after his death that the Catholic paper *The Month* condemned what it called "the narrow-minded bigotry" of Doyle's critics, which marred his artistic ambitions and left him uncertain about the future: "From the moment that Doyle retired from *Punch,* English fanaticism and English prejudice persisted in regarding him as a supporter of the 'papal aggression', and he permanently lost from that moment the ground which his talent and reputation had so honourably won for him."

* * * * * * * * * * * *

In addition to battles with his conscience, Dick suffered the loss of his trusted friend and cheerful confidante Uncle Michael Conan at this time. He had been sent to Paris as foreign art correspondent to the *Art Journal,* and the whole Doyle family greatly lamented the departure from their home of so valuable and energetic a relative. It also meant more of the family responsibilities now inevitably fell upon Dick's shoulders.

One of the most important tasks he set himself was to break his father's spell of bad luck and find him employment. Pausing over his drawings to *The Newcomes* in the spring of 1854, Dick decided to plead to the government on behalf of his father, and wrote a long and masterfully worded letter to the Whig Prime Minister, Lord Aberdeen. It was not as surprising as his father's earlier attempts with previous Prime Ministers; Dick knew Lord Aberdeen had admired his stand over the *Punch* resignation. More recently he had praised Dick's decision to avoid illustrating for political papers which might attack the present government – one Dick once called "quite a triumph for the Catholic body". Moreover, Lord Aberdeen was reported to have exclaimed to his advisors "I wish I knew how to serve him," during one particularly heated discussion about Doyle's career. When Dick was told this, he felt it gave him a decided advantage when pressing home his father's case. He had heard of a new opening for Superintendent of Parks, and hoped, despite his father's meagre qualifications – that he had admired parks and gardens "for many years" – John Doyle might be considered for the post. But all his efforts to promote his father's case among sympathetic politician friends failed, and a week later he received a curt reply from Lord Aberdeen: "I see little probability of being able to carry your wishes into effect."[22] Dick was disappointed but undeterred. He wrote several more letters to Lord Aberdeen, which received polite acknowledgement but little encouragement. He also kept his ears open while at the Houses of Parliament or dining with politician friends, for news of further openings in the government suitable for his father. Unfortunately the government fell in 1855 and with it went all John Doyle's hopes for a governmental career.

By the summer of 1855, *The Newcomes* illustrations were finally completed, bringing to an end two years of accumulated misery. Dick decided he could afford a holiday and not surprisingly he chose Scotland. He wanted first to visit his newly married brother and meet his striking new bride, Mary Foley, whom he had drawn from a photograph the previous year as a wide-eyed seventeen year old beauty. Moreover, with the memory of his own romantic affections for Blanche resurrected during his *Newcomes* ordeal, his thoughts returned to her early invitation to visit her and inspect the grounds of the Airlie family castle.

But Blanche was now very unhappy. Having given birth to her first child in June 1854, she was upset and refused to devote herself to motherhood. Her husband at times seemed to his friends to be almost afraid of his head-strong wife, and he lapsed into bouts of shyness and frustration at being unable to make himself worthy of her. As a result, Blanche preferred to roam the castle grounds alone, with only her two favourite dogs for company; or whenever possible she escaped to her childhood home. There her mother worried about her daughter's peculiar moods. Once she wrote in her diary how Blanche was "in extasies (sic) over the beauty and perverseness of human nature". Her father visited his daughter a month later at Cortachy Castle, and wrote home to reassure his wife, "if at times she may appear to be low it proceeds, I suspect, from a lack-a-daisical sort of moodiness produced from reading incomprehensible poetry".[23] But as Dick was to discover, there was more to Blanche's unhappiness than poetry.

To her friends and houseguests at Cortachy, Blanche appeared bored with her marriage, and in a fit of frustration she told Jane Carlyle she believed Lord Airlie was intellectually inferior to her. It was the expression of a woman trapped by domesticity and she longed for the heady days of society balls and earnest young admirers before her marriage. Whenever possible she returned to London and stayed in her husband's Campden Hill house, where she re-established old aquaintances with Thackeray and inevitably Dick Doyle. There is a Doyle family tradition that Blanche continued to return Dick's affection whenever they met. She was still a beautiful twenty-five year old woman, with the power to attract a group of admirers and to flirt with them. But on the other hand, that same family tradition stressed Blanche's displays of affection were "always from a distance", which suggests well-bred propriety.

However, when Dick visited Cortachy the first time and subsequently, he was cordially welcomed by Blanche and her husband. Dick was obviously delighted by all he saw, and grateful to comply with whatever Blanche suggested he might draw and paint for her. On one visit he painted a portrait of Griselda, one of Blanche's children, and afterwards presented it to Blanche. On another occasion he was shown round the castle grounds and immersed himself in a now familiar legend, which haunted and kept many a fellow guest from sharing the delights of Cortachy. Since Dick relished tales of hauntings and legends, he was willing to accept the fascinating story of the "Phantom Drummer of Cortachy Castle".

Doyle's friend, the ghost story writer Catherine Crowe, vividly described the phantom drummer in her book, *The Night Side of Nature* (1848). It was a ghost which plagued the Airlie family, Miss Crowe explained, since ten years previous to Dick's visit to Cortachy, a woman houseguest had been startled by the sound of drumming outside her window. That evening at dinner, she asked her host, Lord Airlie (Blanche's father-in-law), about the sound but he turned deathly pale and refused to answer. Later she discovered she had witnessed the dreaded return of the phantom drummer, the avenging spirit of a young drummer boy killed by an Airlie ancestor, who announced an impending misfortune or death upon the family. The drumming had recently been heard by Lord Airlie's wife, who died shortly afterwards, and it was this that now terrified him. Indeed, Catherine Crowe continued the story with the fact that this same Lord Airlie shortly afterwards had heard the drumming and cancelled a hunting appointment in his terror; the day after he was found dead trying to escape the drummer. It seems certain, therefore, when Dick arrived at Cortachy his boyish curiosity for such things took over and he pried the haunting legend of the Airlie family from his hostess. Even then, however, he needed to rely on tact and careful disgression, for as his female counterpart of ten years ago had learned, "The drummer is a very unpleasant subject in this family, I assure you!"

The grounds at Cortachy were also filled with unexpected natural delights. There Dick explored the sites of legends he had found so attractive since childhood; those tales of witches, evil giants and most of all the devil, which fired his imagination and provided valuable inspiration for his later books and paintings. On one early stroll beyond the castle wall he crossed the nearby mossy graveyard, walked past the Airlie family mausoleum that led to a single-arched bridge over the River Esk. There he searched for what the locals called the "Devil's Stone", a huge boulder said to have been thrown by Satan in an attempt to destroy the old village church. Dick was immediately struck by the incongruity of the setting – the pastoral beauty of the stream with its theme of inherent evil. It was to become a prominent aspect of his later landscapes peopled with tiny, innocent fairies set in the dark, brooding undergrowth of a forest. He anxiously settled down and painted the Devil's Stone and presented it to Blanche, no doubt as an expression of his gratitude to her. He also had several chances to study the change in her manner and see the mysterious sadness that gripped her. On another walk Dick discovered the ruin and enchanted gardens of nearby Airlie Castle, a favourite place for quiet meditation if one ignored the ominous legends. There among the carefully clipped yew trees and grassy paths was said to live a spectral ram – "the Doom of Airlie Castle" – that made a slow, malign circuit of the gardens whenever death threatened the Airlie family.

If the atmosphere of Cortachy, with its famous ghosts, hauntings and sites of bizarre legends, contributed to Blanche's moods, she eventually adjusted to her new home, and raised six children there. Her considerable energies and gregarious nature were later channelled into politics. Palmerston noted that when Lord Airlie entered the House of Lords, his wife bore most of the responsibilities and became the "joint chief whip" of the House. She found time to work for women's education, to advise struggling artists (she once told Kate Greenaway to produce an illustrated lives of the saints for children), and collected large groups of guests at Cortachy to admire her carefully constructed "Garden of Friendship".

Since Dick was not anxious to return to London, he stretched out his Scottish holiday as long as he could. Apart from Edinburgh and Cortachy, he visited the Pre-Raphaelite painter John Everett Millais, who lived some twenty-seven miles southwest of Cortachy at Bowerswell, near Perth. He and his new wife Effie (the recently divorced Mrs Ruskin) cordially greeted him, and the two artists eagerly discussed book illustration. They agreed an illustrator's career could be made or destroyed by his engraver. Dick noticed some of Millais' fine delicate line drawings and commented, "The Dalziel brothers are the only engravers I know who could do justice to these." This remark hinted at his own recent successes with the Dalziel brothers; but Millais was not then acquainted with the master wood engravers. In fact it was not until the following year when, no doubt remembering Doyle's advice, he entrusted his masterful drawings for the *Moxon Tennyson* to the Dalziels – a work that boosted his own reputation as an illustrator.

After a final excursion into north Scotland Dick faced the uncertainty of his return to London. He loved the mountain scenery and peaceful boat trip on Loch Hourn with his friend Robert Lowe (later Viscount Sherbrooke, destined to become a future object of Blanche's flirtations). When no further excuse could be found, Dick reluctantly returned to London to pick up the pieces of his uncertain career. With memories of Scotland still fresh, he suggested to the Dalziels a Scottish sequel to Brown, Jones and Robinson, which he would call "The Adventures of Brown, Jones and Robinson in the Highlands". He had made enough sketches on his holiday to complete several drawings for this new series, and the Dalziels engraved these. But they were never published, due to "his dilatory disposition and the many and varied engagements we had at that time on our hands" according to the engravers.[24] Like so many of Doyle's projects and plans from now onward, the book fell prey to his debilitating indecision. He needed a direction for his career, and more importantly he needed the will to pursue that direction, once he had decided upon it.

Deerstalking in the Highlands, from Doyle's unpublished series for the Dalziels, "The Adventures of Brown, Jones and Robinson in the Highlands". Victoria and Albert Museum.

Doyle's Bird's Eye Views of Society. No.3:
*A Morning Party. Shewing the Nobility and Gentry playing the
Fashionable Game of the Period, from* The Cornhill, *1861.*

V

Smothered by Society

1856 - 1867

Although Dick Doyle struggled with his career, he was easily diverted by the amusing attentions of his devoted friends. They provided the relief from worry and a chance to escape the Doyle household gripped by indecision and financial strain. Over the next few years, Dick was seldom without invitations to dinners, "At Homes" or country house parties; and in the end, such seemingly indulgent escapes from his work provided the key to his future.

A special friend was Matthew J. Higgins, the "gentle giant" (he was 6′ 8″ tall), of *Punch* days, journalist for *The Times* and *The Cornhill,* whose sympathetic nature proved a great comfort to Dick at this time. Higgins, or "Jacob Omnium" as his friends Thackeray and Leech called him, was often a familiar figure in society drawing rooms, his bearded head towering above the crowds in such an amusing manner that Dick later immortalized him in a Bird's Eye Views drawing. Moreover, Higgins was not afraid of controversy. As a journalist he exposed public abuses under various clever pseudonymns, like "Paterfamilias", "A Belgrave Mother", "John Barleycorn", or "A Thirsty Soul". He also shared Dick's concern over Ireland, and as the son of an Irish nobleman, he had served as agent for the British Association for the relief of destitute Irish during the potato famine. Finally, although he was not a Catholic himself, he had married the daughter of Lady Tichbourne, head of a prominent Catholic family, and was deeply impressed by Dick's *Punch* resignation. Indeed, during the lenten season of 1856, Higgins invited a group of prominent non-Catholic politicians to his house for dinner in Dick Doyle's

honour. Dick was clearly flattered by the gesture, afterwards explaining in a letter to Charles how he "was much amused by his having, although it was all for Protestants except myself, a fish dinner... One guest was astonished, kept saying 'It is not Friday, is it?' "[1]

The Pre-Raphaelite painters were valued acquaintances as well. Since his visit to Millais in Scotland, he had met Rossetti at his house in Cheyne Walk, and enriched his early friendship with William Holman Hunt, which became one of the most important of his life. They had met at a "little dance" given by fellow artist C.R.Leslie about 1850, and Holman Hunt clearly recalled years later the impression Dick made on him then; his "prized friend... standing against the wall, crush hat in one hand, one leg crossing the other... quite young, and his face spoke a happy mixture of interest and humour". By then Holman Hunt shared his friends Rossetti and Millais' admiration of Doyle's Manners and Customs series, which had "made his name a proverb throughout England, and himself a special idol of our Brotherhood". He watched this strange, bushy-haired young man for gestures or indications of his comic abilities to record what he saw around him. He noticed his almost apologetic laugh after combing the room with his sharp eyes for some amusing detail or character. "His eyes were dwelling upon every incident of the room with [a] merry twinkle, and when in facetious talk with another an idea amused him, he bent his face down towards his chest and held up his hat, as a lady might use a fan to hide her laughter."[2]

Thus began the long and valued friendship with Holman Hunt. And when Dick resigned from *Punch,* his new friend admired his princi-

William Holman Hunt was Doyle's close friend for over thirty years.

---

ples, "that while so rigid and consistent a religionist, he was one of the most charitable of men, and would never be a party to any scandal, however much it had been provoked". He was a "unique and delightful" source of entertainment, "overflowing with strange stories", usually about ghosts and witches which captivated Holman Hunt, whose own preoccupations with these evil creatures led to his illustrations to "Witches and Witchcraft" in *Good Words*, 1860. In turn, Holman Hunt could be relied upon for an amusing afternoon escape from London. He and Millais had taken a painting retreat at Worcester Park Farm in Surrey, an idyllic spot said to be the hunting box for Charles II's mistress, set in rolling sheep pastures which proved perfect for their landscape studies. Here Millais sought detail for his famous "Ophelia", while Holman Hunt prepared landscape backgrounds for "The Hireling Shepherd". It was here that Dick brought his brother Henry to visit his two painter friends, who were delighted to show their visitors their favourite haunts, and entertain them with tales of how they had convinced the nearby shepherds to lift and drop their sheep in the pasture to get them to stand still enough for their drawings, despite serious loss of wool. They ate in the kitchen and Dick told them stories of Thackeray's latest literary conquests. Holman Hunt showed Dick his moonlight studies of an ivy-smothered doorway which he eventually used in his famous "The Light of the World". They were strange, ghostly studies which appealed to Dick, and reminded Hunt that he "was not afraid of ghosts, and four years earlier had been restrained by a quaking companion from chasing one across the fields".[4]

Dick had long been an admirer of Millais, especially after the storm he caused with his "Christ in the Home of his Parents" at the Royal Academy in 1850. This painting was a severe, realistic portrait of Christ as a boy in his father's carpenter shop which offended many for its unashamed realism: Dickens declared Mary "would stand out from the rest of the company as a monster in the vilest cabaret in France or the lowest gin shop in England"; *The Times* wrote of a "morbid infatuation which sacrifices feeling to mere eccentricity". The painting in fact gave the Pre-Raphaelites their first notoriety. Dick went to see the work, and afterwards met Millais at the opera during the height of his notoriety. He boldly told him what he thought of the picture but, as he afterwards wrote to Charles, he was more impressed by the painter himself: "He is tall and rather good looking, very young and I rather like him. I am sure he will be one of our greatest painters hereafter. At present his faults are chiefly in 'taste', and that will no doubt improve."[5]

Another new and important acquaintance at this time was Alfred Tennyson, the Poet Laureate. Dick had visited him at his newly acquired home at Farringford on the Isle of Wight early in the 1850s, and during their meetings Tennyson grew to admire his new friend's wit and drawing talent. They met again at the Ashburtons' now famous Christmas country house parties, during the holidays of 1855. Tennyson had then just completed 'Maud', and he willingly read his famous poem to test the reactions of his fellow guests. In the evening after dinner, he guiltily left the table to smoke his pipe among the oranges, lemons and camelias in the Grange conservatory, and Dick followed. He watched carefully as Tennyson stood "tamping his pipe with his forefinger, looking somewhat quizzical at his own inability to quit the habit", and later Dick made a delightful drawing of his friend in this same pose.[6]

It was just one of several portrait sketches he made of Tennyson, mostly done from memory or quick sketches since the poet hated sitting for artists. But Doyle's sketches, however slight, captured the moods and changes of character in his friend better than most of the highly-finished portrait paintings which survive. He concentrated upon the dashing, Byronic image of the long haired Poet Laureate and drew him in a masterful and sensitive pencil line, not unlike a fine miniature of a cavalier or a medieval courtier. In addition, Tennyson persuaded him to paint a long, frieze-like watercolour copy of his favourite landscape view from his study window at Farringford; the wide sweep of pines and rolling hills he called "one of the finest on the island". Dick's painting pleased Tennyson so much he hung it in his study, and often pointed it out to his Farringford guests, among them an enchanted Lewis Carroll.[7]

Doyle's pencil portrait of Alfred Tennyson 9⅛ x 9⅛", British Museum.

Dick's next visit to Farringford caught his friend in the throes of remodelling his house, with packing cases everywhere and rooms in upheaval. Prince Albert had stunned the household a short time previous when he arrived unannounced, looked round the suitably bohemian looking rooms, their disorganized appearance obviously conforming to his ideal of a poet's residence, and liked what he saw so much he promised to bring the Queen next visit. By early spring Dick and the Catholic convert Sir John Simon made the perilous journey across the Solent to visit, having to walk two and a half miles after landing to reach the house. Although Dick was never a good sailor, on this occasion he endured considerable discomfort during the crossing, as Emily Tennyson recorded in her diary. He emerged from "a stormy passage in an open boat, and lost his hat. He wrapt himself in his plaid [Scottish rug] and the woman screams at the grey ghost when he goes to buy a hat".[8] Once there, however, Dick was determined to enjoy himself. He knew the attractions of the island from an early visit with his friend Leech, during a holiday to Bonchurch. But Tennyson showed him the natural wonders while walking upon his beloved chalk cliff paths, staring into the waves below while sea gulls soared overhead. Dick stayed at least a week during March, and even went to the island races with his host. Sadly, this was one of the last times he would enjoy Tennyson's company, as the two men's paths separated. By 1877 Dick had lost touch with his old friend enough to tell Frederick Locker (Tennyson's relative by marriage) how much he longed for the poet to visit his studio, "but I feel a little shy of asking him, it is so long since we met".[9]

One of the high points of 1857 was Dick's new friendship with Charles Hallé the musician and conductor. Hallé had been appointed musical director of the season's most spectacular artistic event, the Manchester Art Treasures Exhibition and he invited Doyle to visit the staggering display of paintings and antiquities, and concerts by international orchestras, as his guest. Although the two men had briefly known each other previously, Dick cautiously accepted the invitation for just three days. But when he met and stayed with Hallé's large family, and toured the exhibition with the nine children, he was so enchanted he stayed in Manchester for two months. Hallé was just five years Dick's senior,

*Doyle's sketches of the
Manchester Art Treasures
Exhibition of 1857,
done for Blanche's sister in
her catalogue.
Victoria and Albert Museum.*

a fine pianist, and most important of all a Catholic; attributes which helped to cement his friendship with Dick and make his visit memorable for them both. "Daily we studied the marvellous pictures together, and he opened my eyes to many beauties which I might have passed by," Hallé recalled. "He was no less quick in seizing upon any comical figure that presented itself in the motley crowd, and many were the pen-and-ink drawings which in rememberance of them he put on paper during our quiet evenings at home, and which I preserve carefully." On other occasions, Dick walked arm in arm with Blanche Stanley's sister Maude, sketching the most humorous exhibits in her catalogue.[10]

The exhibition itself was a celebrated and much publicized success, which collected together in an iron and glass building arranged like a cathedral, examples of English, Old Masters, Continental masterpieces and antiquities. These were to be viewed while Hallé's newly formed orchestra, and others from abroad, gave afternoon concerts on the altar-like platform in the gallery.

Here, as many journalists were fond of pointing out, music and art merged "like a beautiful dream". The papers diligently recorded the impressive list of visitors, who included the Queen, Tennyson, Dickens, Ruskin, Holman Hunt, as well as "Richard Doyle Esquire" – a sign of Dick's reputation at the time. Here Dick strolled each day and carefully studied paintings by artists he had long admired: works by Maclise, Vernet, Landseer, Mulready among the older generation; Millais, Holman Hunt, Arthur Hughes of the new Pre-Raphaelite generation, as well as work by the art world's recent discovery, Frederic Leighton. There were also sixteen Hogarths, numerous Gainsboroughs, Morlands, Constables, Bonningtons, and even watercolours by Dick's less than favourite artist, Turner. These shared the galleries with cases devoted to enamels, porcelain, china, carvings and armour. Dick was especially delighted by the Italian pictures section, which he carefully explained to Hallé. But he found the variety of visitors and the amusing antics of the crowds more to his comic taste, and delighted in over-hearing conversations from less than well-informed spectators. For example, the exhibition catalogue was full of misprints and Dick loved to listen to the bemused comments of visitors who clearly did not realise the mistakes. He watched an elderly man ponder a painting of King Lear on his deathbed, which the catalogue had mis-titled "There is life in the old dog yet", to which the old man nodded, "How true!" and passed on satisfied. Or another elderly gentleman stopped in front of a painting of a madman seated naked on the bare ground, his arms clenched round his knees. The catalogue called it "Portrait of Lord John Russell", to which the rather distinguished looking spectator added, "Probably when he was out of office".

Here too, Dick had a chance to renew his acquaintance with the fairy paintings of Richard Dadd. The exhibition included the now famous "Puck" seated on a mushroom and its companion, "Titania, or A Midsummer Night's Dream", which Dick had seen at the Royal Academy in 1841. Both works were spirited and harmless, and familiar subjects to Dick; but the catalogue thought it necessary to explain why they were exhibited at all, linking Dadd with William Blake as "examples of painters in whom a disordered brain rather aided than impeded the workings of a fertile and original fancy... But do not be deterred by the strangeness of Blake's work, or the sadness of Dadd's, from looking closely at both".[11]

After two months of daily visits to the gallery for the art and concerts, Dick very reluctantly returned to a London gripped by November fog. In such gloomy surroundings, he longed to be back in Manchester; and when he wrote to express his thanks to his friends the Hallés, he added, "Is the exhibition building so changed that its best friend would not know it again? Is my favourite lamp-post as firm and steady in the legs, and as light-headed as of yore?"[12] But his friendship with the Hallés continued, with visits to their home, where he met such distinguished musicians as the outspoken voice master of the Royal Academy of Music, Manuel Garcia, "absorbed in a game of chess". He joined the Hallé family on holiday at their summer home at Cowes, where he sat in the garden which stretched down to the sea and listened to his host's serenades on the piano, and stared into the horizon, delighted by the view. He loved these brief escapes from London, once reluctantly declining their invitation because "I dare not run away for a day, because I know that once in sight of the sea I should not be able to move from it. And oh! the Schuberts, Hellers, and the moonlight nights, how I wish my eyes and ears were among them."[13]

* * * * * * * * * * * *

Despite his *Punch* notoriety, by 1857 Dick Doyle was recognized by some authorities as a successful and influential illustrator. The prestigious *Men of our Time* reference volume of biographical sketches "of living notables, authors, architects, artists", devoted almost a full-page to his career. The entry stressed his early successes as "the son of the reputed author of the celebrated HB sketches" (although curiously John Doyle was overlooked in the book). Despite a wrong birthdate, this article was the first attempt to chart Dick's career as an artist. It stressed De Quincey's praise, "his tone of innocence all are to our mind the work of genius", and Thackeray's defense of his *Punch* resignation; that he was an artist with "wit which had no malice and mirth which has no folly".

Another mark of his popularity among fellow illustrators, was his contributions to the *Merry Pictures by the Comic Hands,* of H.K.Browne, Crowquill, Leech, Meadows, and Hine, which linked him with his successful *Punch* colleagues. And *Punch* continued to publish his drawings from the back stocks he had left at the office.

However, by the end of 1857, Dick had been commissioned to illustrate one of the most prestigious and important books of his career. It was called *The Scouring of the White Horse,* or The Long Vacation Ramble of a London Clerk, and written by a new literary sensation, Thomas Hughes, author of the astonishingly successful *Tom Brown's School Days,* published the year previous. Hughes's publisher, Macmillan, was anxious to capitalize on his reputation as quickly as possible, and urged him to produce a new story of his own choice, which Hughes began within six months of Tom Brown's success. He had been feted by many of Dick's famous friends, was invited to the homes of Lady Stanley, the Hon.Mrs Norton, and Little Holland House as well as entertained by the Tom Taylors. He soon moved to Mayfair to be nearer his society connections. It was here that

Dick Doyle probably first met him, and began a collaboration on the illustrations of the author's book as it was written.

The story Hughes wrote was a confused and disappointing tale, however. It recalled the famous last ceremony of the cleaning and scouring of the chalk horse in the hillside at Uffington, where every seven years until 1857 some thirty thousand villagers and curious spectators gathered to feast and celebrate, with games and contests and a fair, among the ramparts of Uffington Castle. It was an impressive sight, here told through the eyes of a London clerk, who witnessed the final ceremony with a mixture of stirring national pride and nostalgic love of the past. To Hughes, the white horse became a symbol of lost traditions, while in reality it was a 360' long creature stretching across the Berkshire downs, which some called a dragon, and legends called a horse. It had possibly been carved out of the earth (as deep as 130' at one point) by King Alfred; others said it was a tomb, or that it had mystical powers. If you stood on the animal's eye and revolved three times with your eyes closed, your wish would be granted. Such a rich source of legends took on magical dimensions and seemed to come alive every seven years with the animated figures of men picking and hacking at the white stone in the tall grass.

It was undeniably a good subject, and well-suited to Dick's own love of such legends. But Hughes failed to capture his audience with characters which remain mere ciphers, moved about to allow the real interest, the legend itself, to take over. There are familiar class prejudices echoed in Joe, the country lad's hatred of the Squire ("all squires are snobs"), the ineffectual but democratic country parson, and Joe's rather artificial girlfriend, Lucy. Joe watches the ceremony as a symbol of "our own quiet corner of the land of our birth", which stirs in him "the feeling that we are a family, bound together to work out God's purpose in this little island". He and his fellow rustics are glorified by Hughes for their natural goodness and common sense; the parson is a thoroughly human and democratic figure, yet throughout runs the longing – shared by many countrymen – for the lost days of chivalry, "when unpaid magistracy and powerful Church united people in fellowship before God".

Fortunately, although Dick's nineteen illustrations to the story vary in quality, some are striking and inventive enough to make the book appealing. He designed a familiar, intricate border with scenes from legends, like the battle of the Danes and Saxons, embossed in gold upon a bright blue cloth cover. He adopted his rustic style lettering of gnarled branches and twigs to spread across the title and frontispiece. This double-page wood engraved illustration is among his very best. Here crowds of soldiers hack away at the horse he drew sketched across both pages, while a regal looking King Alfred watches in the foreground. But the remainder of the drawings were done in a variety of styles, from simple *Punch* period outline, to dense circular shading of St George and the Dragon.

Part of the reason for Doyle's uneven performance appears in the series of letters he wrote to the book's publisher. These stretched over the unusually long period of eleven months which it took him to complete what became an unexpectedly difficult commission. Dick was in fact uncertain of himself from the start. He first produced a sample drawing at Macmillan's request, to accompany an advertisement for the book, but insisted his name as illustrator should be withheld, "till some further progress be made in the matter". When he started the drawings, he found he was short of money, and like his relations with the Dalziels, he asked a further payment for work as yet uncompleted, "although strictly speaking I am not entitled to receive any more payment... till the drawings for the book are done". He added his assurance that "there shall be no want of activity on my part in bringing the work to a rapid conclusion", if the publisher agreed to the further advance on his fee.

More to the point, Dick's poor health lay at the core of his problems over the drawings. Winter was always a difficult time for him, and by early 1858 he suffered a bout of influenza which left him weak and unwilling to work. He cancelled a plan to visit Uffington with Hughes, but was well enough by February to make the journey. He then told the anxious Macmillan how he wanted "to inspect together the scenes of action and as I am going to make a sketch or two on the spot, of the 'White Horse' fine weather is desirable". But the delays and excuses for missed deadlines increased. In a letter recommending a wood engraver to Macmillan, Dick admitted, "It is certainly most unlucky

Doyle's double-page title design for
The Scouring of the White Horse, *1858-59.*

that twice within a short period I have been stopped from work by illness. I hope this is the last for some time." He grows weak and absent minded, misplaces letters or sends others to the wrong address. Only when Macmillan's urgent pleas for news of his progress reach him does he feel guilty at stretching the drawings over so long a period. But he became indignant when the publisher suggested he simply did not take his work seriously: "I can assure you that I made some great exertions and having been more or less of an invalid for some time back, it was at some personal inconvenience that I endeavoured to meet your wishes."[14]

Moreover, Hughes had endured a nine month silence from his publisher over the fate of his book. When he did receive news, Macmillan told him how Doyle, "that dilatoriest of men" had at last sent all the drawings and the book would "assuredly be out" by 20 November 1858, in time for Christmas sales. But the publisher worried about more than Doyle's

delays by this time. Hughes had been convinced by his literary friends that the story needed revisions and he eventually rewrote a considerable portion of the book to give it more unity. As a result, Macmillan ordered a meagre five thousand copies printed initially: a sign either of caution or lack of confidence in the book. Although six thousand were sold within a fortnight, and by December a second edition was confidently planned, there the book's sales ended. A third edition did not appear until over thirty years later, in 1889. Poor or mixed reviews were partly to blame. Critics were expecting more of a narrative, which had made Tom Brown such a success; instead they found a thin story on which Hughes hung various legends, "most of them lies about the past" according to *The Times.* Hughes accepted this defeat and returned to his proven formula with his sequel *Tom Brown at Oxford* in 1861. But because of the trials of the White Horse drawings, Dick was driven further from his work, and for the next year at least, he refused to illustrate any new books.

* * * * * * * * * * * *

Apart from the White Horse failure, the Doyle family's problems again loomed over Cambridge Terrace in 1859. In particular, news of the troubled life of Charles became a source of great worry and Dick again agreed to visit him in Edinburgh. He hoped to renew his relationship with Charles's wife, and to pass on the family's greetings and love to his new nephew, Arthur Conan, who was born this year. But first he travelled north, to renew his memories of his favourite part of Scotland, the coastal waters around the Isle of Skye. He returned to Loch Hourn, the long, narrow expanse of water which drains into the sea, and travelled further west along its shore, pointing the boat towards Skye. He was especially attracted by Skye's medieval landscape which remains one of its finest features even today. Four years previous, he had taken the same journey with Robert Lowe, and now he longed to compare his memories of that brilliant sea and moonlit coast of Skye, as well as the dense mountain landscapes of the surrounding islands; views destined to reappear in his later fairy watercolours. On board his friend's yacht, "The Dadye", he played at captain, and kept a ship's log filled with comic ink and watercolour sketches of his journey. He made sketches of the coastline, and threw himself totally into what he described to Charles as "cruising about the Isle of Skye, and goodness knows what". But eventually duty cut short his pleasure, and he boarded the train for the exhausting all night journey from Inverness to Edinburgh, which he broke by spending a day in bed in a Perth hotel, and an unexpected meeting with his old friends the Millais and the Leslies.[16]

When he arrived in Edinburgh, he was surprised and saddened to find his brother's growing family living in a shabby neighbourhood, almost oblivious to their surroundings. Charles's strong-willed young wife Mary greatly impressed Dick, however, and he quickly learned to respect her strength and "fighting damn-your-eyes" spirit. It was obvious she "cared not twopence for anybody's opinion", and had set herself the formidable task of running the household and caring for her large family of an eventual ten children. Now just a twenty-one year old woman, she had learned from an even younger age to

Dick Doyle's pencil portrait of his sister-in-law Mary Foley, aged 17, done July 1854.

Charles Doyle, the dreamy, bearded artist and civil servant.

cope with the world, had been sent to France for her schooling and returned "fully grown up". She shared the Doyle family pride in it's ancestry. As a proud Irish Foley, she could trace her own Catholic ancestors back as far as the Plantagenets, and she determined to instil the same dedication to her past in her own family. Moreover, from the moment Dick saw a photograph of his new sister-in-law, he was taken by her distinctive charm. A small (5′ 1″ tall), grey-eyed woman with fair hair pulled back in a practical plait which gathered behind her ears, he thought she had unmistakeable "Irish charm". "She looks nice – decidedly so I should for a 'sun' pictur [photograph] which don't flatter, but the contrary," he told Annette when the photograph arrived just before Mary's wedding. Dick used it for his own pencil portrait of her, which her son Arthur cherished and reproduced in his autobiography. On the other hand, her husband eventually drew her portrait as a beggar woman in one of his later book illustrations to the appropriately titled *Friendly Hands, Kindly Words,* 1860.

Charles's attempts at illustration were half-hearted and full of disappointing struggles not only to get work but to receive payment from publishers after it was accepted. In this he found Dick a sympathetic and shrewd adviser. His letters to Charles are filled with well-meaning advice and practical hints to help place his career on a firm footing. When Charles attempted caricature, Dick wrote obviously delighted that the family traditions were carried on: "I congratulate you on having 'broke out' in the comic character of the Scotch HB." When Charles contributed drawings to an ill-fated magazine which ceased publication and refused to pay for his work, Dick consoled him that it was "a great bore it had not a chance of succeeding, as you might have put 20 or 30 pounds in your pocket. You must have at it again but only take care you don't go caricaturing the office people."[18] When Dick's friend Watts Phillips became chief cartoonist on the comic rival paper to *Punch* called *Diogenes,* Dick secured work for Charles on the paper. Although even here financial worries clouded his contributions: "You had better keep a sharp eye on the £ s d and mind its paid regular, for there is no use working for nothing," he advised after reading in a London paper of bankruptcy proceedings against the paper's publisher. "Of course if he

pays it don't matter whether he is bankrupt or not! Does it? O dear no! Not in the least."[19] Charles thought he might take a leaf out of his brother's successful book and produce his own illustrated volume of "Symbols", but Dick urged caution with the idea he called "an interesting one but of course a very laborious one". He suggested approaching a publisher first, before incurring heavy printing expenses, but of course "any meritorious works you can find time to attend to and publish out of office hours, will I am certain greatly assist your position in the Board of Works, and give you great advantage over the other 'persons' therein. Especially if such work appertains to architecture in any way".[20]

Gradually Charles began to establish himself as a comic illustrator, and published drawings in *The Illustrated Times* from 1856-60. These he preferred to keep a secret at first, but his brother James quickly spotted them, with his "quick eyes of a detective artist", and rushed in to show his father. "Par is delighted with 'em, " Dick reported back to Charles, "and if you are not well payed 'douce' take all the parties concerned in the paper." His own verdict was they were "CAPITAL" drawings with signs of real promise. "I wish to suggest that you should adopt some sign to put in the corner of your pictures so that people will begin to learn your identity though they don't know your name."[21] His illustrations appeared in more prestigious papers, like the influential *Good Words, London Society,* and *The Graphic,* all showcases for the most inventive and exciting illustrators of the period. He was more prolific with the more profitable book illustration commissions, however. By 1859 he had produced drawings for *Robinson Crusoe,* several boys adventure stories, *Pilgrim's Progress, John Gilpin,* as well as a series of colour printed nursery toybooks drawn in a style not unlike Walter Crane. His best work was for those bizarre fantasies which stretched and challenged his own vivid imagination: the illustrations to *Mistura Curiosa,* 1869, or the classical parody of Alice in Wonderland, *Our Trip to Blunderland,* 1877, which sold fifteen thousand copies in a year.

His later illustrations were dominated by his bouts of melancholia and violent anger, as well as the dreamy fantasy world into which he escaped when life became too difficult. There are glimpses of his unsettled state of mind in the

"The Witching Hour" by Charles Doyle.
Pen and ink over pencil, 7¼ x 13⅞"
Huntington Art Gallery.

scenes of wife-beating he drew for *European Slavery,* or Scenes from a Married Life, 1881. Perhaps his most famous drawings were the first ever published of Sherlock Holmes in "A Study of Scarlet" of 1888; Holmes drawn with the unmistakeable bearded features and tall stature of a younger Charles. They remain the only bearded version of the famous detective to be published.

On the whole, Charles developed a distinctive style in his meticulous, spidery ink drawings and pale flat washed watercolours. Like Dick he shared a preoccupation with the supernatural, and drew numerous large versions of seances or spiritual legends, like "The Witching Hour – the Unseen Audience". These were usually full of carefully shaded figures with terrified expressions, or dark shadows picked out in meticulous ink-work surfaces, not unlike the wood engraver's style of shading. And although Charles accepted payment for his published drawings, he rarely allowed his admirers of these large and spooky drawings and watercolours to pay for them, giving them away to avoid the embarassment of setting a price on them.

Many of Charles's drawings were worked up versions from the sketchbooks he kept, since he shared Dick's childhood habits. Together they delighted in word puzzles and puns, experimented with comedy and witty illustrated versions of aphorisms: a spectral horse in blue washes becomes "The jolly night mare"; a flowering branch of currents entwined around a pensive looking woman's head illustrated "The Current Idea". Some of his ideas came directly from Dick's letters, like the time he received a list of new subjects for experiments: "I want to unburden my mind of a little bit of 'facetiae', which weighs upon my (good) spirits. It consists of a few articles culled from a paper, and gathered together for a museum... 1) A garment for the naked eye 2) Eggs from a nest of thieves 3) A buckle to fasten a laughing stock 4) The animal that drew the inference. P.S. The last 2 make me 'laff'."[22]

Dick's greatest concern in advising his brother was to help him earn the necessary extra income he so obviously needed to support his family. Once he proposed that Charles should act as his Scottish agent and try to sell his paintings; it would earn his brother a commission and help his own career as well. Charles willingly agreed, and to Dick's delight he quickly found a buyer for the first painting, and a possible American client for a second. "I wrote to say the other drawing has so much in it that I think you might ask a decidedly good sum, and if the parties won't come up to the mark the drawing can wait a little, and I will send you others. What do you say to trying 100 or 80 pounds?" The paintings were generally early juvenile watercolours like the kind Dick had done for his father's annual Christmas present, many of which remained unfinished. These Dick suggested Charles might touch up and finish before offering them to clients. "I have not the same nervousness about selling unfinished or juvenile works there [in Scotland] as I have 'here', though America, as I said, I like still better. You are a trump, however, it strikes me, and I am delighted that you should make your percentage on the business."[23]

Although Charles and his family would always live in a succession of rented houses in shabby, run-down neighbourhoods in the New Town district of Edinburgh, his salary was apparently insufficient for better housing. Dick decided to join forces with his father and their political friends to get Charles a rise in salary in 1856. This was in way of a compromise, however, since they had hoped Charles would return to London for a better paid post in the Accountant-General's Office. The idea filled Charles with horror, but most of all he feared the return to the daunting atmosphere of London, as he explained in an unusually frank letter to Annette: "I have the greatest horror of being herded with a set of snobs in the London office, who would certainly not understand and probably laugh at the whole theory of construction, as also the technical terms in use among the builders here, to whom brick is an unknown quantity. The Accountant-General's office I simply could not stand. But if the present vacancy is anything in the way of composition, writing, or architecture work – where I would be left to myself, to do my best without any interference till I had done so – I would without hesitation accept the office." In the end, Charles never left Edinburgh, despite the efforts of his family and friends. He remained prey to indecision and melancholia; at one point he even considered a vague idea of going out and digging for gold in Australia.[24]

Meanwhile, brothers Henry and James were slowly finding their professional footings in London. Henry was now by far the most ambitious member of the family, his precocious critical judgements of paintings from childhood now standing him in good stead with his chosen career as an artist. He was a careful if uninspired draughtsman with a meticulous nature, however,

which kept him torn between a career as a painter or an art historian. He started out under Dick's direction, drawing comic initials for *Punch,* then transferred to its rival *Fun.* Here he became known for his decidedly derivative comic characters drawn as diminutive full-length portraits with large heads in his famous brother's style. As a portrait painter he was more successful, and willing to exploit his family's Catholic reputation to gain patronage. He visited the wealthy homes of prominent Catholic families with his friend Cardinal Wiseman and charged £10 or £15 for watercolour portraits of his host's family members. He made a portrait drawing of John Ruskin and practiced his technique on his father, as well as his friend Cardinal Wiseman. This latter work culminated in a highly successful oil portrait of the Cardinal for the Royal Academy in 1858, and a subsequent popular engraving of the painting. He soon became known as a Catholic religious painter and listed among his portrait subjects Cardinal Antonelli, prominent Church dignitaries, "but had no sitting from the Pope", Dick told Charles once. His remark hinted how proud he was by his brother's success. Henry then moved to Ireland, where he decorated a Catholic chapel, and met and married Jane Ball, the daughter of the Justice of Common Pleas of Ireland. In 1866 he turned his back on his painting to become director of the National Gallery of Ireland, and moved to Dublin where he remained for twenty-three successful years at the gallery. There he wrote an illustrated *History of Ireland,* 1868, compiled the gallery's new catalogue, as well as sporadically exhibiting his paintings at the Royal Hibernian Academy, being elected member there in 1874. His keen critical eye led to an impressive number of gallery purchases of works by Rubens, the early Dutch School as well as Rembrandt, his favourite painter. Having been born in Dublin, he felt a distinctive surge of national pride when he initiated a study collection to promote "a truly Irish School of Art" among art students, and he founded a National Historical and Portrait Gallery.

James, on the other hand, was the austere, highly critical head of the family, who took his position very seriously. He was refined, if aloof in society, a tall, long bearded figure who often accompanied Dick, and was nicknamed "The Priest" for his distinctive presence. He had dismissed Henry's early comic drawings as "the merest child's play"; in later years he took over from his father as the dominating figure in the Doyle household. Nevertheless, his accomplishments in his chosen field of painting, illustration and geneology were a further credit to his family. His passion for heraldry and ancestral history was responsible for maintaining the Doyle family name as a prominent force in the higher, aristocratic circles in which he eventually mixed.

James began his artistic career as a painter, as Dick's childhood letters suggested in passages where Dick moaned over his brother's experiments with oil paint, while he still struggled with watercolour. His first major success was indeed impressive, a painting he called "A Literary Party at Sir Joshua Reynolds' " which was essentially a group portrait of famous writers. It was engraved as a large print in 1848, sold for £6 a copy and sold out in two years. A second edition followed in 1851, as well as prints or plans for further similar subjects, like "Caxton and his Press", and a lithograph of the Duke of Wellington's horse. This was no doubt done at

---

Preliminary uncoloured drawing in pen and ink, from the manuscript page to A Chronicle of England *by James Doyle.*

the instigation of his father, the Duke's look alike, to commemorate the Duke's death. James was also a talented fresco designer, whose designs from Walter Scott appeared in the Queen's summer house at Buckingham Palace. Dick was so proud of this that he tried to get Charles to get him further fresco commissions in Edinburgh's public buildings, but this came to nothing.[25]

He turned from painting to writing and illustrating his own books, and to compiling notes for his passionate interest in heraldry and geneology. He had developed a love of history from his childhood, when he and Dick had compiled their comic histories together, although he took a greater interest in historical fact than his brother. His first book, *A Chronicle of England, BC 55 - AD 1485,* was a labour of love, which he illustrated with eighty-one watercolours. These were engraved and colour printed by Edmund Evans and published in one of the most remarkable specimens of Victorian colour printing ever produced. Despite its high price of two guineas, the book sold out in two years. James was encouraged enough by this success to spend the next thirteen years on a more serious work of scholarship. He filled his *Historical Baronage of England,* 1886, with over a thousand drawings in three volumes, but sadly this venture proved a financial failure. And yet it was a

James Doyle's colour printed illustration to A Chronicle of England, *1864, depicting the death of De Montfort.*

monumental achievement, begun under the approving eye of his father, who died before it was published. It also served as the basis for James's friendship with the equally passionate geneologist Mary Doyle, his sister-in-law. He often sent her large elaborately painted cardboard shields of family crests and she would thrust them at her young son Arthur, with a sharp, "Blazon me this shield!" and expect a quick accurate account of the symbols used on each. James remained devoted to his studies and to his family's reputation. He proudly wrote to Charles how during his researches at the Public Record Office the Keeper told him, "You bear a very distinguished name, and as a son of so eminent a man as your father, you enjoy a great advantage over most people". And when he eventually married, late in life, he was invited to spend his honeymoon as the guest of the Duke of Norfolk at Arundel Castle. He clearly was a valued and respected friend to some of the period's most influential figures, among them aristocrats, politicians as well as religious leaders; although in the end, James Doyle remains an elusive, very private member of the family, about whom very little is known.[26]

* * * * * * * * * * * * *

Throughout the 1860s, Dick Doyle's dependence upon his friends and constant appearances with them in society occupied most of his time.

His work suffered as a result, but he was not willing to give up these much valued escapes from obligation and worry. He had collected a number of highly influential acquaintances over the years. As a member of The Stafford Club, he spent a good deal of his time away from home, writing letters and dining with fellow members there. He was also a member of the more prestigious Athenaeum Club. Both served as his base, from which he conducted his social life, entertained friends and relations, and launched campaigns to influence political and religious issues debated in Parliament. He was a much respected member of both clubs, as well as a frequent visitor in Belgravia and Mayfair society, dining there "with no particular object except to spend the passing hour pleasantly and to make it pleasant for others," according to Rossetti's brother.[27] He also occasionally visited his more bohemian friends, like Rossetti at Cheyne Walk, or the famous literary and artistic circles which centred around Campden Hill and Little Holland House; but on the whole he preferred the more influential aristocratic society to struggling artists or overnight literary sensations.

This life of dining out and constant entertainment took its toll upon his appearance, however, and his face began to show signs of strain; his laughter faltered occasionally as his conscience told him to pull himself away from the frivolous customs of society to look deeper at life. But these were momentary lapses, and he continued his taxing social schedule until his death. The portraits of Doyle at this time suggest how much he had changed from his mop-haired, exhuberant youth. Although he seems to have practiced moderation in his eating habits and, as one friend observed, "remained thin at an age when his friends developed middle-age spread" he had a Pickwickian appearance, a high forehead, balding yet handsome greying hair, which gave substance to his generally impish nature. When he laughed, he still delighted his friends and when he lapsed into amused periods of silence, one friend suggested he looked like "a philosopher and the dreamy eyes of a visionary, rather like the head of Oliver Goldsmith".[28]

He was a gracious guest who observed the formalities of society with ease and delight. His favourite position while visiting a crowded room was to stand up against the doorway, his eyes constantly following the traffic in and out, as he moved to let a waiter or guest pass. He called

Dick Doyle
by his brother Henry.
Oil on canvas, 19 x 16"
Courtesy of the
National Gallery of Ireland.

this his "two-way view" which gave him a chance to observe his fellow guests without having to fight his way through the crowd. He suffered from shyness throughout his life; a curious weakness since he never seems to have allowed it to influence or alter his visits in society. Instead he relished the attention paid him by famous hostesses, and tried to reciprocate with amusing stories or anecdotes which added to his reputation as a delightful if childish wit. Once he wrote to comfort Lady Gordon, who was ill in bed, and filled his letter with comic sketches of the recent epidemic of influenza which paralyzed Belgravia but which he refused to allow to influence his social life. He told her how he had dined at the Dowager Lady Molesworth's under most uncomfortable circumstances: "I do assure you in a couple of rooms closely packed with the nobility and gentry every lady was sneezing and blowing her nose, every gentleman sighing and feeling feverish, and feeling 'seedy' (that was the expression), and there was a low murmur on the surface of 'Society' of 'Let's go home'. The conversation of the night was not brilliant, consisting chiefly of the words 'Have you got it yet?' "[29]

The list of Dick Doyle's social engagements at this time is indeed impressive. He continued to visit Mrs Procter's home, where he shared the evenings with Browning, Thackeray, Dickens, Carlyle and Forster. The noted journalist and socialite, Henry Chorley, was often there, or he entertained Dick at his Eaton Place home, where they discussed his music reviews for *The Atheneaum.* Despite Thackeray's ill-fated romance with Mrs Brookfield, Dick was a favourite visitor to her home. Once he graciously acknowledged her invitation: "Always answer when you are spoken to was one of the precepts instilled into my infant mind – when I was an infant, and I am anxious as far as possible to show my behaviour in the direction of good manners."[30] He was equally gracious and witty with politicians, and with Monckton Milnes he was the only non-political guest at Lady Palmerston's exclusive soirées at Cambridge House. He knew dukes and lords, prominent barristers and businessmen in the City. Once the Prince of Wales invited "My dear Doyle" to an informal dinner at his club, "if so inclined".[31] The secret of his popularity was his endearing habit of telling anecdotes and stories, which he began confidently, then paused to chuckle into habit of telling anecdotes and stories, which he began confidently, then paused to chuckle into his cravat before finishing; or he flattered his fellow guests by laughing uproariously at their own jokes, rocking back in his chair in fits of laughter which delighted even more than the story itself. In fact when questioned, few friends could actually remember Dick's stories, only the way he told them and that they had laughed so much. To them he was always "Dear old Dicky Doyle", "Poor dear Dicky Doyle" or "Unique, delightful Dick Doyle"; the subject of praise for his gentle sense of harmless fun, pure nature and sweet disposition, but always without malice. On the other hand, his flawless reputation irritated some more earnest artist colleagues, especially the more outspoken members of the Hogarth Club. Their bohemian habits and willingness to sacrifice comfort for their work were somehow alien to Dick. Among their number was the notorious "thoroughgoing Bohemian", Albert Smith, who admired Dick but with reservations: "Doyle is a good fellow enough – but he's not one of us".

Fortunately a few Doyle stories and anecdotes survive to indicate his peculiar wit and sense of humour. Charles Hallé recalled how Dick had battled the icy streets to reach his club, then burst in laughing so hard he could barely tell the story of what he had just seen. As he clutched his way down the street, he had seen "a gentleman in evening clothes crawling on all fours on the pavement by the Green Park. On looking down he saw that it was the Duke of Devonshire, at that time Lord Hartington. He told Doyle that he had been falling down so

often he did not dare to get on his legs again, and was trying to fetch Devonshire House that way. Doyle said that if a Minister of War, as Lord Hartington then was, did make a progress on all fours along Piccadilly, he was glad he was there to see it."[32] Another time Dick was the only passenger on an omnibus and as was his habit he carefully listened to the conversation between the driver and the conductor. The conductor goaded his companion into driving faster, and the bus raced forward for a time, then slowed up, until the conductor again objected. The driver, hinting that his bus was now fit for a hearse, imitated the slow rhythm of the bus with his voice: "Well, Will-i-am! After all, – I don't see why you *should worry!* We've plenty of time. We shall do-it-easy. The cemetary – don't – shut – till – five!"[33] Such was the quality of local humour which had amused Dick from childhood.

Dick was the frequent guest at two rival London salons: the artistic evenings at Arthur Lewis's Moray Lodge on Campden Hill, and the teas and dinners at Little Holland House, in nearby Holland Park. Moray Lodge was the home of the rich silk mercer turned patron of the arts, Arthur Lewis. A friend of the Pre-Raphaelites Millais, Holman Hunt and Arthur Hughes, he had helped to establish the young illustrator Frederick Walker, (destined to replace Dick Doyle as Thackeray's illustrator). Lewis's monthly bachelor evenings were famous, with "Music 8.30, Oysters at 11", and an assortment of seemingly incompatible guests, who ate and sang the night away. Here Dick eagerly enjoyed meeting his old friends Tom Taylor, Leech, Millais and Thackeray, as well as some of Lewis's own discoveries, like the horsedealer Tattersall, or Poole, the famous tailor rumoured to have once lent Louis Napoleon £10,000. Here in summer the parties spilled into the garden, with entertainment by the "Moray Minstrels", those talented singers and actors among Lewis's friends. By 1863 a wide-eyed young illustrator, George Du Maurier, was amazed at how lavish these evenings had become, "more and more gorgeous; half the peerage will be there tonight and very likely the Prince of Wales". In addition to such entertainment and the chance to renew old acquaintances, it cannot be overlooked that from Dick Doyle's point of view, Moray Lodge was tantalizingly close to Lord Airlie's London residence (second in the road), where his beloved Blanche often stayed on trips to London.

One guest whom Dick met at Moray Lodge provided his entrance into the rival world of Little Holland House society. Valentine Prinsep was a struggling painter whose mother kept a covetted salon in the grounds of her house, in the idyllic depths of woods and countryside two miles from Hyde Park. Mrs Prinsep loved to assemble the famous and the recently discovered on the lawn of her home, to serve them tea or occasionally dinner under the tall elms in the garden. Here Holman Hunt recalled the "leaders of English society" flocked at her invitation: "Aristocrats there were of ministerial dignity, and generals fresh from flood and field, appearing in unpretending habit, talking with the modesty of real genius... Mrs Prinsep was cordiality itself, and surrounded by her sisters, could not but make an Englishman feel proud of the beauty of the race." These were memorable events, when "many artists were present and literary stars shone in brilliant scintillation", many of whom had crossed the border from Moray Lodge to infiltrate the more genteel world of Holland House. Here Tennyson, Swinburne, Rossetti and Browning were entertained with Leighton, Millais, and Frederick Walker of the Moray Lodge world. Dick had met his friend Charles Hallé here, and renewed acquaintances with Manuel Garcia, as well as listened to music provided by the famous violinist Joseph Joachim.

During the 1850s Dick had been drawn to Little Holland House by his painter friend George Frederick Watts. Watts was then a struggling artist with a brilliant future, a mural painter, illustrator, sculptor destined to earn the epithet, "England's Michelangelo". He had been rescued from poverty in 1851 by Mrs Prinsep and given a studio in her home, where he remained for twenty-four years. Dick had admired his friend's grand historical designs for the Houses of Parliament and shared a common disgust with Irish poverty (Watts had visited the country during the worst of the upheavals) and the doomed plight of the people of Ireland. He also shared high-born friends from among Mrs Prinsep's relatives, like the Earl and Countess of Somers. They had ordered Watts to design frescoes for their dining room at Carlton House Terrace, and Watts had chosen "The Elements" as a theme, using figures he borrowed from

Greek mythology and Venetian painters. Dick knew the Earl and Countess as well, and having eagerly followed the progress of their dining room decorations, he was invited to the grand celebration at their completion, along with forty other guests. It was a typical, if somewhat tedious social event. The young George Du Maurier, who was also invited, was delighted to escape, and by the comic antics of Dick (whom he called "a stunner") and Mrs Prinsep in the carriage going home: "Jolly Mrs Prinsep drove me nearly home though quite out of her way; so droll – she and Dick Doyle in the back seat, Val Prinsep and I on the other smoking two enormous cigars we had stolen from Milor [Earl of Somers], and Mrs P [rinsep] cuddling poor Doyle because he couldn't bear the smoke or the window being open."[34]

During the twenty or so years Dick Doyle frequented the most famous drawing rooms of London, he noticed the gradual changes in social custom. The era of restraint and careful selection among guests which was practiced during his father's heyday, which he had seen during his childhood, had been replaced by a new wave of radical reform in the drawing room, based upon egalitarian principles and the cult of the famous. Hostesses vied for the most famous personalities to grace their parties, and filled their homes with people to display their talent for lionizing. "The tendency of Society in England is to grown large: indeed, to be unwieldy. London has become the centre of the civilized world. It is the fashion to know everyone and to go everywhere and the struggle to accomplish this feat inevitably expands Society," remarked one of the period's grandest and most successful hostesses. Lady Jeune attacked the regrettable custom of inviting too many guests, "packed together in a hot room, much too small for half their number, a surging crowd composed of the most opposite elements... an assemblage of people more or less interesting and distinguished, none of whom they know by sight, in whose experience, indeed, they never interested themselves until it became the fashion to invite the Lions and make them roar."[35]

This frantic and generally ridiculous celebrity hunt became the subject of Dick Doyle's new drawings. He knew too well the scenes of defenseless new discoveries feted and made to look ridiculous by gloating hostesses and their bored husbands. He had seen too many furious

"Lionizing" a Doyle pencil frieze depicting the hollowness of notoriety in Victorian Society.
2 x 12⅛"
British Museum.

---

dowagers as they jealously guarded their inno-cent daughters from the unsuitable fortune hunters and inept swells who crowded round such beauty like bees to a honey pot. Such

---

Doyle's preliminary title design for "The Present State of Parties" inspired his later Bird's Eye Views of Society, *1861-62. Here the margin sketches are just as telling as the roundels.* Christie's.

subjects preoccupied him from now onwards. They filled the series of delightful pencil friezes he experimented with, filling the small, 2" wide borders with dowagers curtseying to an ass, ladies bowing to a society lion, or swells racing after bags of money. They were satiric jabs at society's injustices and echoed Thackeray's views on the lamentable marriage market. The gentle pencil humour of Manners and Customs had now turned sour, after his years of watching society from the edge of the room. In fact Dick planned a new book of such illustrations, which he hoped to call *The Present State of Parties*. His title design alone suggests the idea was to include the current dances, yet women and men dressed in eighteenth century fashions. His talent for sharply observed detail appears in the

characters – from a wide-eyed innocent girl, a bored woman of the world, and an aging old footman – he sketched at the base of the title design. Dick completed twelve drawings for the book, each about folio size ("of all varieties of 'English Nights Entertainments' ", he told Charles); then he tried to find a publisher who would give him "a share in the work". But he was "put off" by other projects, until Thackeray asked for a series of illustrations for his *Cornhill* magazine. Dick returned to his original idea and completed sixteen masterful satiric studies of society he called "Bird's Eye Views of Society". They were given prominence as fold-out plates, wood engraved by the Dalziels in issues from 1861-62, accompanied by Doyle's complementary initial letters and brief articles written by Dick to describe the scenes. Later the whole series appeared in book form, like a splended photograph album which he entitled *Bird's Eye Views of Society taken by Richard Doyle,* 1864.

The Bird's Eye Views were based upon his own experiences in society. They echoed his

Manners and Customs themes, yet were drawn in a more refined, carefully detailed style. His crowded drawing rooms are filled not with cutout figures but a sea of faces, well-rounded and expressive caricatures of familiar society "types": the demure young innocent beauty in frills and flowers, the haughty, frowning connoisseur, or bored philistine. And where these figures were crudely drawn in the previous series, here they are meticulously developed; in a dense crowd every face has a personality and recognizable pose. For example, in " 'At Home;' – Music" he drew an elegant drawing room, with marble columns and crystal chandelier flooded by a sea of guests, some attempting to sing while others merely attend to make up the audience. It is a scene of sophisticated chaos, as more guests flood through the curtained doorway, adding to those already forced into the very corners and up the columns of the room. Among them, Dick drew familiar faces: his own self-portrait peering behind a column; his father attentively listening in the foreground, while the most clearly drawn woman is a strikingly beautiful Blanche, Countess of Airlie, who sits demurely behind his father, toying with her fan. It was one of several scenes in the series which Dick described in his accompanying text as "chiefly for the information of country cousins, intelligent foreigners, and other

Bird's Eye Views of Society, *1861-62:*
a) "At Home – Music. And what makes it the more gratifying is that the Chorus is composed exclusively of Amateurs."

remote persons; also young ladies and gentlemen growing up, and not yet out, to let them know what and where they might expect to go if they should 'give up to parties what is meant for mankind'." His descriptions are comic attempts to initiate his largely middle-class readers into the "delights of society", just as he had so successfully done with his early Brown, Jones and Robinson series. But here he adopted the role of the critic as well as the storyteller; with scenes in which, as he put it, "a philosopher may, although a stout lady be standing upon each of his patent-leather feet, in agony... he may, I suggest, still if he has any pluck find amusement and instruction".

Other drawings depicted the delights of a children's party, not unlike those he had experienced at Dickens's house. Here he draws the children for which he was often praised, with round, cherubic faces and sharp features, engaged in a party dance, while their mothers and governesses politely supervise the proceedings. What amuses Dick most by such occasions is the unexpected comedy between the young guests when forced to play decidedly adult roles: a small girl he calls "that little fairy" is

finally lured onto the dance floor by a suspicious little boy, who afterwards remarks, "I enjoyed myself very much, but I am full of kicks". In "The State Party", Dick attacks the over-indulgent diners at a most "solemn, pompous, and profuse banquet", with a waiter for every guest and almost as many courses to the meal. "I would humbly submit, that if there was only half as much at dinner, one might be invited twice as often," he notes at the end of his attack. Another View represented "A Picture Sale", in which an auction room lined with paintings is crowded out by a group of fashionably dressed philistines, members of what his father once called "the new breed of art patron". To Dick they were ignorant of the arts but "most valuable to look at" as personalities. As members of "the unemployed classes of the West End", they were out to enjoy "one of the most fashionable modes of passing an hour or two after breakfast... Perhaps you are not aware how exquisite is the pleasure some people find in 'buying' an article they don't want for less than its proper value." He borrowed his Manners and Customs subject of life in Belgravia, and drew a Bird's Eye View of Belgrave Square, which he fills with idle young ladies "not yet out"; "some at play, others reading the mild emotional domestic novel, and not having found their lives as yet a bore".

b) "A Juvenile Party".

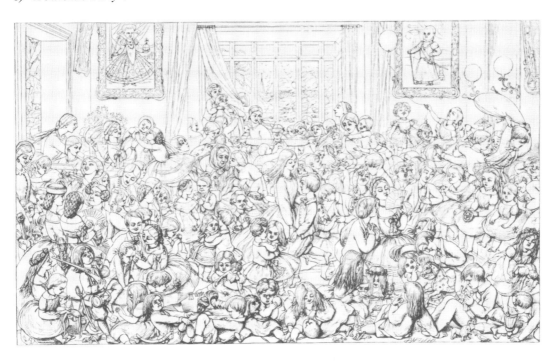

Doyle's friends and period celebrities appear in "Science and Art Conversazione", from Bird's Eye Views of Society, *1861-62.*

Dick was especially fond of including portraits of his friends in these drawings. In the first "At Home" in the series, he drew the bearded Matthew Higgins towering above a mass of hungry fellow guests, while he himself appears in his familiar doorway pose. In "Science and Art Conversazione", the scientist Michael Faraday is drawn in the centre of a crowded gallery, while the throngs of eager spectators rush to tables filled with scientific instruments and documents, maps and even a wartime cannon. In such a setting Dick declared "more useful knowledge could be acquired than in all the balls in the season, or out of the season". To the far left he drew a demure if sad-faced Holman Hunt with his unmistakeable long bushy beard as he showed a group of guests his portfolio of draw-ings presumeably of his latest journey to the Holy Land. It was clearly a difficult experience for the young artist, as Dick's portrait suggested; with Holman Hunt standing beside his work, explaining drawings to "admiring amateurs, or pompous collectors, or purseproud patrons". In the opposite corner, gathered around a table

filled with stereoscopic slides, Dick drew the figures of Tyndall, Harriet Martineau and Thomas Carlyle. Miss Martineau at least was clearly unfamiliar with the device as she stares into it with both eyes open. Finally Dick Doyle concluded the sixteen drawings in the series with a pet hate – cigar and cigarette smoke. He never indulged in this popular habit; and certainly one of the reasons he preferred the edge of a crowded room, close to the doorway, was the chance it allowed him to breathe gusts of clean air, untainted by smoke. He drew a room of a gentleman's club with its members immersed in clouds of their own smoke, and he introduced it by saying it was "not the result of personal experience of smoke, but conjecture derived from contemplating mankind's expression of face and attitude when under the influence of a weed". And the addiction was a mystery to him: "When the curls of cloud go wafting slowly upwards, perhaps they sometimes obscure for the moment a misfortune, or shut out for the time some of the worries of life; or it may be that the smoker, his head thrown back and his eyes turned up towards the sky and to the ceiling, beholds a whole panorama of splendid castles in the air. But they begin in smoke and end in smoke."

When the sixteen drawings were published in

book form, in time for Christmas 1863, the critics greeted them with mixed responses. The conservative *Athenaeum* (16 January 1864) strongly objected to Doyle's limited choice of subjects from " 'Society' in its narrowest sense. To look at these 'Views' one would think man existed only at the 'West-End'. Mr Doyle's taste denies him the range of many a fine expanse of thought and ourselves the happiness of enjoying his experiences in them." But the paper's critic praised his abilities to capture all too familiar social foibles and faux pas. Of the "Science and Art Conversazione" the *Atheneaum* critic asked his readers, "How often do we see the self-conscious artist displaying his drawings, the ladies pretending to try to look through microscopes with both eyes shut or both open, the dismal woman with her hair let down about her shoulders, and the obsequious folks making way for the venerable peer?"

Doyle's *Bird's Eye Views of Society* echoed many of the prejudices and outraged reactions to society he shared with his valued friend Thackeray. In fact its publication late in 1863 was followed by the tragic announcement of Thackeray's death on 24 December. The book then served as Dick's tribute to their friendship; one which had been at times dogged by anger and argument but which never broke down. (Dick had been invited to Thackeray's home as late as April of the year he died.) And his friend's death signalled a period of personal trauma and grief over the next few years.

Thackeray's death was followed by that of another close friend and much loved colleague, John Leech. His sudden death the following year shocked the many *Punch* colleagues and artist friends who flocked to the funeral and unashamedly mourned the passing of a remarkable man. "We all forgot our manhood and cried like women," Millais later explained, after standing silently with his fellow artists at the graveside. Here Dick joined his *Punch* colleague John Tenniel, as well as Landseer, John Gilbert, Dickens and Arthur Lewis, and after the ceremony he and Millais organized a benefit sale of Leech's drawings and paintings for his destitute widow and children. They also campaigned hard for a pension for the family. Dick lobbied his influential political friends and countered their objections that pensions had never been given to artists – only literary figures – by arguing "Leech's drawings were 'literary' in one sense as what was written under them was a considerable element in their success".[36] Needless to say, he won his case, and the Leech children were given £50 a year by the government.

By the end of 1864 the Doyle family had regretfully moved from Cambridge Terrace, to a smaller house further north at 54 Clifton Gardens, Maida Hill (now Vale). The family's serious financial state had probably forced the decision to abandon their favourite home, where so many happy times had been spent. The new house was certainly in a more remote and less fashionable district; although more countrified and near Regent's Park, it was also closer to the notorious St John's Wood, of "kept women" and secret rendezvous in a district of leafy lanes, small cottages and suburban villas. And although all Dick's brothers moved with the family to Clifton Gardens, it was not long before Henry moved away to Ireland, and eventually Dick abandoned the house for his own studio in Fulham. This would leave only his father and eventually only James to share the small new house with Annette, who continued to housekeep in her own exemplary manner.

Fortunately the move was marked by a new book commission which Dick agreed in principle to take on. He did not then know the troubles which lay ahead but he must have sensed the impending difficulties when he learned more about the book's author. Frederick Locker was a popular poet of slight, though inoffensive verses, the best known of which were compiled in *London Lyrics*. These clever if overly sentimental verses in the *vers society* style, were highly praised by his famous artistic and literary friends, among them Thackeray, Trollope, George Eliot, Browning, Ruskin, and Tennyson – to whom he would become related by his daughter's marriage to Tennyson's son Lionel. Locker was, above all, a society dandy, who loved to lionize and collect famous personalities, just as he loved to buy rare books and pictures. His first marriage to the daughter of Lord Elgin lent credence to his social aspirations, and although he became a civil servant, his heart was never in his work, and he suffered chronic ill health which forced him into premature retirement. This gave him the leisure to pursue his real love, socializing and endearing himself to his more talented literary and artistic friends.

Moreover, Locker was especially fond of young illustrators. He had befriended the talented but difficult Cruikshank, and persuaded him to illustrate *London Lyrics*. Later he would become the personal confidante to Kate Greenaway as she struggled with her career, as well as her rival Randolph Caldecott. In each instance Locker tried to monopolize each artist's work, offer criticism and business advice which, however well-meaning, usually was based upon only a slim knowledge of what an illustrator actually did – technically at least – to produce a book. And so it was that in 1864 Dick was sent a copy of Locker's *London Lyrics* with a proposal for illustrations to a new edition. It was flattering alone to think he might replace his favourite Cruikshank's drawings for the book, and so he

---

Children and romance dominated Doyle's illustrations to A Selection from the Works of Frederick Locker, *1865:*
a) "On an Old Muff"

b) "A Wish".

agreed. "I have read the 'Lyrics' with very much pleasure," he told Locker on receiving the book. "I must also express my admiration at the very pretty and tasteful manner in which the volume is got up as to paper, printing &c."[37] The commission was in fact for an illustrated edition in the "Moxon Miniature Poets" series, for which Dick was at first given fairly free hand choosing which poems to illustrate. He re-read the poems with this in mind, and chose those with simple, direct themes. Locker's passion, if not obsession with infants appeared in several poems he felt suited his own talent for juvenile drawings. There were poems on the theme of young love, like "A Wish", which Dick drew as a pair of child lovers in a churchyard, the boy crowning his love with flowers. There were poems of fairyland, like "My Mistress's Boots", with the lines: "The fairy stitching gleams, On the toes and in the seams"; as well as sentimental and melancholic lines on the passing of time, as in "On an old Muff": "Time has a magic wand!" Here Dick drew a chubby cupid emerging from a musty hand-muff upon a book covered table. Other verses dwelt upon the hollowness of society, as in the aptly named "Vanity Fair".

In the end, Dick chose sixteen of these poems which he felt were "the most pictorially 'suggestive' and therefore worth illustrating". He then sent his list to Locker for approval. "I think that a 'literal' illustration of a poem is likely to be prosy, and that, so long as it does not run counter to the sentiment, that what I may call a free translation of the idea into art is the right principle. For instance in many of the subjects I should like to put the figures into costumes of former days for the sake of picturesqueness. What do you say?"[38] He was obviously enthusiastic and pleased to be working upon a new book. But sadly the commission went the way of the ill-fated Dalziel commissions and suffered from Dick's intransigence, infuriating delays and excuses and most of all Dick's refusal to allow the book to interfere with his social life. He sent Locker a number of feeble excuses for not working or meeting a deadline; the most frequently used was his "absence from town". These understandably angered the author, who was easily irritated whenever the slightest upset damaged his plans. When Dick showed signs of diligence, he was encouraged enough to try to forget the excuses, however. Once he wrote to explain why he changed a clown's face, so as "not to let it resemble a little jester with a mask that Thackeray put in Vanity Fair". Another time he asked for photographs of famous country houses to use for background drawings.

Eventually he completed all the drawings on the wood blocks and on 1 March 1865 he sent them to be engraved. But even this seemingly simple act was plagued by mishaps. Dick had apparently misplaced the address of the engraver, and instead of waiting to get it, he sent the valuable blocks by messenger to first the *Illustrated London News* offices, then *Punch,* hoping the engraver would be working there. It was all guesswork, and extemely slip-shod on Doyle's part. But it was typical of his lackadaisical attitude toward work once it was finished. Eventually the parcel of blocks was returned with the messenger to Dick's club, and was left there, "the servant who took it having forgotten to give it to me", Dick told an infuriated Locker afterward. He tried to apologize, but the damage was already done. Dick sent several letters in explanation, just as he had done with Macmillans over the *Scouring of the White Horse* delays. In one he explained, "my only object being that the illustrations should please you and the public. I wish you to know this because it is so natural to judge by results only the fact is that after the hardest day's work I have produced less than nothing because I end up destroying all I have done. These are the sorrows of an artist who is above all desireous that you should not think he had been wanting in attention to a book of poems to which in the course of the work of illustrations he has taken a great fancy."[39]

The eighteen drawings he produced were wood engraved by his old *Punch* mentor Joseph Swain, as well at W.T.Green. Each drawing introduced a poem, some with Doyle's familiar rustic-styled lettering for titles as well. The best of the works are undoubtedly his children, while the backgrounds on which Dick had spent so much time, sketching from photographs, were faintly engraved and poorly printed. And yet the book went into a second edition three years later, and became a covetted collector's item. However, after publication Dick's relationship with Frederick Locker remained strained. Locker was especially keen to obtain the original sketches for the book, knowing Dick had taken such care with them, working out each composition in pencil as well as watercolour and ink. At first Dick refused to sell these, explaining "there

were too much work in them to part with". He did send Locker a selection of brief pencil sketches which he offered for a pound each, but Locker refused these as too slight and much too over-priced. Eventually, however, an agreement was reached and his nineteen preliminary water-colour drawings were sold.[40]

The Locker volume shared the limelight with another ill-fated Doyle project which appeared at the same time. Dick's Sleeping Beauty drawings for the Dalziel brothers appeared as *An Old Fairy Tale Told Anew,* with a new text written by the prolific dramatist J.R.Planché. Although fifteen years later than the time they were commissioned, the drawings now helped to restore Dick's flagging reputation as a fairy-tale illustrator, and they remain among his finest

---

Doyle's successful fairy drawings to An Old Fairy Tale Told Anew in Pictures and Verse, *1865, recall the days of his beloved Blanche. a) Frontispiece: "And o'er his head, and round the bed, By the protecting Fairy led."*

b) The Blanche-inspired Fairy Queen, from
An Old Fairy Tale, *1865.*

---

work. The frontispiece, which depicts the Sleeping Beauty kissed by her Prince, encircled by a flurry of highly suggestive nymphets and marauding elves, is a masterwork of sensitive line and expert engraving and printing; the Prince and Beauty standing out from the swirling figures. The wide-eyed Fairy Queen which introduces the first page is a typical Doyle invention, with devilish elves and vine leaves again carefully engraved in a tapestry of dense detail. Here too is the Blanche-inspired face, drawn at the height of Dick's love for his "Miss Stanley": "A Beauteous face with starry eyes. And streaming hair, with blossoms wild, Crowned as a Fairy Queen should be." She reappears peering from behind a curtain, all wide-eyed innocence and beauty, as the book's tailpiece and lasting reminder of Dick's beloved Blanche.

The appearance of these illustrations, after so long a period, fired Dick's ambition to attempt another fairy-tale book. He wrote to Macmillan – itself a bold act, considering his past strained relationship over the *White Horse* – and suggested a new edition of classic fairy-tales with as many illustrations as they could afford. He planned to charge £10 a drawing, and noted "I am struck more than ever with the excellent subjects they afford for pictures humorous grotesque and poetical."[41] Sadly, this new proposal never materialized. But the seeds were sown for Dick's most famous fairy illustrations, and now helped to steer him toward a new career as a fairy painter.

Giants, dragons and dwarfs dominated Doyle's fairy-tale drawings, from unpublished sketches. Private collection.

VI

Summoned by Fairies

1868 - 1883

hile the last fifteen years of Dick Doyle's life were spent in half-hearted pursuit of his new career painting fairy subjects for the galleries, worries over his family members, as well as his own uncertain direction plagued what little progress he made. Above all, he refused to sacrifice his position as valued guest at house parties in the country, as well as At Homes, lavish dinner parties and receptions in London, all of which took primary place over his painting. It was as if he was trying to escape from reality, and the bitter lesson that without continual hard work and dedication even the most celebrated artist – in his case child prodigy – might lose his reputation and his public. Clearly Dick had experienced the overwhelming phenomena of success and public acclaim from too early an age; his career had peaked too soon, and now, as he reached his early forties, he, like his father before him, suffered from the threat of premature retirement. And while John Doyle sought a totally new direction for his later years, Dick was less ambitious. He preferred to coast along on past successes, altering proven formulas and turning early fairy subjects into large gallery watercolours.

Significantly, the year Dick chose to launch his gallery career was also the year of his father's death. John Doyle died on 2 January 1868, and five months later Dick's newest watercolour, "The Enchanted Tree" appeared at the Royal Academy. Based upon those familiar fantasy subjects perfected under the stern direction of his father, the painting was a clear tribute to John Doyle, whose influence Dick never escaped, even after his death. This was to be HB's greatest legacy – the influence he

maintained over his talented sons' careers, shaping their futures as surely as if he were still alive. On the other hand, his faded reputation as an artist himself was acknowledged by his obituaries. The *Art Journal* waited three months before publishing its substantial tribute, by one of his friends. It claimed as HB he was "one of the most remarkable men of the remarkable epoch in which he lived". Like most of these accounts, it concluded HB's reputation had died long before its originator. By 1886 the historian and critic Graham Everitt noted of HB's Political Sketches, "it is surprising how completely they have passed into oblivion". Friends tried to preserve his reputation, notably Prince Metternich, who presented his collection of over nine hundred HB Sketches to the British Museum, while John's family sold the government three or four more for the astounding price of £1000. But when they attempted to sell their father's studio works at Christie's, shortly after his death, the response was shattering. On the day of the sale no buyer even bothered to appear, and the sale room itself stood empty, except for one curious spectator. Needless to say the sale was cancelled.

This was especially disappointing to his children, who could have used the money from the sale. But it was a bitter blow to Dick Doyle's special efforts to preserve and revitalize his father's reputation. As late as 1855 he had persuaded his father to attempt a new series of political sketches, to coincide with the General Election held that year. He told Charles how he intended to promote these drawings from several quarters. "The fine political sketches which he has done and which, keeping in our hands we are trying to circulate by means of an agent and

Richardson of Derby" were not a success, however: "Things are not brilliant as yet, but they have not been well 'put about', and especially it was unfortunate they were not well over the country before the elections."[1]

By the end of a year spent mourning for his father, Dick had produced another curious tribute, this time in the form of a book based upon his father's greatest love, the family religion. It was called *The Visiting Justices and the Troublesome Priest; or Irish Biddy in the English Gaol.* An Easter Carol for 1868 too well founded on fact, and published by his friend Richard Bentley. It was a most uncharacteristic piece of work; more a political tiraid than a serious piece of illustration, with its theme of the unjust trials and persecutions by English police of Irish Catholics sent to Middlesex gaol. Taking the form of a popular broadsheet song, the discrimination and unfair prison regulations were laid down, with Dick's rather crudely drawn illustrations. Here the poor, beleaguered Biddy suffers for her beliefs, and Dick draws her in the courtroom where she is sentenced to prison, when all she wanted was to be allowed to sit quietly and say her rosary. The booklet itself was largely overlooked by the press, and his biographer later dismissed it for the poorly drawn illustrations (only acknowledged on the title-page "By R.D.") which "indicate that he was shy of such polemics, as indeed he had some reason to be".[2] Indeed, he was taking a risk in stirring up old arguments about his religion especially now, at this crucial turning point in his career, when he depended upon public support from all quarters. The *Visiting Justices* was then an extremely brave, if perhaps fool hardy book to publish.

* * * * * * * * * * * *

More to the point, Dick returned to the fairy subjects he loved from childhood, although even these familiar sylvan scenes of fairies and puckish elves dancing in the moonlight had begun to lose favour with a fickle public. As a book illustrator of such fantasies he was often dismissed now, as a member of a faded era, placed alongside Leech, Phiz and Cruikshank as representatives of the largely self-taught school of sketchy, expressive drawing based upon imprecise if inaccurate detail. Meanwhile a new school of expertly drawn and superbly

engraved illustrations, later called the "Sixties School" had supplanted them. Their surfaces were filled by dense, jewel-like detail and correctly drawn figures. Many of these young illustrators had made their names as painters; some were Pre-Raphaelites who brought to the wood block a passionate love of detail from hours spent studying Nature. Although Dick's own intricate style was admired and his imaginative fantasies were studied by this new generation, he found himself relegated to that older generation of illustrators Dickens had once dismissed as lacking in "fancy and imagination" which made their drawings examples of "merely a sophisticated trade". It was a mark of his fading reputation that he failed to interest Lewis Carroll, when Carroll called in January 1867, to ask about Doyle illustrations for *Through the Looking Glass.* Having been first refused by his original illustrator John Tenniel, and the fairy artist Noel Paton, Carroll was encouraged at first by Dick's early powers of invention. But after the visit he wrote to a friend how much he had been disappointed by Dick's old-style humour and poorly drawn figures. He would have "to try my luck again with Mr Tenniel, and if he fails me I really don't know what to do. Doyle isn't good enough (look at any of his later pictures) and Arthur Hughes has not, as far as I know, any turn for the grotesque".[3]

Lewis Carroll had probably been shown Dick's latest struggles to paint for the galleries, for which he had chosen subjects of proven merit; those grotesque gnomes, fairy sylphs in diaphanous drapery, and creatures he borrowed from his vast store of ghost and folk legends. A favourite was a Fairy Prince, whose Nordic-looking regal appearance included a tall crown on his flame red hair and long beard which he trained into tendrils for his maidens and courtiers to keep trimmed and combed. He appeared in several paintings at the time as a compositional device, which allowed Dick to use his long beard lengths to tie together the disparate creatures of his fantasies. One of these was "The Fairy Tree", in which a cherubic-faced young boy (not unlike a young Charles Doyle) stares into the bare branches of a tree, where the Fairy Prince holds court over the creatures of Dick's early fantasy world.

Dick also associated the ghostly world of fairies and spirits with the high, powdered wigs and elaborate embroidered gowns and waist-

"The Fairy Tree".
Watercolour, 29 x 24½"
Private Collection.

coats of eighteenth century dress, and some of
his newest inventions were clothed in this style.
He loved the "picturesqueness" of the period,
as he had once told Locker, and how the pale
glow of powdered wigs and silk stockings enhanced his vision of spectral beauty. The idea
reached its height in "The Haunted Park", a
watercolour he exhibited successfully at the
Royal Academy in 1871. The painting combined
a recent preoccupation with landscape, here in
the bare branches and trunks of a winter wood,
with a new sense of atmosphere and a remarkable
use of light. The scene is set at dusk, just as the

sun paints the horizon pink and purple, and the moon softly glows through the veiled cloud. In the centre a pair of startled country children peer round an old bare lime tree in the avenue set before an old red-brick mansion. They stare in amazement at the ghosts of its former inhabitants, dressed in fine silks and high wigs, enjoying a pic-nic and dance in the early moonlight. It is a wonderfully evocative study of light and enchanted atmosphere; the landscape alone suggests how much care Dick put into his paintings, when not worrying about the engraver's harsh lines re-interpreting his original designs. Indeed, such competent atmospheric effects were a special preoccupation at this time, one he shared with his occasional visitor, John Tenniel, who especially admired Dick's skill at painting the effect of moonlight through a thin layer of cloud. It was not the traditional idea of a full moon like a globe, with a halo effect so long

"The Haunted Park"
Watercolour, 18¾ x 27½"
Sotheby's Belgravia.

associated with the supernatural, but a new pervasive glow which was much more exciting for Doyle's watercolour evocations of the spirit world. His fairy figures become phosphorescent in the ghostly light of such a moon, and they swirl and dance about in the darkness of their haunted wood. Indeed, Dick was so pleased with "The Haunted Park" that he painted a second version of the ghostly pic-nic, omitting the juvenile spectators, and called it "A Fairy Celebration"; as well as adopting the idea in a book illustration to *Higgledy-Piggledy,* 1876, in which young Billy watches from the castle door as a crowd of ghostly wigged and frock-coated dancers cavort in the moonlight.

Another favourite subject for his paintings was the violence associated with elves and puckish gnomes; the sadistic element in fairyland, which had attracted many Victorians to the fairy legends and their paintings. And Dick's thorough knowledge of these legends had been extended beyond his childhood love of cruel giants and terrible dragons. He painted a large and equally violent view of "Elves Battling with Frogs", with all the spirited invention and anthropomorphic style made famous by his

friend Edwin Landseer; but here instead of dogs, it applied to elves and frogs. The centre-piece to this long, frieze-like painting was the gory death of an anguishing soldier frog "receiving full in his yellow stomach the thrust of a spear of grass", according to one shocked critic when he saw it exhibited at the Grosvenor Gallery in 1880. Dick provided a long and telling account of his picture, to accompany and clarify the subject. It deserves to be quoted in full, for it gives some indication of his passion for fairy legends even at this late period in his career. He was like an excited schoolboy redis-covering lost toys, and he clearly relished every possibility these new paintings offered him:

"This event, it is supposed, took place in pre-historic times, or it might have been added to the fifteen decisive battles of the world – making sixteen. The cause of war is wrapped in obscurity, and the mystery is not now likely to be cleared up. At present the fortune of war varies in different parts of the field. The King of the elves seems to have delivered the world of command, 'Up Guards, and at them!' and a desperate charge all along the line is the result; the troops advancing in three divisions, the third of which, to the extreme left, is com-posed of reserves, who are taking a hasty drill at the last moment. Some are very young children at arms, and even in arms, while warlike mothers urge them on to action. A portion of the light troops of the frog army under stress of a heavy fire of stones, seek shelter, by a temporary move-ment, under water. On the right, in the middle distance, may be seen the frog-king, surrounded by his family, looking on with anxiety depicted on his countenance. On the other hand, in the foreground to the right, many frogs of great personal strength are getting the best of it. Prisoners taken by the elves are seen in the foreground to the left; one, evidently a frog of distinction, lies on his back while his limbs are put in chains. Near this group a wounded frog is bandaged by an elf-surgeon, showing that among these little people, and at that distant time, the civilities of warfare were not unknown. Just in front of the elf-king, who sits on 'a coign of vantage', surveying the scene, there is going on a fierce 'battle of the

standard', the result of which is in doubt. An incident in the thick of the fight, in the centre, may be of interest to the student, as showing that the warlike manoeuvre known in modern times as getting an adversary's head 'in chancery', was familiar to the primitive frog. Personal valour, and the weapons provided by nature, may do much, but cannot in the long run save the frog-army from defeat. The superior civilization of the elves must tell in the end."

Such scenes were popular among the gallery visitors, who loved to explore his convoluted surfaces for clues to the story to unravel the jig-saw puzzle like compositions. Another, on a similar theme, was a battle between elves and crows. Here Dick concentrated upon the gloomy atmosphere of a darkening sky, and put the decisive tug of war between the swooping black shapes of the crows and the tiny prostate elves defeated in the leafless wood below, set against a haunted hillside and dominated by an ancient tower. He was especially fond of monkeys, and planned an illustrated story, "The Sailor and Monkeys, a Story of Imitation". He completed six watercolour chapters, which he exhibited at the Grosvenor Gallery in 1881. Monkeys were creatures of uninhibited habits, as Dick had seen so often at the zoo; and yet they made perfect subjects for anthropomorphic paintings and illustrations as Landseer and Grandville had discovered. He painted them in "The Manners and Customs of Monkeys" in 1877, a delightful work with the following explanation: "According to a recent letter from Darfur, in Africa, the monkeys in that region are inordin-ately fond of a kind of beer made by the natives, who use the beverage to capture simian poor relations. Having placed a quantity of the beer where the monkeys can get it, the natives wait till their victims are in various degrees of inebriation, and when they then mingle with them, the poor creatures are too much fuddled to recognise the difference between Negro and ape. A Negro then takes the hand of one, the others follow, holding on to one another, and they are led off into captivity."

These animal paintings were hung in the galleries alongside his more numerous fairy inventions. Dick was particularly fond of fairy family subjects; generally with a fairy king or prince and his queen or princess. The maternal

The Battle of Elves and Crows, 1874, exhibited
at the Grosvenor Gallery 1885.
E.Joseph.

"The Manners and Customs of Monkeys
(Darfur, Africa)", 1877.
Watercolour, 9½ x 17¾"
Victoria and Albert Museum.

queen is sometimes nursing a changeling in her arms surrounded, as one enchanted critic noted, by "young maids-of-honour, equerries, descending, no doubt, from the ancient families of Cobwebs, Peas-blossom, and Mustard-seed, while grey beard officers of state are not wanting, figuring as Masters of the Ceremonies and old Sticks-in-Waiting".[4] They were taken from his knowledge of fairy legends, descriptions like those he had found in the classic Thomas Keightley's *Fairy Mythology,* 1828, with W. H.Brooke illustrations, or Thomas Croker's *Fairy Legends and Traditions of the South of Ireland,* 1825-28, with Maclise illustrations. Both entered several editions and were favourite childhood reading. And he dipped into them freely now, in search of painting subjects. Both Keightley and Croker had introduced the English-speaking public to the delights and mysteries of the fairy world, peopled by strange named creatures with bizarre if alarming customs. Dick was especially fond of the shefro, "a gregarious fairy who wears a foxglove as a cap", or the puckish Phouka said to be responsible for spoiling blackberries after Michaelmas. Croker described the elves with which Dick filled his paintings; creatures "a few inches high, they have an airy almost transparent body; so delicate is their form that a dewdrop, when they dance on it, trembles indeed but never breaks".

The fairy haunts of Scotland, a country where fairies were its original inhabitants, provided him with numerous subjects and landscapes for backgrounds. He was fascinated by the Scottish mountains, where it was said the fairies drove newcomers and forced them into retreats on their snowy peaks. Here he learned to seek out the sites of these legends, just as his friend and fellow lover of Scottish landscape, Edwin Landseer, declared his favourite spot in all the country was near a fairy hill. For the Scottish fairies were the most descriptive in their dress and habits, and best suited to Dick's needs. According to the famous account by John Gregson Campbell in *Superstitions of the Highlands and Islands of Scotland,* the Scottish fairies "are a race of beings, the counterpart of mankind in person, with its occupations and pleasures but unsubstantial and unreal, ordinarily invisible, noiseless in their motions and having their dwellings underground, in hills and green mounds of rock or earth..." One could best find these creatures at night, "at dusk and during wild and stormy nights of mist and driving rain when streams are swollen and 'the roar of the torrent is heard on the hill' – " and usually they lived in the hills. They "were said to come always from the west where blood-red skies combined with deep blue hills, grey clouds and greenish lights which were sometimes known as fairy fires. They invariably dressed in green robes, were fond of music (there are numerous legends of villagers being given green violins and taught to play tunes which the untutored could not duplicate), and dwelt in regal palaces under the hills and within domed earthen mounds. They worshipped Truth, Justice and Equality and had endless magical rituals and festivities."

The West Country and Welsh borders of England were the source of some of the most stirring if not violent legends of fairies and their relations. The famous Cornish legends were first set out in Mrs Bray's *Legends from the Borders of the Tamar and Tavy,* 1838, which opened a rich vein of folklore and legend that Dick borrowed for his work. He discovered a religious basis to fairyland here, in the legend that Cornish fairies were said to be the souls of good Druids, or pagan giants who had been shrunk by a shower of Christian holy water. On the other hand, the famous Cornish pixies, or piskie, were more malignant creatures, wizened and meagre, more threatening than their sturdy, earth-bound Somerset relatives, or even the pale white naked pixies of nearby Devon. Here for example, it was said that Oberon and his fairy army were defeated in their attempt to gain control of the pixie stronghold over all the West Country. This was the region Dick loved to visit; steeped as it was in essential atmosphere to set his vivid imagination going. Here, for example, the region's most recent historian and collector of legends, the Reverend Sabine Baring-Gould, Rector of Lew Trenchard in Devon, had spent his later years collecting legends which Dick avidly read and recommended to his young nephew Arthur. In Baring-Gould's most recent work, *Curious Myths of the Middle Ages,* 1866-68, he included the stirring account of how, at the age of four, he had seen goblins running beside the horses on a country estate. More recently, one of his sons had seen a little man wearing a red cap, green jacket and brown knee breeches among the pea pods in his own vicarage garden. These were the sort of stories which made Dick long to visit and see for himself, and on several occasions this was exactly what he did.

Unfortunately by the time Dick Doyle made his bid for public acclaim as a fairy painter for the galleries, the vogue for fairy subjects was almost over. Throughout the 1850s and 1860s, the Victorian preoccupation with the spirit world, seances, ghostly beings and drawings and paintings of the fairy world had swept into some of the most astute and respected homes in the country. The Queen and Prince Albert gave their approval by buying the expert fairy compositions of Daniel Maclise, and of Noel Paton, who was appointed Her Majesty's Limner and was later knighted for his paintings. Enterprising young artists soon jumped on the bandwagon and the vogue for elaborate canvases filled with fairies, mostly inspired by Shakespeare, was well launched. In a world plagued by increased industrial desolation, stilted religious dogmas, and repressive customs which played upon the Victorian psyche, the fairy artist offered a brief glimpse of escape. His intricate evocations of a new world, peopled by strange and oddly familiar creatures whose habits often reflected their human counterparts, were a welcomed change. Here too, in intricately detailed studies of nature inspired by the Pre-Raphaelites, the fairy artist convinced his viewers of the importance of fairyland. There were hints of the era's new attitudes towards sex in its evocatively posed nymphs and lecherous pixies, as well as glimmers of the new passion for the unseen world of spirits, which rivalled the most serious scientific studies of the age. Under Thackeray's editorship of *The Cornhill,* numerous works of psychic literature were reviewed in its pages, as well as his publishing articles like "The Fairyland of Science" (January 1862), which set out to link science with the fairy world.

Many of Dick's friends and fellow artists had contributed to the fairy painting vogue. Even the famous historical painter C.R.Leslie surprised his devoted friends when Thackeray discovered his last work was an unfinished "beautiful fresh smiling shape of Titania, such as his sweet guileless fancy imagined the Midsummer Night's queen to be". Others were captivated by the vogue's more startling manifestations, notably the practise of seances and table-turning. This opened up the equally fascinating world of spiritualism, and Dick was a frequent guest in homes where the practise was taken very ser-

iously. "Tea and table-turning" parties led to spiritualist societies, spirit photography, and books of strange tales from the other world. Dick's friend George Cruikshank produced delightful comic parodies of the vogue in *Holidays with Hobgoblins, and Talk of Strange Things,* 1861 (with a hilarious frontispiece "Shaving a Ghost"), and poked fun at the spiritualists in *Concerning Ghosts, with a Rap at the Spirit-Rappers,* 1863. Others, like Dickens, Rossetti, Holman Hunt, and Tennyson took the spirit world very seriously. To Tennyson it represented a "great ocean pressing round us on every side, and only leaking in by a few chinks". When Dick attended seances, he often met such noted disciples as Captain Marryat and the ghost story writer Catherine Crowe, at Mrs Loudon's famous seance evenings. But he tried to maintain a distance from the most ardent believers. There was too much conflict with his own devout Catholic faith to take spiritualist ideas too far. As his friend Henry Chorley exclaimed after one of Mrs Loudon's seance evenings: "To play with the deepest and most sacred mysteries of heart and brain, of love beyond the grave, of that yearning affection which takes a thousand shapes when distance and suspense divide it from its object, is a fearful, and unholy work."[5]

But the public enthusiasm for the strange evidence of spirits – spirit photographs especially – was shared by Dick, and later by his nephew Arthur. Such photographs gave the final sanction to fairy painting, and it was rumoured that the Queen herself was interested in them. The Royal Academy judges received a series of spirit drawings in 1872, which were said to be "done by spirits". One judge called them "quite indescribable, resembling nothing in heaven above or on earth beneath"; but added how they "were necessarily laughed out of the rooms".[6] On the other hand, spirit photography contributed to the falling off of interest in fairy painting; for what better proof was there of the "other world" than actual scientific photographs, rather than some artist's wild conjectures? And by the 1870s, the vogue for fairyland scenes was forced out of the galleries and into the nursery and children's world of illustrated literature, where it had originated in its earliest stages.

It was with this fact in mind, that Dick alternated his fairy paintings with scenes painted

Doyle's version of "Rumpelstilskin".
Watercolour, 8 x 5½"
Sotheby's Belgravia.

from favourite fairy-tales and nursery stories. The obvious source was the Brothers Grimm, and he borrowed heavily from their tales. He concentrated upon tales of dwarfs and goblins, which gave him a chance to combine fantasy with realistic landscape backgrounds. For example, his version of Rumplestilskin shows a wide-eyed maiden innocently confronted by the hunch-backed goblin in the dragon infested garden of a mountaintop castle. He chose the delightful tale of "Rose-red and Snow-white" for the painting he exhibited at the Grosvenor Gallery in 1878. According to the long summary of the story which accompanied the painting, Dick chose the moment when the two young girls "went into the forest to gather flowers, they saw an ugly dwarf with an old shriveled face, and a white beard a yard long, which had caught

A favourite Grimm fairy-tale, "Rose-red and Snow-white", 1877, exhibited at Grosvenor Gallery 1878.
Watercolour, 8 x 9½"
Christie's.

in the roots of a tree, and he was skipping about and struggling violently to get it free. And when he saw the girls, he fixed his glaring eyes upon them and cried out, 'Why do you stand chattering there, you simpletons, cannot you come and help me?' The children tried all they could to pull the beard out, but it stuck so fast all their efforts were in vain. 'Only do not be impatient,' said Snow-white, and so saying she pulled her scissors out of her pocket and cut off the end of his beard. The dwarf then clutched a bag of gold which was in the hollow of the tree, and, grumbling to himself, "Ill-bred creatures, to clip off a piece of my beard!' walked away without thanking or even looking at the children."

Another favourite subject Dick borrowed from fairy-tales was the familiar dragon. A Doyle dragon took many forms, however. His earliest *Punch* dragons were generally sea serpents with long, snake-like bodies and sharp fins. They had wide mouths of teeth and tried to look fierce, but they were really rather inoffensive and preferred to smile instead. And so were his recent painted dragons; creatures which on the whole were more whimsical than ferocious. He painted a two-headed creature tethered by its groom like a horse to await the witch who used it for transport. It had wings "like holly leaves", green leaf-like scaly skin, and an arrow-head sharp tail, and a forked tongue which slipped out when the animal breathed fire from its mouth. Dick especially liked the idea of a witch owning a dragon, and he painted several versions of the theme. In one a witch returns from a palace ceremony to her dragon-pulled carriage. There her groom and driver, a smartly dressed goblin, waits patiently while, "a few minutes walk away, playing with its tail" was a crowd of mischievious boys. As one delighted critic noted of the painting, "the reptile's length was such that, although he extended along an entire street, his tail was still round the corner. No living naturalist knows so much about dragons as Doyle. Next to fairies, he has studied them more than any province of animated nature."[7] Such versatility with dragon themes led to further paintings; of a dragon playing chess with a princess for her liberty; a witch driving her domesticated flock of young dragons to market. He painted a group of these young, scaly creatures waddling along the moonlit shore of a Scottish loch in a dense, carefully detailed style, and the work was eventually engraved as "A Tailpiece" in *Puck on Pegasus*. Although Dick was at first reluctant to allow the engraving, he wrote to Frederick Locker, who owned the original drawing, "I do not think for the style of the drawing that it would be well reproduced by an engraver unless I put it on the wood myself."[8]

Legends with dragons as the protagonist, or more commonly the symbol of evil, provided subjects for numerous other paintings. Dick was especially fond of the Dragon of Wantley, a true dragon (as opposed to the Scandinavian "worm" variety) with reptilian characteristics, the ability to belch fire over its victims, and a long history of victimizing children and cattle, which he ate in equal quantities while terrorizing the countryside. Legend said that this ferocious beast was eventually slain by the strange knight More of More Hall, "of whom it was said that so great was his strength that he had once seized a horse by its mane and tail, and swung it round and round till it was dead, because it angered him". And if More was the traditional version of the chivalric knight so loved by the Victorians, the Dragon of Wantley was the very embodiment of evil. According to legend the beast was "the terror of all the countryside. He had forty-four teeth, and a long sting in his tail, besides his strong rough hide and fearful wings. He ate trees and cattle and once ate three children at one meal. Fire breathed from his nostrils, and for long no man dared come near him."[9] Similarly, Dick painted versions of the symbolic St George and the Dragon, as well as "The Return of the Dragon-slayer". This last work was a strange mixture of comedy and carnage: a triumphant knight drags a dead dragon by the tail while others are led as captives in various states of injury, the victorious knight's handkerchief tied carefully around one poor dragon's injured eye.

Haunted landscapes with ghosts and spectres of evil also featured in Dick's gallery paintings. His favourite subject was "The Knight and the Spectre", in which a Scottish loch is painted in shades of blue – an unusual monochrome device for Doyle. Here a knight in full armour and his dog cower on the shore under the spell of a rising spirit – a beautiful woman in gossamer drapery and long flowing hair who rises over the reflections of the snow-covered mountains in the icy water. The knight's horse breathes a frosty breath and the dog twists away in cowardly fear, but the entire scene is bathed in the evil atmosphere of moonlight – now a favourite

a)

b)

The Doyle witch: a)b) Preliminary ink sketch and engraved illustration to An Old Fairy Tale, *1865. "And, lo! upon the sands hard by She sits and mutters moodily On the kingdom's coast in a lonely tower Blackened by time and rent by blast. A fairy of prodigious power."*

The Dragon of Wantley.
Watercolour, 14 x 20"
Courtesy of the National Gallery of Ireland.

Doyle device. [Colour Plate II]

Hauntings also meant witches, and the Doyle witches were carefully developed creatures praised by his critics. Although they generally had gnarled faces and hands, stringy hair and glared with evil eyes and toothless grins, occasionally they could look beautiful. A long-haired maiden of the Pre-Raphaelite type was given a deceptive, wide-eyed beauty in Dick's "Stirrup Cup" series, but this only enhanced her role as a deceptive mountain sorceress with the powers to lure knights to their doom when they drink from her evil brew. Other witches were chosen for their legends more than their appearances. The famous Dame Blanche of Normandy was painted in several versions as she crouched alongside a woodland tarn, wearing white to attract unsuspecting victims to her watery home. "She sat upon a wooden bridge and would not allow any one to pass unless he went on his knees to her," Dick wrote to accompany one picture. In another version Dame Blanche was painted in a merry mood: "The Dame Blanche requires him whom she thus meets to join her in a dance". This caught the eye of the Doyle family friend, the Duke of Norfolk, who eventually brought it.

As with most of his new paintings, the landscape backgrounds were carefully developed from actual places Dick visited. His country house friends often showed him their favourite views so that he could make brief sketches for new works; or they took him to nearby sites of legends, to ruined castles or haunted woods, where he could free his imagination and create his own versions of the tales. For example, he visited the legendary Dunstanburgh Castle in Northumberland, to see the impressive ruin standing on cliffs that rise a hundred feet above the North Sea. It was once the site of a stirring ghost story, the castle said to be haunted by Sir Guy, a valiant knight who had been bewitched by "a serene beauty... a lady with tears glistening on her cheek" who lived in the cavern under the castle. In the thick of battle, Sir Guy escaped there with a hundred knights and horses, and when the enchanted witch blew her magic horn they all disappeared.

Yorkshire was especially rich in legends and folk tales and Dick often took his subjects from there. He painted two versions of the famous Raby Castle, set in the Yorkshire Durham borders and reputed to be the most splendid medieval castle in Britain. With its high battlements and massive blood-red marble baronial hall built by the Neville family (large enough for seven hundred knights), it was an ideal subject for painting. Dick also loved the cathedral city of York, with its fine eighteenth century streets and surrounding countryside. He visited Castle Howard on one occasion and painted the elegant, sprawling building in its grounds. He was a frequent house guest of the Marquis of Ripon on his estate at Studley Royal. There he made several landscape paintings of the deer park, and the fine old oaks he later incorporated into his fairy painting, "The Enchanted Tree". He visited the medieval Fountains Abbey nearby and painted the ruins, inspired by the rumours that the abbey monks combined Christian beliefs with magic. Yorkshire was also the well-known site of fairy sightings, and while in the district Dick kept a close eye out for signs of his favourite subjects. Here, for example, as early as 1815, William Butterfield had reported seeing fairies at nearby Ilkley, and that story was now a respected local legend.

Although Dick tried straight-forward landscape paintings from his travels, those which were most often brought in the galleries were the fairy subjects, or at least a landscape with a witch, ghost or spectral being inserted. But then on the whole, his landscape watercolours were never completely successful. His choice of subjects was occasionally influenced by his friends. He painted the deer park at Egerton Castle, near Ledbury, as the guest of the Earl of Somers. When John Tenniel visited his studio to look over the new paintings, he was especially intrigued by Dick's spectral subjects, and the two artists often exchanged favourite tales of the supernatural. These culminated in Dick painting, "The Wraith" – his attempt to capture the spectral appearance of a living being said to portend another's death. But however good his invention, the subject was more grotesque than picturesque, and the painting failed to find a buyer.

Fortunately, Dick chose subjects from folklore with less grotesque or threatening characters, and these paintings eventually sold in the galleries. He had collected a large number of legends, not just of Britain but of Scandinavia and France as well. Some of the most enchanting came from Wales, the land of brooding mountains and hidden valleys. A favourite Welsh mountain legend he turned into one of his most delightful paintings. This was "the goat legend": "According to the Welsh legend, the goats have their beards combed by fairies on Saturday nights, to make them decent for Sunday." He painted several versions of the tale; the best was a group of fairy maidens with flower wreaths on their heads, combing the long grey hair of the mountain goats while two red-coated pixies watch attentively from a nearby rock. Dick sold one version to Lady Brownlow, who was delighted with the sylvan scene, although she first returned it to Doyle for "finishing some parts more".[10] [Colour Plate III]

The Scandinavian legends were among the most horrific. Dick had discovered some while working upon his illustrations to *Fairy Tales from all Nations*. Here he drew the bloodthirsty nature gods, trolls and other violent spirits of the fjords which kept the stories from becoming popular children's reading. Dick painted one version as "The God Thor, Drives the Dwarfs out of Scandinavia by Throwing his

Hammer at Them", which appeared at the Grosvenor Gallery in May 1878 with the following explanatory text: "The Trolls have a great dislike of noise, from a recollection of the time when Thor used to be flinging his hammer at them; so that the ringing of bells in the churches has driven them almost all out of the country. He, Loki, the Fire-God, gave the hammer to Thor, and said it would never fail to hit a Troll, and that at whatever he threw it, it would never miss it, and that he could fling it so far that it would not, of itself, return to his hand." Dick liked this subject so much that he painted two versions; one was eventually bought by the Duchess of Cleveland. Fascinated by the Scandinavian mythology of nature gods, he toyed with his own version of other tales. "The Knight and the Jotun", remained an unfinished watercolour, possibly part of a planned series of similar themes, but it was a delightfully whimsical look at the spindly-legged frost giant. He stares out of a deep wood and terrifies a knight, who has fallen from his horse and is left at the mercy of the nature spirit.

The Danish legend of the Altar Cup of Aagerup, which appeared in Keightley's *Fairy Mythology*, was painted in several versions, and remains the most extensively documented of all Doyle's folk tales. When Dick hung one

"The Altar Cup in Aagerup", originally owned by Doyle's brother James.
Watercolour, 6⅝ x 11¼"
Christie's.

a)

b)

A new version of the Aagerup legend:
a) "The Witch".
Watercolour 10 x 13¾"
Huntington Art Gallery
b) "Horseman and Gnomes".
Watercolour, 12 x 18"
Huntington Art Gallery.

---

version at the Grosvenor Gallery, he attached the following excerpt from Keightley to explain the story: "One Christmas Eve, a farmer's lad at Aagerup, Denmark, rode out to watch a troll meeting and danced with the dwarves all night long. When he finally remounted to return home, a girl offered him a golden stirrup-cup and invited him to drink. In a moment of suspicion the lad threw the liquid over his shoulder, it landed on his horse's back – from which in an instant it singed all the hair. The boy clapped spurs to the horse's sides, and, still clasping the cup, galloped cross the ploughed fields, the dwarfs tripping and tumbling in pursuit over deep furrows. He flung the cup into the churchyard as he passed and just reached the farmyard in safety, thus thwarting the trolls of victim and stirrup-cup alike."[11]

"Dame Julianna Berners Teaching her young
Pupils the Art of Fishing", one of the last works
Doyle exhibited at the Grosvenor Gallery, 1883.
Watercolour, 8 x 19¾"
E.Joseph.

Dick's version depicted a race of trolls stumbling across a furrowed field, with a low Scottish-inspired landscape in the background, not unlike those he loved on Skye. A church spire rises immediately behind the terrified farmer's lad. This sacred symbol emphasized Dick's addition to Keightley's version of the tale: "if he escaped he would bestow the cup on the Church". But in other painted versions of the story, Dick veered even further from the original. He was apparently intrigued by the wild-eyed sorceress who offered a cup to unsuspecting strangers. In one version, she confronts an elegantly dressed knight on horseback. She holds out her forbidden cup to coax him into evil, with open arms and a glazed expression. Only the knight's terrified horse, and the pair of ecstatic dwarfs dancing in the distance, suggest the evils to come. Dick added the lines, which accompanied the picture: "If the knight drinks the cup offered him by the 'wild woman', he becomes insensible, and is led off into the mountains." And the resulting scene of the knight's doom at the hands of the dwarfs, after having succumbed to the wild woman, is one of Doyle's most striking fantasies. In an orgy of elfin revelry and torture, the unfortunate knight and his horse are plagued by swirling pixies; bearded gnomes clasp hands to block their path, and one ogre pulls at the terrified horse's reins.

Of those English legends he chose to paint, the greatest number were set in Tudor times. Dick loved the period's elaborate and romantic costumes; the women with veiled hats and

"The Triumphal Entry of the Queen. 'Now she's coming!' "
Watercolour, 20 x 34"
Courtesy of the National Gallery of Ireland.

---

embroidered and jewelled dresses, the men in brocades and colourful stockings, as well as elaborately engraved designs on their armour. Much was left to his imagination in these early legends, and he loved to combine historical accuracy – here he must have borrowed from James's vast historical knowledge – with flights of his own fancy. One legend involved the earliest known angler's treatise, written by the beautiful Dame Julianna Berners, prioress of the nunnery at Sopwell, Hertfordshire. Her book first appeared at St Albans in 1486, and not only did Dick paint the prioress teaching her young pupils on the shore of a stream, but he also attempted to write and illustrate his own angling treatise, which remained unpublished at his death. Dick's painting of the Dame is a delightful stream-side landscape, with a row of cherubic pupils in various states of their lessons.

In the background of the painting lies a half-timbered Tudor style house, typical of Dick's preoccupation with period detail. This reached a climax in one of his most famous later

paintings, "The Triumphal Entry of the Queen. 'Now she's coming!' ". Here he adopted his familiar processional device, set in a Tudor street, for the arrival of the fairy queen in some mythical village. The street is lined with hundreds of figures in meticulous detailed period costumes; others hang from the overhung windows of half-timbered shops and houses. Down a crooked back street hung with elaborate shop signs of lions and dragons, a castle tower rises among the hills with a flag waving for the arrival of the Queen. The painting was acknowledged as a masterwork, a culmination of Dick Doyle's fairy visions and boyhood love of history. It remained in the Doyle family, owned by his brother James, until years later, when it entered the collection of the National Gallery of Ireland.

Processionals gave Dick a chance to fill his work with as many characters from history, fairy-tales or his own imagination as there was room. In "Prester John's Promenade", he crowds an amazing number of these inventions under the palm trees. There is a squat Napoleon and a bemused St Nicholas, some elephants, a giraffe, lions with barristers' wigs, and camels led by a pair of elegant cranes. Prester John was the legendary "Priest John", a Middle Ages Christian king and priest said to reign in the extreme reaches of the orient, beyond Persia and Arme-

Prester John's Promenade.
Watercolour and ink, 24½ x 38¼"
Private Collection.

---

nia. The legend of this mythical king was a favourite among the Victorians; Baring-Gould included him in *Curious Myths* as the king Marco Polo called Un-Khan, who was slain by Genghis Khan.

* * * * * * * * * * * *

When left to explore his fairy inventions unhampered by publisher deadlines or worries about the most saleable subjects for the galleries, Dick produced a series of fairy illustrations for his most famous book. It was called *In Fairyland,* and originally was conceived as a fairy album of favourite creatures, posed in characteristic settings and dressed in legendary costumes. He hoped to call it "Fairyland – Pictures from the World of Fairies, Elves, & Goblins, Dwarfs, Sprites". He produced sixteen watercolour drawings as well as initials and binding designs, and borrowed his brother's colour printer, Edmund Evans, who wood engraved and colour printed the large, folio-sized plates. By so doing, Evans earned the accolade of producing one of the largest colour printed books of the period – a

landmark in the art of colour printing from wood blocks.

However, it had been almost five years since a Doyle illustrated book had appeared in the bookshops, and the publisher of *In Fairyland,* Longmans, took the precaution of special pre-publication advertising. It was, after all, an expensive and lavish production, to sell for one and a half guineas. They settled upon the following poem which appeared in their forthcoming books catalogue, *Notes on Books:*

"Where had Dicky Doyle been
All this length of years,
Since Punch wept to miss him
From his merry peers?

* * * * * * *

Now last, we know
where Dicky Doyle has been! –
He has been to Elf-land
With the Fairy-Queen

* * * * * * *

Yes, Dick has been in Elf-land
And the pictures which he took
The worthy Messrs Longmans
Have published in a book."[12]

[155]

On the whole, Dick chose woodland settings for his elves, sprites and fairy maidens. They huddle under dock leaves, lie in the sun upon lily pads, or shelter beneath toadstools or tree branches. It gave him a chance to suggest the miniature world to scale, as it might appear in any natural woodland setting. The predominate theme for his fairies was romance, and the book opens with a fairy prince on bended knee, appealing to his "wayward fairy princess". Dick wrote below the drawing: "He also offers her his heart, and his hand; and besides he begs her acceptance of priceless gifts." It was a familiar homage to fairy beauty, while the princess's courtiers, the wicked pixies rustling in the undergrowth, wait to see if their spears and arrows are needed to protect her. This set the scene for further romantic themes. In "Flirting", he drew a fairy prince charmed by his princess in the roses. He also devised a three act

The genesis of In Fairyland, *1870:*
a) Pencil sketches for illustrations, 9¾ x 13¾″
British Museum.

romantic tragedy of forsaken love, played out under the toadstools. Far more interesting are the drawings of elfin antics. These creatures of torture tease birds and force butterflies into harnesses to carry the Queen's carriage. They ride beetles and battle with grasshoppers in a mock medieval tournament. Some climb onto the slimy heads of snails to race in the annual fairy competition to find "the swiftest snails in Fairyland". These were the antics of the wicked fairies, symbols the Victorians associated with the human spleen. But the most effective plates were the large fairy compositions. Here nymphs and elves, a fairy prince and his princess, are scattered over a woodland clearing, or lie dozing in the moonlight alongside a lake. There is a fairy dance to celebrate a romantic reconciliation: "But it is supposed that the little creature whispering in her ear brings a message of reconciliation; and that is why the Elves, an amiable race, are showing their joy by dancing like mad," Dick wrote below the plate. The book ends in a delightful silhouette scene: the dancing elves and water nymphs, exhausted by their revels, fall asleep in each other's arms on a

lakeside tree branch, lit only by the grey-green of the moon reflected off the water. As for the fairy couple, they "are evidently friends again and let us hope, lived happily ever afterwards", Dick concluded.

Perhaps the most successful plate in the book was "The Triumphal March of the Elf-King". [Colour Plate IV] It fulfilled Dick's original plan to collect together all the most striking and his favourite fairyland inhabitants in one drawing. Here for example, the now familiar elf-king, with his long strands of red beard and gold crown, heads the procession. "This important personage, nearly related to the Goblin family, is conspicuous for the length of his hair, which on state occasions it requires four pages to support," Dick wrote below the drawing. "Fairies in waiting strew flowers in his path, and in his train are many of the most distinguished Trolls, Kobolds [German spirits of the mines], Nixies [water elves] Pixies [West Country fairies with green capes and red hats], Wood-sprites, birds, butterflies, and other inhabitants of the kingdom." Like a finale to a ballet, this one drawing brought all of Doyle's fairyland together for his public's delight.

The genesis of such an influential book is just as interesting as the published result. Dick took great care with the first preliminary pencil and

ink drawings, experimenting with various poses and fairy antics. He turned some of these into watercolour studies, just as he had done with Locker's poetry illustrations. The technique allowed him to study colour as well as tonal contrasts which he knew to be essential when working for wood engraving. When his drawings were submitted to Longmans, they felt there was a lack of cohesiveness; despite Dick's brief captions, the drawings lacked a narrative thread, a storyline like all good fairy-tales. As a result, they commissioned the poet William Allingham to write a verse story around Doyle's drawings. Allingham was the author of the famous fairyland verse, "The Fairies" – "Up the airy mountain, Down the rushy glen, We daren't go a-hunting, For fear of little men" – and shared Doyle's sylvan view of fairyland. His fairies lived among the reeds in a mountain lake, ate only "crispy pancakes of yellow tide-foam", kept frogs as their watchdogs, and were ruled over by an elf king. Allingham was a favourite guest at the Tennysons, and among the Pre-Raphaelites, who enjoyed his Irish humour and sentimental poetry. Once he even read his verses to Dick's beloved Blanche, who had invited him to her London home.

Allingham's verse story used the device of a single day in fairyland and the changing light and duties of the inhabitants to form the structure of his plot. It was essentially a romance, intro- duced by the cry of a night watchman: "Fairies

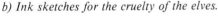

b) Ink sketches for the cruelty of the elves.

c) Original title-page design.
Watercolour, ink, pencil
Christie's.

---

and Elves! Gone is the Night, Shadows grow thin, Branches are stirr'd." Then followed the prolonged tale of the fairy courtship and marriage between the foreign Prince Brightkin of the Purple Helm, son of the King of the Blue Mountains, and the Fairy Princess, "the lovely lady of Elfin-mere". Although an uneven and at times annoying story, there are some beautifully poetic passages, as in most of Allingham's poems. But when the book was published, both author and illustrator were far from pleased. Allingham wrote his disgust into his diary: "In Fairyland comes – *a muddle,* no consultation having been made or proposed between artist and poet. The former (in a huff probably) has put his own prose descriptions to the pictures." He did note that *The Daily News* had found his poem "charming", but he remained disgruntled by the publication.[13]

Nevertheless, despite the book's high price its sales were good enough for the publishers to re-issue it in a cheaper edition four years later. Critics praised Dick's drawings which served as the basis for a new edition in 1884, this time with prose story by Andrew Lang. It was called *The Princess Nobody,* and while it omitted several of Dick's original illustrations for the sake of telling the story, it was the most pleasing attempt to bring order to Dick Doyle's fairyland. For this Lang had been influenced by Thackeray's successful *Rose and the Ring,* and he told the story of the Princess Nobody's rescue from the grips of a wicked dwarf. She meets the kind but ugly Prince Comical, who protects spiders from wicked fairy torturers and is made into a handsome prince by the Queen of Mushroomland. He falls in love with Princess Nobody, and after she vanishes at the sound of her name, she is restored by a kind water fairy and the two live together happily, *au temps jadis.*

The plight of Dick's *In Fairyland* illustrations, re-arranged and later republished in new sequences, points out how vulnerable and defenseless he was to control his work's future publication. Indeed, this was just one of several instances in which previously published Doyle illustrations were re-issued in new guises, often shockingly printed or poorly engraved to misrepresent the delicate Doyle style. The greatest culprit was the enterprising publisher Dean & Son, a pioneer in the field of cheap picture books and second-rate gift volumes. They had obtained the blocks for Dick's *Juvenile Calendar* illustrations, and in 1871 they produced four compilation volumes of foreign fairy-tales, each with equally familiar Doyle illustrations. They were taken from books like Montalba's *Fairy Tales,* and were poorly engraved with disastrous colour printed frontispieces. These were generally intended to illustrate lurid tales of torture and murder. Most notable was Dick's "The Feast of the Dwarfs" drawing, to fit the Norwegian title tale of witchcraft and evil. He drew a striking scene here: the witch Guru embraces a bearded statue while a crowd of ecstatic dwarfs dance round in their own torchlight. They were showing up their "pale earth-coloured faces, with large noses and red eyes, in the forms of birds' beaks and owls' eyes, surmounted on mis-shapen bodies. They waddled and shuffled here and there, and seemed to be sad and gay at the same time."

Other publishers followed suit, like the enterprising juvenile publisher Griffith & Farran, who borrowed Doyle's *Jack and the Giants* illustrations for *The Attractive Picture Book,* 1875. To combat this piracy, Dick agreed to provide some new drawings for wood engraved editions throughout the 1870s. Most notable were eight drawings based upon his fairy paintings and recent painted landscapes, to E.H.Knatch-bull-Hugessen's *Higgledy-Piggledy* in 1876.

"The Feast of the Dwarfs", from the Dean series, 1871.

Here appeared a version of Dick's recent painting, "Elves in a Rabbit Warren", although it was a poor reworking of a favourite theme. [Colour Plate V]

* * * * * * * * * * * *

By the mid 1870s Dick Doyle had completely abandoned book illustration. He preferred instead to struggle sporadically over watercolour paintings for the London galleries, and to surrender to the continual demands made upon him by the invitations of his well-meaning friends and their constant bids for his company. When he found time to work, he gradually modulated his early watercolour style. Those first carefully painted compositions, clogged with intricately drawn figures and smooth even washes now gave way to an erratic stippled effect. It was as if he was uncertain of himself; or perhaps he had seen works by the recent scourge of the art world, the Impressionists. Whatever the reason, his landscapes, with their unevenly built-up tree trunks and layers of dotted foliage, were not a success, and failed to find buyers in the galleries.

It was generally admitted that Dick Doyle was an inventive draughtsman, but not a skilled painter. After all, he had not been trained to know about colour or the techniques of fine brushwork. When he used colour it was generally for garish effect rather than subtlety. He loved bright, almost pure colour, and as his spectral monochromatic paintings indicate, his favourite colour was indigo and other shades of blue. But a watercolour's success depended upon transparency, a fine blend of light and pigment. Unfortunately, in his later pictures Dick forgot this cardinal rule, and clogged his surfaces with thick pigment. He was fond of opaque body colour, the stark white some purist dismissed as a crutch to those incapable of using the white of the paper. Worse still, he would paint over the white in pure bright colour, perhaps inserting a blue kingfisher in a dense woodland setting, or making a figure's drapery heavy, uneven and chalky in texture. He might have learned the value of even, transparent wash from Charles, whose expertly drawn watercolours depended upon an almost elemental use of colour, had he studied his brother's paintings. Instead Dick muddled along with his tight dots of colour, building up an object much like his wood engraver colleagues had done. And in the end,

Doyle's later impressionistic watercolour style:
a) "View in Studley Park".
Watercolour, 14 x 20"

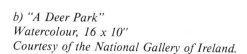

his critics largely dismissed his paintings for their glaring technical faults. "To the last he remained amateurish," one remarked. Sadly, this remains quite true.

Apart from two appearances at the Royal Academy, Dick chose to exhibit exclusively at the Grosvenor Gallery, where some twenty-five landscape and fairy paintings were exhibited from 1878-83. The Grosvenor was a major venue for established painters of the period, and among its directors was young Charles Hallé, son of Dick's great musical friend, and an avid admirer of the Doyle style. The subjects he and Dick agreed over for exhibition reveal the diversity of Dick's interests as well as how he

b) "A Deer Park"
Watercolour, 16 x 10"
Courtesy of the National Gallery of Ireland.

now searched for a subject which might attract a new public. His Scottish loch-side landscapes, painted in rather garish ochres and bright indigo with pure purple mountains, hung alongside the darker, somber views, like "On the River Derwent, Cumberland". This had been inspired by Tennyson's line in *In Memoriam,* "The rooks were blown about the skies". Here too appeared the familiar fairy subjects, the Aagerup legends, the finished watercolours from book illustrations. All were hung at the Grosvenor annual summer exhibition, alongside works by such famous painters as his old friend Watts, Poynter, as well as struggling newcomers like Burne-Jones, and the illustrator Walter Crane. But he had little success selling his work at the Grosvenor. One critic concluded his work had "a primitive childishness, sometimes, which suggested pathetically that this man was not in touch with these days and ways".

Most of his patrons were the wealthy friends who had collected his work over the years. He, in turn, had dined at their country estates or in their London homes. A large number came from that new breed of art patron, the industrial baron of the North, from places like Yorkshire and Cumberland, or the Midlands. Many were aristocrats, with large estates and fine houses filled with growing art collections. Lord Egerton of Tatton Park in Cheshire had commissioned Landseer to paint portraits of his daughters, and afterwards asked Dick for similar portraits; he also purchased his "The Return of the Dragon Slayer" painting. The Earl of Granville was the head of the hunts throughout the southern counties and a valued friend. He had often invited Dick on his shoots, although Dick was never a huntsman, and preferred only the social aspect of the sport. But the Earl was also a valued patron who commissioned portraits of himself and his family. Similarly Lord Aberdare was a political ally, who had bought Dick's first Royal Academy picture, and the Dame Berners angling painting. Sir Robert Inglis was another political friend of the whole Doyle family. He was the author of "On the Roman Catholic Question" and a member of various artistic commissions, who had watched Dick's career and offered his patronage whenever possible.

Among his valued country house friends, the most notorious and endearing was Lady Dorothy Nevill. Dick was a frequent guest at her Hampshire estate, Dangstein, and he loved to visit this enchanting and redoubtable hostess in her Berkeley Square home in London. It seemed Lady Dorothy knew everyone of consequence, from politicians to writers and artists. Each had a peculiar story to tell, and she mixed her guests like an expert, maintaining their confidences and delighting in their intrigues just as her guests delighted in her "old world ways and 'new world' eccentricities". Frederick Locker had fallen under her spell at an early stage: "When Lady Dorothy ordains, we nib our quills and rack our brains". At Dangstein, she had fascinated Darwin with her curious collection of botanical specimens. There she maintained a silkworm enclosure as well as her model farm and dairy where she trained "wayward" girls from London. She became a valued friend, who often invited Dick to Dangstein in the hopes he might find new patrons for his work. There, for example, he met the Leveson-Gowers, whose portraits he was commissioned to paint; as well as his old Scottish travelling partner Robert Lowe (now Lord Sherbrooke). There was even the suggestion that Dick's beloved Blanche might appear, since she too shared Lady Dorothy's friendship, and was known to visit Dangstein whenever she was down from Scotland.[14]

On other occasions, Dick was entertained in some of the country's most famous country houses. He loved Wilton House, near Salisbury, where he had been invited by Lady Herbert, a kind but prickly dowager, who led him round the estate. James I had called Wilton "the most beautiful house in England". With its Inigo Jones interiors and large rolling lawns and huge cedar trees, Dick easily agreed with the claim. He joined a large party for the shooting season there, and his hostess graciously sent a box of game to Dick's brother Charles in Edinburgh before he could arrange payment for carriage. Here he renewed his acquaintance with Gladstone, then Prime Minister, and the two men argued amicably over "Jews and their eminence in music". Dick dismissed the popular rumour that Beethoven was "to some extent a Hebrew", and later sent Gladstone a list of fourteen musicians, "probably the greatest names in musical composition and it seems that only two are Jews".[15]

Although Dick was perhaps too willing to accept popular prejudices in society, his remarks were never unkind or spiteful. On the whole he was a respected and charming guest who was as much sought after for his fund of witty stories as his friendships and reputation as an artist. Sometimes he combined these attributes: when he accidentally spilled wine over a lady he sent his apologies with an elaborate decorated fan. On one he drew "The Seven Ages of Shakespeare". On other occasions he sent fans with elves and fairies taken from *In Fairyland,* or a comic clown stealing apples and disturbed by a police-man painted upon them – subjects which would have delighted a lady's children as much as herself.[16]

And yet by being so frequently in society, Dick continued to view its customs and unfor-tunate victims with a sharp if disapproving eye. Some of this disapproval surfaced in the eight illustrations he made for the satiric novel, *Piccadilly, A Fragment of Contemporary Bio-graphy,* 1870. Its author, Laurence Oliphant, presented a catalogue of the false values and pitfalls one might encounter in Society. It was essentially a familiar story of romance among the high-born, or as *The Athenaeum* called it, "good society". It was the story of the ill-fated love between the aristocrat Lord Grandon, and

the wealthy daughter of Lady Broadhem. This domineering dowager rejects Lord Grandon for his poverty and his poor prospects, but the marriage is secretly arranged by the saintly Lord Frank Vanecourt – the essential chivalric figure in this drawing room romance. The story was divided into six symbolic chapters, each given a clever illustration by Doyle. They were his versions of the horrors and temptations offered by Society: "Love", "Madness", "Sui-cide", "The World", "The Flesh" and finally the ominous "The ----" In "Suicide" Dick drew Lord Grandon tormented by a crowd of poison-bottle bearing fairies with a nightmarish fantasy of Lady Broadhem racing after sacks of money and a group of society swells hoisting aloft the bubble of wealth and success. In "The World", a procession of dancers in elegant gowns and evening dress pass through the arms of cunning fairies and dance to the tune of a devilish fiddler. And the drawings end with Dick's own moral comment: a drawing of a beautiful woman with a fishing pole hoping to catch a husband from among the school of eligible suitor-fish, with "At Home" cards clutched in their hands.

While the drawings are clever fantasies on their own, coupled with the some-what weak story, the book should have failed. Instead it entered a second edition the same year it was published, and was reprinted in 1874. Readers

Doyle's fan design in the style of In Fairyland. *Christie's.*

clearly enjoyed the vicarious thrill of entering "polite society", as Oliphant and Doyle pictured it, and the strong moral tone attracted even the most pious. Was this the reason *The Athenaeum,* that conservative barometer of middle-class taste, found the book's moral misguided and offensive? Its critic argued polite society was not as lurid and evil as Oliphant had pictured; people had changed, society was "better, more honest, and appreciative of others". But by now Dick Doyle knew otherwise.

Although Dick never married, he was fond of children and loved to entertain them with stories and drawings. It was a valuable asset when visiting the young members of his patrons' families, if only to keep them quiet enough for portrait sittings. The Percy Wyndham family in particular he adopted as his favourite, and he was a frequent guest in their home. They lived in a magical crenellated, castle-like house Isel Hall, tucked away in the Cumbrian hills on the edge of the Lake District. It was an enchanted

setting which Dick painted like a medieval castle set among haunted woods beneath the gentle slopes of mountains in the distance; an Avalon where he could imagine Arthur might have lived. The Wyndham children were equally delightful, especially young Madeline, a six year old charmer who wrote a story about a pig which Doyle illustrated. The family had it privately printed years later, but the quick ink sketches of Madeline's "motherless" pig and the tragic death of its young girl owner who loved it, remain enchanting evidence of Dick's abilities to captivate his young audiences. Moreover, Madeline's mother was the famous patron and model for many of Dick's friends, "one of the queens of the art world" who had sat for Watts, and befriended Burne-Jones and Rossetti. Her classic beauty was not unlike Dick's beloved Blanche, and he found her a delightful hostess and a willing and sympathetic patron. Under her roof, he met future patrons for his own portraits, like the Tennants, Madeline's sister-in-law Lady Elcho, and Arthur Balfour.[17]

One of the joys of visiting the grander country

Doyle's version of the temptations in Society: original pencil and ink designs for Laurence Oliphant's Piccadilly, *1870.*
a) "Suicide".

---

b) "The World".
Christie's.

*Isel Hall, Cumberland, home of Doyle's friends
and patrons the Wyndhams.
Watercolour, 19 x 30"
Courtesy of the National Gallery of Ireland.*

houses of his friends was the possibility of
discovering an unknown painting or drawing by
an Old Master. It gave him a chance to study
some of the country's finest private art collections
and he had developed a well-trained eye for
quality over the years. At Chatsworth, for
example, where he stayed in 1877 at the
invitation of the Duke of Devonshire, he was
delighted to be allowed free access to its overwhelming collections. On this occasion, Charles
Hallé had arranged for him to select works he
thought suitable for a special Grosvenor Gallery
exhibition of Old Masters. To Dick's amazement, as Hallé recalled, "he found some beautiful
things – Raphaels, Michelangelos, Leonardos,
hanging about in dirty frames in corridors and
most unexpected places. The Duke of Devonshire
did not know that he possessed them, and gave
Doyle permission to send us anything."[18]

Dick once toyed with the idea of painting
architectural studies of the largest of the country

houses he visited. He had painted views of
Castle Howard as well as Cortachy Castle. But
he found in Longleat House, seat of the Marquis
of Bath, his most agreeable subject, and produced
several views of the house and grounds on his
visit there. He had known the marquis from his
early days and produced a charcoal portrait of
him in 1852, possibly through the invitation of
Thackeray, also a mutual acquaintance. In
1874 Dick made a visit to Longleat to meet and
draw the marquis's family, and he produced
eleven charcoal portraits of the children, as well
as an amusing nursery parody of a moon
jumping over a cow. He was most delighted with
the majestic house, especially the famous Old
Library with its rows of precious leather bound
volumes and the various oil portraits of Dryden
and Shakespeare as well as the country's kings
and queens, like Henry VIII and Queen Elizabeth.
It was a treasure house to delight his boyhood
fantasies. He painted the room and its collection
of armour and weapons, and in courtesy to his
hostess, he included portraits of the marchioness
and librarian, Canon Jackson, although he was
clearly more interested in the cavernous room
and its treasures.

* * * * * * * * * * * *

Doyle's watercolour of the Fourth Marchioness of Bath and her librarian, Canon J.E.Jackson in the Old Library at Longleat, 1874. Doyle painted several views of the house and drew portraits of the family while a visitor to Longleat in the early 1870s.
Marquis of Bath.

Dick marked his fiftieth birthday by moving house with his sister Annette. He chose a smaller house in the less fashionable district of Fulham, at No.7 Finborough Road. It was a long street, full of uniform three storey terraced houses with tiny back gardens and steep staircases at the front door. But it was the first house in which Dick could arrange his things as he wanted them, and he took great care with the furnishings and decorations. Pride of place was given to the famous mahogany dining table his father had willed to him; the table round which so many famous guests had once dined. He kept his violin in the window seat where it would be always ready to console him during his periods

of increased melancholy. In fact the window where he played became his favourite spot in the house; he spent hours there playing and watching the view onto the street. His studio was a different matter. Here he stacked his many unfinished watercolours, set up his easel to catch the variable light, and quickly discovered that only the early morning light was suitable for his painting. On the walls he hung the many unsold exhibition watercolours and along the edge of the ceiling he painted a bright frieze of mischievous elves, goblins and fairies to inspire him and delight his occasional visits from friends and patrons. Shortly after he settled in, his brother Henry called to admire his work and see the new house. Henry had been on leave in Italy, and on his way back to Ireland he spent several days in London renewing old acquaintances. Some he hoped he might interest in Dick's newest paintings. He wrote to one prospective purchaser, the politician Austin Layard, "Dick had been making some charming sketches from Nature (landscape) during his autumn holiday, which I am sure you would like."[19]

By far the greatest worry to Dick and his

sister and brothers was the continued report of Charles's poor health. His moods plagued his career and worried his growing family, to which a new son, John Francis, had been added. Arthur, now a fifteen year old schoolboy, had been sent away to boarding school in Lancashire. This was a strict Jesuit school which forbade holidays and taught strict obedience to religious dogmas. But after consultations between his uncles and aunt in London, it was agreed Arthur should have his first taste of London. He was given permission to visit for three weeks over the Christmas season, from the end of November in 1874. Arthur was over-joyed by the prospect of his visit to London, and wrote to his Aunt Annette, describing himself so she would know him at the station: "I believe I am 5' 9", pretty stout, clad in dark garments, and above all, with a flaring red muffler round my neck."[20] James and Henry agreed to help entertain their favourite nephew, and the Doyles prepared for his arrival by planning excursions and explorations of the city.

But it was Arthur's Uncle Richard who most delighted and captivated him during the visit. Dick's boyish sense of fun, the jolly games, and seemingly endless stories, not to mention his freedom with pocket money, left a lasting impression on his nephew and they became good friends. Dick took him into his studio and showed him the paintings and the friezes of goblins and fairies, and filled him with his favourite stories of supernatural beings and ghosts, until the young schoolboy had been thoroughly indoctrinated into the ways of the "other world". It was an important initiation which would surface many years later in Arthur's own role as a champion of spiritualism. Arthur had remembered his uncle's famous *Punch* drawings, which he had seen as a child, and how Dick once drew his portrait as a round-faced, cherubic-looking lad with deep, saucer-shaped eyes and thick hair. They shared a mutual delight in London's tourist attractions, from the Tower of London to Madame Tussaud's waxworks. Together they marvelled at the Hall of Kings and the Chamber of Horrors which Arthur wrote home to his mother was his favourite. Dick took along a sketchpad to entertain Arthur and drew the tableau of Marat in his bath, while Arthur took great interest in the equally lurid descriptions of the crimes in the catalogue – an interest which would surface

Doyle's trip to Canna Island inspired the barren landscapes in his series, "The Witch's Home", here "Broom at the Door-Witch Coming Out". Watercolour, 13½ x 19"
Sotheby's Belgravia

---

later in his Sherlock Holmes stories.

Dick also took him to concerts and Hengler's Circus, while brother James reserved a box and took Arthur twice to see the celebrated performance of Henry Irving as Hamlet at the Lyceum Theatre. They took him to Westminster Abbey, to the Tower of London to admire the crown jewels and armoury, and brother Henry stayed in town to take him to the Crystal Palace and Regent's Park zoo. The visit was an exhausting time for them all, but in the end it was a complete success. Arthur's aunt and uncles warmed toward their favourite, and carefully watched over his future, eagerly awaiting news from Arthur of his progress at school, and subsequently at his medical college. On the other hand, the experience had opened Arthur's eyes to a tempting new world unfettered by rules

---

Arthur Conan Doyle by his Uncle Richard.
Pencil and ink
Private Collection.

"She's off!"
Watercolour, 13¾ x 20"
Victoria and Albert Museum.

and school regulations, and he returned to Lancashire confused and disillusioned with the sacrifices forced upon him there. It was a dangerous discovery with repercussions soon to affect and startle his doting relations.

The news from Edinburgh the following year was not encouraging. Charles suffered increased bouts of melacholia and depression which culminated in his forced early retirement in June 1876, with an annual pension of just £150, despite twenty-seven years of government service. Dick decided to visit his brother and see if there was any advice he could give, although financially he was not in a position to offer much help. As if to prepare himself, he first returned to his familiar Scottish haunts, toured the waters round Skye, and this time landed upon nearby Canna Island. He was fascinated by the stark landscape, the rocky coast and far off Cuillin hills of Skye in the distance. It served as the background for a striking series of witch paintings, in which he inserted the ruins of a castle and the hag-like witch attended by her faithful

dwarf, Broom. He then travelled east to stay with his recently widowed friend Mrs Ellice and her family at Invergarry, and painted a view of her house on Glen Quoich. On the way to Edinburgh he stopped to pay homage to the Dumfries home of Robert Burns, and painted the River Nith from the famous Duchess Walk on the Duke of Buccleuch's estate. He also painted the nearby waterfall at Drumlanrig. All these Scottish landscapes were destined for the Grosvenor Gallery over the next few years.

When at last he arrived in Edinburgh, he found his brother a dreamy, long-bearded stranger, shabbily dressed and in the habit of escaping home and his family responsibilities. He declared how he liked fishing best, "because when you fished the nagging world let you alone", and he found brief comfort in his fantasy drawings and watercolours which became more grotesque in theme. "The Saving Cross" was an eerie nightmare, in which a child clutched a celtic cross in a churchyard, chased there by a demonic "night mare" with rolling eyes and sharp, angular body. When young Arthur saw these, he was reminded of his Uncle Dick's stories, but he thought them much better paintings than his more famous uncle. Later he declared his father's artistic skills were "the greatest, in my

Charles Doyle's "The Unseen Audience".
Pencil and ink, 10½ x 17⅜″
Huntington Art Gallery.

opinion, of the family. His brush was concerned not only with fairies and delicate themes of the kind, but with wild and tearsome subjects, so that his work had a very peculiar style of its own, mitigated by great natural humour... His originality is best shown by the fact that one hardly knows with whom to compare him."[21]

Sadly, Charles continued his rapid decline toward a tragic fate. "My father's life was full of tragedy, of unfulfilled powers and undeveloped gifts," Arthur later explained in his autobiography. Charles was prey to bouts of uncontrollable emotion, like the time John Doyle visited him a few months before his death. Afterwards Charles was certain he had helped to cause his father's early death. He suffered in such a way that drink seemed the only answer, and he became an alcoholic. When he became too difficult for his wife to handle, he was placed in a series of hospitals where epilepsy was discovered as well. Moving in and out of asylums over the next few years, he clung hard to his skill as an artist for comfort, and created some remarkable watercolours and sketchbook drawings. [Colour Plate VI] During this time he felt remorse and toyed with his sense of guilt. While at the Montrose Asylum at Sunnyside, he wrote in one sketchbook: "Keep steadily in view that this Book is ascribed wholly to the produce of a MADMAN". He continued his word games and the visual puns he once shared with Dick, and filled many pages with bizarre fantasies of animals, a "Fairy Whisper" given to a baby, or ghosts in a field. Throughout it all however, he remained true to the family religion. He noted on a self-portrait drawing in which he shakes hands with a skeleton: "Note. I do believe that to a Catholic there is Nothing so sweet in life as leaving it. Glory be to God." He died after prolonged illness, at the Crighton Royal Institution at Dumfries on 10 October 1893. It was a tragic end to a talented and tormented soul.

* * * * * * * * * * * *

Sadly, by the late 1870s, Dick Doyle began his own slow and premature decline as well. Although prey to fits of less severe melancholia and depression – mostly centring around his fading ambitions as an artist – he had learned to channel his gloomy feelings into his work, or to escape into society. But soon debilitating bouts of illness took even this away from him. He suffered attacks of painful lumbago, which limited his movements and sapped his strength. During winter months especially, long battles with bronchitis ("my old enemy") forced him to visit desolate seaside resorts for the bracing sea air. Even more serious, he was victim to attacks of apoplexy, which increased in number and alarmed his family, and frustrated his defiant plans for social engagements. Perhaps the most tangible indication of his suffering survives in his handwriting, where the fine, carefully formed copperplate of his journal now gave way to a spidery scrawl. Even his closest friends must have found his letters difficult to decipher, despite the exaggerated size of the characters, carefully drawn but disconnected to form each word.

His friends noticed the change as well. He seemed to age more quickly now. One friend simply noted he was "a man who seemed rather tired". Henry's late portrait of his brother showed a sad, rather haggard looking man, almost totally bald, but with the unmistakeable twinkle still in his eye. His illnesses kept him away from his club, which he deeply regretted, for he had virtually used it as a second home. He became known for his elusive habits, out of necessity rather than choice. One admirer had hunted for him diligently throughout London, but always seemed to miss him: "Like the elves too he was not always easy to find in person." This led to rumours that he was dead. "Not a bit of it, he's as willing as ever," snapped Lord Granville to one of his doubting guests when the subject of Doyle's work came up. When he appeared at The Athenaeum Club the older members noticed how much his familiar wit and spirit had faded; one whispered after he left the room, "Ah, poor fellow... I feared he was losing his masterfulness, and that would indeed be a bad sign."[22]

Certainly the most unfortunate aspect of this decline was the falling off in the number of friends and social acquaintances in his life. Since he was obviously unable to fulfil his social obligations in his familiar ebullient style he was passed over by hostesses making up their guest lists. But his closest friends remained devoted, among them Holman Hunt. Dick had given his name to a Life Assurance Company as a credit reference, and the painter willingly supported his friend in the claim that he could make a guaranteed income from his painting. Other devoted friends continued to visit his studio in search of new paintings to buy to help him through his obvious financial difficulties. By 1882, for example, he could offer his beloved Arthur no money to help set him up as a doctor, only well-meaning advice and lunch at his club. It was clear that the rumours which had circulated after his *Punch* resignation – that the proprietors offered him an annual annuity for life – were simply not true.[23] Dick depended wholly upon his picture sales, and because of his poor health, his output decreased from twelve exhibition works in 1878 to a mere two in 1882.

When illness prevented him from visiting friends, he wrote to them and looked forward to their news. Holman Hunt's young wife became a valued correspondent at this time. She was a delightful, spirited woman twenty-one years her husband's junior, who sent Dick flowers, news of her husband's latest painting triumphs, and the love of their child Gladys, who Dick called "the Fairy". With a mixture of envy and admiration, Dick had followed the prolonged progress of Holman Hunt's biblical painting, "The Triumph of the Innocents", over the nine years it took to complete. He was especially intrigued by the painter's use of bubbles for the spirits of the slain children ("they shine with inner beams"), as well as the intriguing tale that Holman Hunt had to conquer the devil which he was convinced possessed him during the painting, before he could complete it.[24]

Dick's bronchitis attacks forced him to the seaside each Easter. These were lonely times, when he stayed in hotels in which he was unknown to his fellow guests. He spent hours staring out at the sea from his room, or on mild days from a bench on the front. At Eastbourne during the Easter of 1879, he wrote to Mrs Holman Hunt how much he longed to be home among his friends. He couldn't work in his hotel room, although he had tried, and "as I am cut off from speech knowing nobody, I take refuge in observing". Among the temporary delights was a "tearful and wonderful" pretty young girl dressed in a large bonnet which he thought was probably the latest fashion. He also listened to the seven man band in the band shell and attended an evening performance of Mendelssohn's "St Paul" oratorio. To another valued friend, Thackeray's daughter, now Mrs Ritchie, he described the small details and snatches of conversation he continued to collect, even on these lonely convalescent holidays. He was amused by the antics of the local school children and how a large dog had raced into "a mob of little boys. It was only his desire to join in the fun, but one boy was quite frightened and ran crying towards where I was. He stumbled at the curb stone, but was so pleased to find, after falling on his face, that the dog was not following that he forgot to begin crying again. A gruff but kindly work-king (sic) man passing said 'What's the matter' when a wee little girl about half the size of the crying boy said – 'A dog barked sir, and the 'child' was afraid'."[25]

The seaside tonic usually worked, but was often followed by Dick's rush back to London in time to prepare his watercolours for exhibition at Grosvenor Gallery, usually in May. Then the bronchitis inevitably returned by the following winter, despite the efforts of his doctor who prescribed a diet of beef tea and "good old port", no solid food and "sleep by artificial means". This left him frustrated, weak, and unable to paint. All he could do was "sit in my painting room and try to read the paper". He tried various seaside resorts, generally the less fashionable, like Dover or St Leonards on Sea, near Hastings. He loved the unspoilt clutter of the seafront, and the unexpected encounters with local people, whom he loved to watch, but mostly avoided talking to. It was more fun to overhear bits of conversations than to force himself upon them.[26]

He returned home after his rest at the sea in 1880, revived but still too weak to send in more than two works to the Grosvenor. The cheering news that Arthur had passed his medical examinations but seemed unable to plan his future forced his relatives into immediate action. Although Dick and his brothers and sister had not seen Arthur for some time, they still felt responsible for his welfare, and they quickly arranged a family meeting with him in London. It proved a disastrous plan, which left the rebellious Arthur more determined to resist his well-meaning relatives' assistance, and the Doyle family were shocked by his rejection of their coveted Catholic religion. "Never will I accept anything which cannot be proved by me. The evils of religion have all come from accepting things which cannot be proved," Arthur later wrote, still firmly convinced of his decision to reject the Catholic church. Although James and Annette were deeply upset, Dick was the most willing to understand Arthur's position. He argued that since they had no money to spare, they were offering their nephew only introductions to their influential Catholic friends, who might help him set up as a doctor. Arthur called this "moral fraud". He was an agnostic, and unwilling to accept their beliefs. "*We* are speaking of the Catholic church," Dick argued. "What we believe is true." Eventually James, Henry and Annette dismissed his agnosticism as "a perverse whim" and gave up. But Dick persisted, and when Arthur set up his practise in Portsmouth, Dick sent him a series of uninvited recommendations to the Catholic bishop of the city and also the Duke of Norfolk, which Arthur promptly tore up. He then invited Arthur back to London, to lunch at his club, but these new tactics proved unsuccessful. "I fear that I was too Bohemian for them and they too conventional for me," Arthur later recalled. He refused to alter his religious views, and even influenced his devout Catholic mother's decision to switch to Protestantism – proof that she was devoted to her son.[27]

The argument and rift between Arthur and his Uncle Richard could not cloud the fact that Arthur remained in his uncle's debt. For Dick had taught him about the world of legends and ghosts, fairies and spectral beings, and this peculiar strain was something Arthur was willing to accept from his relations, not only Dick but his own father as well. In time Arthur developed his own means of expressing his uncle's spirit obsession. First he tried drawing himself, but gave that up for writing stories. One of his first published tales appeared in the appropriately titled anthology, *Dreamland and Ghostland*, 1886, which was attributed to "the nephew of the late Richard Doyle". His more famous Sherlock Holmes detective stories perhaps borrowed from his uncle's influence as well: Holmes played away his depressions with his violin, just as Uncle Richard; he lived in Baker Street, not far from the sight of Arthur's unforgettable excursion to Madame Tussauds with his uncle. Arthur took a closer look at his father's fantasy paintings after learning more about the world of fantasy from his uncle. In 1924 he even organized an exhibition of these to help revive his father's reputation. He framed each work and took a keen interest in the reception, inviting his most influential friends to attend and review the pictures. It was also a tribute to the Doyle family's tradition of fantasy, which Arthur grew

to believe was a major influence in his own spiritual quest.

The exhibition was hardly a success, partly because of the unfortunate title, "The Humorous and the Terrible". *The Times* wrote a moderately encouraging review, but concluded "the terrible did not terrify us. The more deliberately humorous did not amuse us. But nearly everything charmed us." George Bernard Shaw gave it a typical double-edged remark; that the pictures "deserve a separate room in the National Gallery". But by then Arthur was determined to prove his own theory of the existence of a volatile yet important spirit presence in the world. His experiments with spirit mediums enhanced that view, and shed a fascinating light upon his uncle's fairy preoccupations as well. Arthur in fact contacted his Uncle Richard, as well as his famous grandfather HB, through the spirit control Black Hawk, and received encouraging messages from his mother: "Uncle Henry is here. All the uncles and all the other Catholic relatives are very much in sympathy with you in your work."[28] When he introduced the famous Cottingley fairy photographs as "The Coming of the Fairies", these blurred images of fairies and winged sylphs in sylvan glades were compared with his uncle's *Punch* drawings by critics who were familiar with the fantasies of his famous uncle. And although recently these photographs have been declared fakes, they remain telling evidence of the Doyle family's preoccupation with the spirit world, and Arthur's attempt to prove his father and his uncle's fairy preoccupations had been more than mere artistic whims.[28]

* * * * * * * * * * * *

Among the five watercolours Dick exhibited at the Grosvenor the year of his death was a melancholy view of his favourite author, Charlotte Brontë's Haworth Parsonage. It was a significant painting for an ailing artist; a gesture – perhaps even the result of a premonition – which inspired Dick to attach a quotation from Mrs Gaskell's biography of Charlotte Brontë to the frame: "A strenuous soul keeping itself alive amid the gloom of decay and death". It was a gloomy, death-like work according to the critics who saw and described it: "Nothing could be more gaunt and melancholy than Haworth Rectory, the home of Charlotte Brontë, where a wilderness of blanched grave stones fills the

"Frances and the Fairies".
Cottingley fairy photograph, published in The
Coming of the Fairies, *1922.*
Brotherton Collection, Leeds University.

churchyard and on its boundary stands a stark, ugly brick-house, that looks as if it were set to guard them and must needs be more depressing than they. A wan light is in the windows distinct from that of the low moon, unseen behind the building. The whole chills while it repels, and makes one think of the cold, pinched lives and embittered hearts of the inmates who lived in such a place, perched high on the barren York-shire wold." Another critic simply decided it was Dick's "reply to the question, 'Tell me, where is Fancy bred?' ".[29]

By the autumn of 1883, however, Dick was well enough to leave London on an ambitious painting tour of the West Country. But first he travelled north and stopped again at Chatsworth, this time to look again at the treasures he had discovered there. "It requires such an effort to leave a house so full of pictures, fine books, and above all, sketches of the Old Masters," he wrote to a friend, but then hurried on down to Devon. There he renewed his memory of legen-dary haunts, and stopped to make sketches in a haunting Lynton churchyard, for what was destined to become his last painting. Again one wonders how much premonition played in his choice of subjects. For he selected the gravestones huddled together in the churchyard which over-looked the Bristol Channel and the church, whose spire nestled in the tall trees which sheltered it from the cruel sea winds. He inserted an old man mowing the long late summer grasses between the graves and two young children who scatter flowers over one particular

stone. The painting was discovered in Dick's studio, unfinished and framed in black: a symbol of his approaching death. "There it remains on his easel, unfinished still, as if to tell of one cut off so suddenly, not indeed in the summer of life, but in a mellow autumn, which seemed to give promise of many years of good work still to be done."[30]

When Dick returned from his painting holiday, he was over-joyed to hear that Arthur had agreed to meet him at his club for lunch. He was excited to explain his travels to his nephew, but the trip had taken its toll upon his weak heart and during lunch he collapsed in an apoplectic seizure. Fortunately Arthur, the trained doctor, was there to help and he rushed his uncle off to St Bartholomew's hospital, where he quickly recovered and was sent home. He was well enough to visit his old friend Charles Hallé at the Grosvenor Gallery Reynolds exhibition where he was "much interested" in the paintings. But Hallé noticed how tired his friend looked, how he complained of weariness yet refused to go home to rest. Instead he returned to his club where he was delighted to find Edward Burne-Jones, with whom he spent a pleasant time discussing pictures. Burne-Jones then left him for the library, and according to his wife's diary account, "on coming down again about half past nine, he told me, he saw a knot of men clustered round his companion of an hour ago lying already unconcious from the siezure which preceeded his death".[31] An ambulance rushed him home this time, and despite a slight improve-ment he never regained his speech, although the priest who accompanied him "thought he detected some traces of a joyful acquiescence" during the Sacrament of Extreme Unction.

The following morning, on the 11 December 1883, at 4:00 a.m. Dick Doyle died. He had just reached the age of fifty-nine. He was buried six days later at Kensal Green cemetary, where his friends Thackeray and Leech lay. It was a sad, yet peaceful end to a gentle artist, who had given the world over forty books illustrated in his inimitable style and over a hundred delicate watercolour paintings. But most of all, he left a memory of the "Delightful Dicky Doyle": "He will long be remembered not for the playfulness of his wit alone, but for that superadded charm and attractiveness which were due to the purity of his character, and for his many noble qualities of heart and mind."[32]

Epilogue

 he obituaries and later critical assessments of Richard Doyle, the artist and champion of the Catholic Church, make fascinating reading. His earliest obituaries outlined his contributions to book illustration but said little about his later attempts to gain recognition as a painter in the galleries. To some it was as if his career had come to an end after his *Punch* resignation; to others he was most important as one of Thackeray's and Dickens's illustrators.

The first substantial notice of his career appeared in *The Athenaeum* (15 December 1883), four days after his death. The paper had often reviewed his books and given long descriptions of his paintings exhibited at the Grosvenor, so it was fitting that the article should stress his abilities as an artist. Unfortunately the facts were not always correct. The article perpetrated the false idea that Dick had attended art school – not only Sass's art school but also the Royal Academy schools. This, in their opinion, made Dick "a much better and more learned draughtsman than his father" and allowed him to get "beyond the rudiments" of illustration. He was "the most graceful and genial as well as the wittiest of our satirical designers, and since Cruikshank's decease the most fanciful of our illustrators of fairyland". Equally inaccurate was the claim that he had received a pension from *Punch,* "and thereafter contributed to no other periodical of the kind". But like other obituaries and tributes, the paper felt Dick Doyle's influence could only be expressed in verse, and the article ended with the following:

"On the death of Richard Doyle"
A light of blameless laughter, fancy bred,
Soft-souled and glad and kind as love or sleep,
Fades, and sweet mirth's own eyes are fain to weep
Because her blithe and gentlest bird is dead.

Weep, elves, and fairies all, that never shed
Tear yet for mortal mourning; you that keep
The doors of dreams whence nought of ill may creep,
Mourn once for one whose lips your honey fed.

Let the waters of the Golden River steep
The rose-roots whence his grave blooms rosy-red,
And murmuring of Hyblaen limes be deep
About the summer silence of its bed,
And nought less gracious than a violet peep
Between the grass grown greener round his head.

A week later *Punch* (22 December 1883), published the following extract from the laudatory tribute by E.J.Milliken, the chief *Punch* poet:

"Richard Doyle (In Memoriam)"
Dropt the wizard pencil, resting
That unchilled, untiring hand!
Should some sorrowing Fay come questing
From the Court of Fairyland,
Come inquiring among mortals
For another fit to pass
Through those dim sequestered portals,
Fit that realm to the type and glass,
Of its wealth to be possessor,
Humour's harvest, Fancy's spoil,
Where should she find right successor
To the unrivalled *Richard Doyle*? . . .

Olden ties unknit too quickly
Take new charm as we review
Fancy's wit-world thronged so thickly.
Mors, who has so much to do.
Night, one dreams, give longer tether
Unto lives that keep so young.
Heads of wood and hearts of leather
Freely in his way are flung.
No! He will not be cheated
Of the choicest of his spoil,
To the further shore has fleeted
Fancy's favourite – "DICKY DOYLE"

More objective if critical reviews of his life and work appeared in papers like the *Illustrated London News* (5 January 1884). Dick had worked only sporadically for this paper, and the article was frank and perceptive. It divided his post-*Punch* work into two categories: popular social themes for Thackeray and others; and fantasy and fairy subjects. The *Punch* work dominated the assessment, however, since Dick "never again got an equally suitable and constantly remunerative vehicle for his graphic designs". And yet his resignation, once so controversial, now commanded the paper's respect: "a rare example of self-sacrifice and fidelity to conscience".

Three months later Dick's greatest champion and future biographer, Lewis Lusk, better known as the novelist W.D.Scull, published the first of a series of assessment pieces about his favourite artist. It was a brief notice of his death for the *Art Journal,* and surprisingly was full of factual inaccuracies – a poor showing from the magazine which once had reviewed Doyle's books in its Christmas book pages with such frequency.

Among the most substantial critical assessment articles about Doyle's life and work, the most biased was the eight-page article in the Catholic paper, *The Month* (March 1884). As a guide to "Richard Doyle, Painter and Humorist", it remains the most valuable contemporary account. Unlike previous or indeed subsequent articles, this one unashamedly took the view that Doyle was an influential artist as well as a true and admired Catholic, "a Christian who carried his religion with him unobtrusively, but more the less really into every scene and every company; a Catholic faithful to his religion with all the faithfulness of his loyal heart, and ready to make any sacrifices rather than even appear to throw in his lot with those who ridiculed or misrepresented it. Such a man ought not to pass unnoticed in the pages of a Catholic magazine." On the other hand, Doyle's influence went beyond the limitations of his family religion. The article also pointed out how his Protestant friends mourned his death, especially "a Protestant lady of rank, in whose house he often stayed" [possibly Lady Nevill], who wrote to a friend: "Your news had indeed saddened me. One of the rare ones of the earth is gone: for he was indeed unique. When shall we, or any one else, see again such a combination of childlike simplicity and warmth of heart, joined with such sparkling genial humour, such high honour, and such instructive good sense and judgement?"

Doyle's death touched those who only knew his work as well. The distinguished traveller and scholar, Sir Richard Burton, had never met Dick personally, but he admired his drawings and noted in his diary, writing from Trieste: "Richard Doyle died Dec.11". Among his younger artist admirers was the seventeen year old Beatrix Potter, who took the occasion of Doyle's death to write a wistful, longing passage in her diary: "Deceased, Richard Doyle the designer, died age sixty (sic). I have always from a little child had a great admiration for his drawings in the old Punches. He left the paper in 1850 when the stir against Papal agression began. He designed the Punch cover. I consider his designs as good and sometimes better than Leech's. He must have been little over twenty when he made those drawings. How time does go, and once past it can never be regained."[1] Interestingly enough, young Miss Potter's animal drawings borrowed much from her admired

a)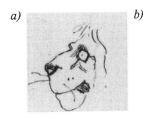
b)
c)

a)b)c) Doyle's animal inventions echo his colleague Randolph Caldecott and recall the work of his later admirer Beatrix Potter.

Dick Doyle. His quick ink sketches of comic dogs, horses and plants could easily be mistaken for her work, or her other great favourite, Randolph Caldecott.

* * * * * * * * * * * *

Meanwhile Dick's brothers and sister were determined to guard and preserve his reputation. At first Annette refused to disturb Dick's studio. where the poignant Devon churchyard painting still stood on his easel in its black frame. But within a year James had taken control and sifted through the unfinished book manuscripts, paintings and published drawings, in an attempt to find what might be publishable. He discovered Dick's childhood journal, and negotiated for its publication, securing a brief but valuable introduction by Dick's Catholic friend, J.H.Pollen. He reworked his own early collaboration with Dick on the *Scenes from English History,* wrote out the text in fine copperplate and had Dick's colour illustrations lithographed to make a splendid tribute volume to their boyhood days working together. Dick's early *Homer for the Holidays* appeared the following year, "for the

imitation of the rising generation", according to its publisher, the *Pall Mall Gazette,* who also published Dick's *Jack the Giant Killer* in 1888. But then the paper's proprietor, H.Yates Thompson, had always been a Doyle fan, and owned Dick's original Tournament drawings.

When Dick's *Journal* appeared in facsimile in 1885, less than two years after his death, it was reviewed as a memorial to Doyle's career; *The Portfolio* noting perceptively how sad it was that "the artistic promise of the boy did not develop into a larger and more impressive maturity in later years". It also coincided with the memorial exhibition of Doyle's studio, since Annette had at last relented and allowed her brothers to sort through Dick's paintings. Over one hundred and seventy-six watercolours, drawings and manuscripts were framed for the Grosvenor Gallery, and although some were borrowed from friends, most came from the studio and were to be sold with the copyright. It was an impressive show, but not large enough to fill the gallery, which was shared with an exhibition of Gainsborough's work – surely an anachronism. But the *Athenaeum* gave it full coverage and urged its readers to visit and perhaps buy Doyle's works, which "deserve long and searching examination". Unfortunately many works were left unsold, and reappeared the following year in the estate sale, held at Christie's on 7 June 1886 – the very rooms where Randolph Caldecott's estate sale was held just four days later.

The underlying reason for the family's concerted efforts to keep Dick's work before the public was of course financial. Dick had left a mere £1,500 in his estate, and at least two members of the family still did not have the means to support themselves. Annette had been Dick's devoted housekeeper until the very end, while James tried to live from his books, and had stayed on in the family home at Clifton Terrace with his books and research. In fact it was there he put the finishing touches to his monumental *Baronage of England,* which was soon to become a financial disaster, despite a second cheaper edition. Brief respite from money worries had come within two months after Dick's death, when the British Museum offered the family £1,000 for a collection of Dick's work, although James was disappointed since he had asked for £2,000. Moreover the government bureacracy only inflamed his anger. There was obviously an immediate need for the money, and yet the government agent's intransigence was infuriating, as James hinted to his agent. "As to the commission, I shall cheerfully pay it though the conduct of the government made the case a hard one for the family".[2] More revenue was raised when Annette agreed to sell the British Museum the manuscript of Dick's *Journal* for the princely sum of £200.

All these efforts to guard over Dick Doyle's reputation and reap some benefit from his posthumous fame, came to an abrupt halt within ten years of Dick's death. By that time all three of his brothers had died: Henry from a sudden heart disease on 17 February 1892; James on 3 December 1892, and Charles on 10 October 1893. And to a large extent, with them went the reputation of their most famous and revered brother Dick.

Through the efforts of Henry Doyle and his brother James, many of Richard Doyle's watercolours were added to the collections of the National Gallery of Ireland. Here a version of Doyle's favourite subject:
The Knight and the Spectre.
7½ x 14"
Courtesy of the National Gallery of Ireland.

Richard Doyle and the Critics

Apart from his family, Dick's publishers kept many of his illustrations in print throughout the first few years after his death, although some were reprinted in different contexts. When his *In Fairyland* drawings appeared in *The Princess Nobody* in October 1884, it was praised as the work of an artist who was "surely, among modern Englishmen, the most able to give life and tenderness as well as playfulness to a magic story of children and sprites". But, as the *Athenaeum* critic pointed out, "Unless some loving hands gather the scattered works of that genial artist, this is likely to be the last specimen we shall have of his skill". It proved a perceptive prediction, for apart from *The Doyle Fairy Book,* 1890 (itself a tribute volume with biographical introduction and reprinted illustrations from Montalba and his *Juvenile Calendar*), later editions of *The Enchanted Doll,* 1903, and *Brown, Jones and Robinson,* 1904, most of Doyle's work was out of print by the turn of the century.

The reason for this was generally the rising new generation of competent, and many agreed better trained, young illustrators of the elaborate and lavishly produced colour-plate gift books. These artists, like Rackham, Dulac, the whimsical Robinson family, especially William Heath, recognized Doyle's influence over their work. But they and the new generation of critics who promoted them could not help but relegate Doyle to a past era, of gentle, inoffensive and sometimes slight fantasy. Too many articles stressed "this singular sweet and noble type of English gentleman", as if he had been a curiosity rather than an innovative artist. His entry in the *Dictionary of National Biography* was typical. Here a substantial amount of space was devoted

to his career, but critical remarks were left out, in favour of rather limp praise of his personality: "the kindliest of pictorial satirists, the most sportive and frolicsome of designers, the most graceful and sympathetic of the limners of fairyland. In Oberon's court he would at once have been appointed sergeant-painter." He was too easily lumped with the Cruikshanks, Mulreadys and Grandvilles of the past. *The Athenaeum* compared his posthumous Grosvenor Gallery exhibition with Cruikshank, although Doyle's "ghostly imaginings had nothing miserable and mean in them". When Thackeray's daughter was asked about Doyle by his biographer Lewis Lusk, sometime in the late 1890s, she lamented Doyle's neglect: "I don't think Mr Doyle's work is appreciated seriously enough, and I am always glad to hear him praised. How people admire Fra Angelico! But Dicky Doyle's fancy and beauty are as great, and his fun is perfectly irresistible. I was laughing again only yesterday over the Brighton series in *The Newcomes.*"[3]

It was too easy to dismiss Doyle as an early example of the woodblock illustrators who spawned the more successful Sixties School, as Chatto does in his revised chapter to John Jackson's pioneering *Treatise on Wood Engraving* in 1861. There Doyle was given space alongside fellow artists of the woodblock, like John Gilbert and William Harvey, with a Brown, Jones and Robinson illustration which "fairly exemplified" his style. Other critics were less satisfied with his technical abilities. "I never regretted the hard necessity which forbids an art critic to shut his eyes to artistic shortcomings more heartily than I do in speaking of Richard Doyle," P.G.Hamerton explained in

1868. He found Doyle's Newcome etchings "full of wit and intelligence, so bright with playful satire and manly relish of life, that I scarcely know how to write sentences with a touch at once light enough and keen enough to describe them". And yet technically they were flawed by his "feeble" use of light, and under-developed "sense of the nature of material", an absence of "imitative study", which gave them "no value as works of art".[4]

Critics and historians of the illustrated book at first did not know what to do with Doyle. Gleeson White cited several Doyle books in his pioneering *English Illustration, The Sixties,* 1897, but years later Forrest Reid in *Illustrators of the Eighteen Sixties,* 1928, failed even to mention him (although Leech and Gilbert were given). Clearly the definition of a Sixties School artist had changed. Much later Percy Muir, in *Victorian Illustrated Books,* 1971, firmly took the view that Doyle was neither a *Punch* school nor a Sixties School artist, but a unique pheno-menon. Many of Dick's friends would have agreed, and cited De Quincey's elaborate claim that his was "the work of genius". Among them was *The Month,* which agreed that Dick had genius. On the other hand, P.G.Hamerton and fellow critic Graham Everitt thought genius was too generous a term for Doyle's talent, though "we who are strictly impartial will cheerfully admit that if he had not positive genius, – which we somewhat doubt, – he was certainly one of 'the most genial and graceful of comic designers' ".[5]

Such was the confused state of opinions immediately after Doyle's death. By the turn of the century, his work was largely forgotten while his role as a social butterfly was duly recorded in the numerous books of memoirs by society hostesses and artist friends. The Dalziels gave an affectionate assessment of their turbulent business relationship in their history of the firm in 1901. Lady Nevill quoted from his letters and added her own praise of his personality. It was also the period when Doyle's biographer began work, publishing his first assessment of Doyle the artist in the *Art Journal* in 1902, (which is reprinted here). It began with the claim that "although the *Punch* cover is one of the best decorative designs ever placed upon a magazine which stares the British Empire in the face every week, Doyle had rarely been taken seriously as an artist". Then it set out to do just that, under

the title "The Best of Richard Doyle", aided by a selection of his lesser known illustrations.[6]

Confusion also centred around the question of Doyle's public. Even during his lifetime, critics often had been unsure whether his drawings were intended for children or adults – especially the more horrific giants and torture scenes in the fairy-tales. "Was it to children only that his productions gave, and still give, pleasure? Have they not proved a source of delight to the men and women of his generation – more fully appreciated, perhaps, by the 'used up' and disillusioned than by the young?" asked J.H. Pollen.[7] Others, like *The Month,* stressed the harmless qualities of Doyle's vision: "We can put everything he ever drew into the hands of a child without the slightest fear. He liked to show

---

Doyle's quick ink sketches delighted the children he entertained with them:

a)

b)

his pictures to children, and to listen to their childish criticisms. He himself ever retained many of childhood's sweetest characteristics." This was a view shared by Doyle's more recent biographer: "Childishness was an undoubted misfortune for the man described by a contemporary as 'just the sort of artist a child would ask to do a funny man upon paper', or who, being shown a cave on a Welsh hill called locally the 'rocking stone', drew for a friend's children the sketch of a mother dragon smiling indulgently as she treated her brood to a see-saw on the stone."[8]

Another problem in preserving Doyle's reputation as a social satirist was the topicality of his drawings. Like his father, whose reputation suffered with the passing of those political heroes he drew, Dick Doyle's impressions of

fashionable drawing rooms, full of famous faces, lost their appeal when fashions changed and the famous passed from the limelight. His friend Holman Hunt believed this was the greatest single factor in Doyle's decline after his death; his "designs in gentle satire of the manners of the day will not be appreciated to the full in succeeding generations, from want of knowledge of the individuality of each figure in the various groups".[9]

Nevertheless, Doyle's fairy illustrations and his distinctive sense of comedy – the antics of Robinson on his horse, or mischievous elves cavorting down a page – are timeless. Even the sternest editor and critic recognized this, as did the rising generation of artists who borrowed unashamedly from his fairy visions. Throughout the 1880s magazine reviews of new artists' works often acknowledged this debt: Keeley Halswelle drew "firmly in the tradition of Richard Doyle"; Thomas Maybank's fairies were "inspired by Doyle". Kate Greenaway had launched her career as a greeting card artist on fairy designs inspired by *In Fairyland,* and

c) "Girls and a Bear".
Pen and ink, 6½ x 9½"
Huntington Art Gallery.

owned a copy of *Brown, Jones and Robinson* (given to her by Frederick Locker). Other fairy painters who had been recognized during Doyle's lifetime and continued to exhibit into the 1890s were acknowledged as "capable of carrying on the traditions of Doyle": artists like Arthur Hughes and especially the elusive John Anster Fitzgerald. This was the era of William Heath Robinson, who had gained much from his early study of Doyle's *Punch* cover.[10] Even at *Punch,* the new generation of illustrators worked under the shadow of their inventive predecessor. John Tenniel, who began in Doyle's style, continued on as chief cartoonist until 1901, while his colleague Harry Furniss was often called "the Doyle of our days", despite his famous break with the paper in 1894.

The rise of the so-called Nineties Decadents – artists like Aubrey Beardsley, and his circle of exotic illustrators – put pay to the last popular remnants of Doyle's innocent and wholesome fairy world. Public taste had changed and sentimentality and sprightly fantasy gave way to the grotesque, the distorted and the cynical. Rudyard Kipling could write of Doyle's alien fairy visions in *Puck of Pook's Hill,* 1906, "Besides what you call *them* are made-up things the People of the Hills have never heard of – little buzzflies with butterfly wings and gauze petticoats, and shining stars in their hair and a wand like a schoolteacher's cane for punishing bad boys and rewarding good ones." The little interest there was in Doyle's illustrations and paintings came inevitably from collectors.

The first hints of this new and encouraging direction in his reputation came in an article, "The Demand for First Editions" in *Publisher's Circular* (29 July 1893). Among the list of books for bibliophiles to look for was the first edition of Locker's works illustrated by Doyle, "which is worth a good deal more than its original price." A few years later Gleeson White published the first attempt to list Doyle's illustrations in "Children's Books and their Illustrators", a *Studio Special Number,* Winter 1897-98. It was a brief list, with the comment that Doyle's books "enjoy in a lesser degree the sort of inflated popularity which has gathered around those of Cruikshank".

For the benefit of collectors, as well as students of illustration, some Nineties critics tried to analyze Doyle's style. Gleeson White offered the first attempt in his *Studio* article:

"Doyle lacked academical skill, and often betrays considerable weakness, not merely in composition but in invention. Yet the qualities which won him reputation are by no means despicable. He evidently felt the charm of fairyland, and peopled it with droll little folk who are neither too human nor too unreal to be attractive." Similarly, the expert pen draughtsman and critic Joseph Pennell placed Doyle in the "old-school" of self-taught illustrators, who now suffered for their glaring inadequacies: "I suppose that among artists and people of any artistic appreciation, it is generally admitted by this time that the great bulk of the works of 'Phiz', Cruikshank, Doyle, and even many of Leech's designs are simply rubbish."[11] M.H.Spielmann, historian of *Punch* and an art magazine editor believed Doyle's primary weakness was his poor draughtsmanship: "as a draughtsman he is usually feeble, though graceful; his efforts, technically speaking, were constantly false, and his drawing often as poor as Thackeray's. He was saved by his charm and sweetness, his inexhaustible fun and humour, his delightful though superficial realization of character, and his keen sense of the grotesque."[12] Finally his first biographer Lewis Lusk attempted to categorize his drawings: from the "sylvan style" of the rustic borders of ivy and branches seen in the *King of the Golden River;* the "gothic beauty and fine angles like medieval armour" of his so-called "fresco style", which borrowed from what Lusk called a "teutonic strain" in Maclise and Phiz; to the fairy drawings of woodlands inspired by his own "love of the woods and their mysteries". There were hints of medieval illuminated manuscripts in his dense watercolour and ink border designs, and in the delicate scenes of chivalrous knights and their damsels in distress. But on the whole Lusk's categories were too loosely based upon impressions, and he lacked the knowledge of his more educated critics.[13]

Doyle's style of draughtsmanship on a variety of subjects:
a) Cut-out silhouette style used in Bird's Eye Views of Society.
b)c) Watercolour and ink cross-hatched style learned from drawing for wood engravers.
d)e) Fine etched-line style used in his Newcomes *etchings.*

b)

a)

c)

d)

e)

Plans for a biographical study of Doyle's life and work met with disinterest by publishers, and frustration by his friends. They watched helplessly as his reputation faded into obscurity. According to Rossetti's brother, he was merely the "dainty designer of fairy fantasies of queer comicalities". This was the only mention of Doyle's friendship in his autobiography. Charles Hallé lamented the fact that, like so many of his closest friends, Doyle would be "also consigned to the limbo of the forgotten past".[14] Indeed, Lewis Lusk received little encouragement from publishers for his planned biography of Doyle, which he admitted to a Doyle relative in 1903 had been a crushing blow: "My only desire is that Richard Doyle should have his proper appreciation as *Artist,* and to that end I have written my little treatise". Seven years later he was still at work on the book, aided by a collection of Dick's private letters given to him by a relative. But in the end Lusk gave up the task, and wrote to "My dear Mrs Doyle": "The letters were sent, but after further consideration, I thought that I had better regard them as strictly private and not read them, as I have come to the limit of what I can do on the subject of Richard Doyle. This is what it seems to me what he would have done had he been in my place." His only wish was to "live very quietly and merely keep in order what remains".[15]

It was not until almost fifty years later that a new attempt was made at Doyle's biography, by Daria Hambourg. Unfortunately the book was part of an illustrated series, "Art and Techniques – Master of Black and White", which left out Doyle's paintings, and only briefly summarized his life, despite the access the author was given to Doyle's letters. More recently *Dick Doyle's Journal* has been republished (sadly from the 1885 facsimile, and not the original manuscript now in the British Museum). His paintings and drawings are best known by reprints of *In Fairyland,* and the numerous greeting cards which came at the tail-end of the recent revival of interest among collectors in fairy artists. But Dick Doyle's life, with its inextricable links to the fairy world, which were carried on by his most famous nephew, Sir Arthur Conan Doyle in his own spiritual quest, have been largely overlooked until the recent centenary exhibition at the Victoria and Albert Museum.

REPRINTED ARTICLE

The Art Journal, 1902.

The Fireside Fairy. By R. Doyle.
From " The Lady's Companion " (1850).

The Best of Richard Doyle.

IT is not usual to attribute greatness to "The Tour of Brown, Jones, and Robinson," or to the author thereof. In this case the popular verdict has its usual rough justice. Often it happens that a man of delicate genius gives himself to the public in a cheaper form than his best,—makes a hit with it, and goes on in the same style ever after, so far as the public is aware. Doyle did that very thing, very early in life, since the majority of the "Pips hys Diary" cartoons and some of the "Brown, Jones, and Robinson" appeared in *Punch*. Guided by the warm applause which greeted these, he came to work chiefly in that manner. And although the *Punch* cover is one of the best decorative designs ever placed upon a magazine which stares the British Empire in the face every week, Doyle has rarely been taken seriously as an artist. Mr. P. G. Hamerton (in "Etching and Etchers," first edition) praises Doyle's wit, but says that his etchings have no value as works of art. Other writers dwell on his delightful qualities, chiefly from a literary standpoint, as witness De Quincey, Thackeray, and the kindly French critic Chesneau. But, just as those who would know the best of "Phiz" must study Mr. Croal Thomson's fine monograph, so those who would know Doyle's true position must study the article by Mr. Austin Dobson in the "Dictionary of National Biography," which alludes to "Dick's Journal" as a

NOTE.—The writer's thanks are due to Col. R. Holbeche (of the Camera Club), and to Mr. S. J. Hodson, R.W.S.

marvel of fresh and unfettered invention. This, again, is only to be rightly understood by a sight of the original, which is in the Print Room of the British Museum. It is an MS. journal kept by "Dick" in 1840. That it was kept entirely in the family circle would appear from the fact that even Mr. Holman Hunt, one of Doyle's oldest and most valued friends, never saw the little volume during the artist's lifetime. It is now one of the treasures of the Print Room, and would be a remarkable work for anyone to produce at any age. For a boy of sixteen to have produced it is surprising. In 1885, after Doyle's death, it was reproduced in facsimile, with an introduction by J. Hungerford Pollen, but the reproductions, good though they are, cannot equal the delicacy of the originals. Some of the best are 'Beethoven's Concerto, performed by Liszt and Eliasson,' 'Braham in Masaniello,' and the street scenes at the time of Queen Victoria's marriage. Very lovely also are the portraits of his sister in the family groups. At that time Doyle had a fine, nervous style, rather like the work of the Parisian Tony Johannot, or certain early illustrations by Meissonier. It is a lively style, and often implies sunlight. He kept it on in *Punch* for a certain time, becoming paler and freer and more decorative by degrees. Just when he was between his earlier and his later manner he did some illustrations which are remarkable for simple beauty. These were the drawings for Leigh Hunt's "Jar of Honey from Mount Hybla," in 1848. And, with a curious

THE BEST OF RICHARD DOYLE.

return to this central manner, after a number of works in his looser style he illustrated " A Juvenile Calendar," by Mrs. Hervey, in 1855.

Mr. F. G. Kitton, in " Dickens and his Illustrators," has done a real service to Doyle's memory in pointing out the illustrations to the "Chimes" and the "Cricket on the Hearth." The "Battle of Life" drawings are in Doyle's cheaper manner, but nothing could be better than the scene of the estrangement between John and Dot. The attempted suicide of Margaret is almost as impressive.

Mr. Holman Hunt, to whose kindness I owe much information about Doyle, tells me that even in early struggling days the Pre-Raphaelite Brotherhood took pleasure in buying—when they could afford to do so!— the "Manners and Customs of Ye Englyshe" as they appeared in *Punch*, and studied with real appreciation the artistic arrangement of the groups, and the character. Later on, Doyle became their warm personal friend. For Ruskin, as is well known, he executed a very fine title-page, "The King of the Golden River" (p. 252). It is about the best of his looser manner; though simple, it summarises Doyle's finest fancy—all his freedom of line; as much of his irresponsibility as shall give lightness, but no more; a wealth of gentle suggestion. For another man's three lines he has put one; with the very fewest of these simple instruments of expression he has given the pure spirit of Ruskin's fine prose. It is a line-poem of a noble and smiling valley, with the glen of the Golden River seen behind its forests, placid kine straying across its breast, and fields of corn waving in the breeze; in the distance is an ancient farmstead, one of those mansions so hallowed by long years of rustic ceremonial, of spinning, of shearing, of harvest festival and Christmas gathering, that it has acquired a flavour of homely aristocracy. Far behind rise the shoulders and cliffs of a mighty mountain range, the light clouds lying by their peaks. All is golden peace and happy labour in the fresh air, a theme which has inspired some of the finest passages in Art and Literature. Perhaps it is small wonder that Doyle should have been inspired too. For, under this inspiration, Virgil wrote the "Georgics," Jean-François Millet painted the 'Sower,' his masterpiece of breadth and suggestion of rhythmic movement, and under this inspiration did Mrs. Barrett Browning pen that finest of all her stanzas, which describes Millet's picture with curious fitness.

> " His dews drop mutely on the hill,
> His cloud above it saileth still,
> Though on its slope men sow and reap.

> More softly than the dew is shed,
> Or cloud is floated overhead,
> ' He giveth His beloved sleep.' "

Particularly in this "Golden River" drawing does the stragglesome tendency of Doyle's line help the spirit of it; even does it create a sense of atmosphere. Aided by the wild woody waving of the lettering, one can hear the fresh highland breeze go crooning down the vale. Whistler, in some of his later etchings, has used his lines in a similar spirit, to convey an impression of the blur of moving mill-sails, and we know that Rembrandt was a master who had this resource at command, when he was working without reference or deference to the stiff taste of his time.

The other drawings in Ruskin's book do not arise to so high a plane; to find others one must refer to the first edition of Frederick Locker's "London Lyrics."

A Composition. By R. Doyle.
From "The Life of Oliver Goldsmith " (1848). By John Forster.
By permission of Messrs. Bradbury, Agnew and Co.

The gem of these illustrations is ' The Old Oak at Hatfield Broadoak,' in which Doyle's style appears at its very best, being simple and strong, like the pen-work of Millais in "Once a Week."

The size of this Titan of old Britain is suggested by two graceful little figures on horseback, pausing beneath its masses of foliage, and a fleeting herd of deer; nor does the style anywhere destroy the breadth of the effect by any attempt at over-minute detail. The figures give an instant impression of refinement, but no more. Anything more would lessen the poetry of the sentiment into the prettiness of a vignette. Without hesitation one classes the work as large. The sensation of an ancient, stately forest is there. Such a tree creates a neighbourhood for itself, an historic neighbourhood, through which have passed the Roman legions and the hosts of the King-maker. And this again is a noble theme, which has inspired great workers, this of " the forest primæval, standing like Druids of old." Doyle's study of elves and squirrels in a tree has almost as fine a feeling ("A Jar of Honey"). His impressible nature seems to have been profoundly stirred on these occasions of meeting with these two great themes, the Mountains and the Forest, being brought to them by some mind more dominant than his own. When he has set himself to the themes one does not see an equal measure of inspiration, as witness "Brown, Jones, and Robinson on the Lake of Como,"—a nice but not great drawing, as it might have been. Evidently Doyle depended much upon the companionship and sympathy of his fellow men. They could depress him, they could inspire him. Without them his work flows tamely, and yet he cannot lose his manner in the rendering of humanity or of nature; he must be Doyle, not as are the

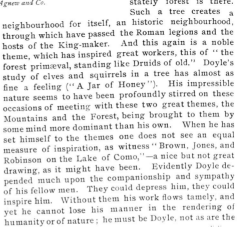

K K

Realists. He goes to nature, but to a limited extent; he dare not take much from her, but only just so much as his gentle style can bear. There is one curious exception to this, which shall be noticed later. With the fanciful creatures of old legend and superstition he is at home; the Fairies he draws are quite convincing.

This brings me to another of his finer works, hidden away in the obscurity of an old periodical long dead, *The Lady's Companion* for 1850 (p. 248). It illustrates a very beautiful and touching story, which is all in the

The King in disguise. By R. Doyle.
From "The King of the Golden River." By John Ruskin.
By permission of Mr. George Allen.

spirit of "The King of the Golden River," and such a noble fantasy has given Doyle just as strong an inspiration. I often wonder who wrote the tale. Perhaps Holme Lee, the authoress of the Tuflongbo stories, which have much the same dignity and sweetness, or Mrs. Gatty. For the Mrs. Loudon who edited the magazine was a remarkable woman, and commanded the best talent of her time.

In water-colour, Doyle tends to be trivial and somewhat resourceless, and is frequently gaudy where he meant to be rich in hue. But in the National Gallery of Ireland is a very large composition of several hundred figures entitled 'The Triumphant Entry, a Fairy Pageant.'

Dublin is rich in Doyle's work, in various media, one of the best being a drawing hung in a dusky corner—which suits it; the subject is a fairy form arising like mist out of a mountain tarn in the moonlight, and a knight on a scared horse. This is a very beautiful work, very serious in feeling, very fine in its simple treatment, though it does not quite entitle Doyle to rank as a master in the art. The Print-room of the British Museum has a similar work, which almost makes me place his technique in the first-class, it is so fascinating. But it is the business of the critic to speak proportionately, and for all the peculiar merit of this work, and of another very large dream of a Fairy Dance in a glen, one cannot seriously consider the craftsmanship as more than good second-class. The 'Fairy Glen' deserves description, being a very large water-colour, dated 1878. It is all foliage, with peeps of pale yellow evening light through, and a great slope of burdock leaves down to the water's edge. A crowd of dainty tiny figures is flittering around like a wreath of smoke; in the foreground a blue kingfisher flies up, his vivid hue giving a greyish look to the little blue wraiths beyond.

The composition is somewhat crowded, and rather clogs the great sweep of the Fairies' circling movement. Quite often Doyle has to fall back on body-colour for little bright touches of limbs and drapery, and so his work suffers the usual penalty of being a trifle chalky and garish in those places. Of course, Sir Noël Paton's 'Oberon and Titania' pictures are supreme; otherwise this of Doyle's, and a large and much more artistic 'Fairy Dance' in William Allingham's book, are the finest renderings of Fairyland known to me by British hands. This latter fairy dance is of a tender grey, suggestive of young moonlight and poetic mist, and while the wholeness of the great circular movement is carefully kept, certain figures and groups are emphasised with real Greek beauty, and suggest that Doyle had cast an observant eye over Flaxman's 'Homer' designs before setting to work. There is a dryad grace about certain of these fairy maidens, such as one perceives in Flaxman's exquisite divinities (notably his 'Morning'), and it gives the whole a serious claim to high artistic rank. This, of course, is barring the strict technique of the full wash, for there Doyle so often fails—so often is he persistently dotty in his foliage, so streaky everywhere. The 'Fairy Glen' suffers thereby; but the Print Room has one study of a noble Scottish mountain range (Loch Quoich), all rich greens and dusky purples, which is not unworthy to rank with similar work by the great men, being broad and clean of colour, the strong tones hit off at once and not muddled with any after touches.

Caledonia in her wild stern moods has a way of exciting certain artistic fibres, as might the boom and twang of some gigantic harp. The artist has, so to speak, in his sudden eagerness to get right up close to Nature in this excitement of her strong beauty, absolutely cast aside his usual timidity, and flung his arms round her and

THE BEST OF RICHARD DOYLE.

The Shepherdess and Flock.
By R. Doyle.
From " A Jar of Honey."
By Leigh Hunt.
By permission of
Messrs. Smith, Elder and Co.

hugged her. As a rule, if one does this to Nature, one gets a box on the ear and considerable discouragement. But here Nature has rewarded her lover kindly enough, and has additionally helped him with a group of waterfowl in the foreground, which are gracefully touched in and happily assist the sense of wild repose. Doyle has rather mistakenly inserted a modern piece of lawn and a lawn shrub, part of the property of his host; but then he was so absorbed in the study that he forgot the picture. Quite as often as not, this is a fortunate forgetfulness. In this instance it rather mars the effect of solitude. Possibly the beauty of Absolute Solitude was a theme which never did appeal overmuch to Doyle the sociable, who drew crowds so easily and effectively. There *is* a Solitude (so-called) which is in reality the most crowded hour of glorious life, and Doyle understood that condition very well, and sympathised with it wholeheartedly, as I will show. But he has drawn so many crowds —he began at sixteen in his Diary by drawing so many crowds, and drawing them so remarkably well for a man of any age—that one must always consider him an eminently

The Repentance of King Robert
of Sicily. By R. Doyle.
From " A Jar of Honey."
By Leigh Hunt.
By permission of
Messrs. Smith, Elder and Co.

social being. Life made him happy, evidently. He rejoiced in the whirl and sparkle of its stream, its quaintness, its prettiness, in the general shape of it. He had not been like many another man of genius, compelled to fight his way, to conquer opposition, to make the public accept and understand and finally approve of his Message. I use a capital M, for surely all originality is a Message of a greater or lesser sort. Doyle fitted in with the social taste very early — though he had a sufficient share of character, on certain occasions—and he seems very early to have felt that the best life for him was that of absorption in the simple art which happened to suit society also ; he managed to live very sociably, and yet to be also of the life of J. J. Ridley in " The Newcomes." This is a good life all round, if a man can find its white light sufficient. A man of such temper is always likeable, and is always becoming more likeable, seeing that he is nobody's rival, nobody's enemy. . . .

But this is preaching, not criticism. I do not consider Doyle as a complete J. J. Ridley, and we are told that J. J. attained to high rank in the craft of painting, which Doyle did not. But Doyle could sympathise entirely with that character, as may be seen by his etching ' J. J. in Dreamland ' (frontispiece of " The Newcomes," 1854).

It is suffused with poetry, and though Doyle's hand wavers at the task, that task is so pleasant that he cannot fail. J. J., that personality so near and dear to Thackeray's heart also, sits by the piano, listening to music played by a beloved hand, at whose touch his spirit is uplifted into a realm of romance. All round the dingy room floats the phantasm of fairy legend, terrible monsters, brave knights, beautiful ladies, joys of battle and festival, and true love triumphant. A pleasant and most noble palace of Dream ! Happy they, the rare ones, who never have to quit it for the sordid world of greedy minds and mean streets. Happier they who can carry it always in heart, like the Perpetual Light of the Rosicrucians, who can guard its flame undiminished by the gust and buffet of common cares. Doyle's art was to him just such a sanctuary, despite his social tastes, and so he very fitly has used his own face as model for that of J. J.

Of the same tenor is a small initial drawing of a stricken knight, attended by his faithful squire and his lady-love. It would seem as if she has come too late, for she presses her hands over her eyes as if to shut away the harsh sight of the dear face suddenly gone cold to her. Much mute eloquence is in the simple study, and the insolence of Victory is symbolised in the crowing cock. Doyle is not often so tragic in fantasy.

The best drawing of this set is ' The Old Love again.' It hardly conveys the idea of a chance meeting of two persons, once lovers, separated by social destiny, who now, with outward calm and inward agitation, desire that if they cannot be friends, at least each shall think well of the other. Such is Thackeray's suggestion. Probably the thing is impossible to convey by any mere draughtsman's effort. Life itself does not show its own tale so, rather would it hide it carefully in a genuine case of such an anxious moment. The artist has not the means of the writer, who can state what is really felt. But the drawing is more in the spirit of Millais than the others, and it is a pity Doyle could not have conveyed the same truth into his studies of Ethel Newcome. Ethel is lovely, but not quite fully and rightly drawn, as Millais or Du Maurier would have drawn her. Colonel Newcome is well enough rendered.

Another man of genius whom Doyle illustrated to his own great profit is Leigh Hunt, as stated earlier. The initials of "A Jar of Honey from Mount Hybla" (p. 251) are marvels of beauty, but the severe style of the engravers, W. J. Linton and E. Dalziel, has added a Flaxmanesque quality which rather divides the honours. The 'Robert of Sicily' and the Arcadian scene are as dainty as a cameo, and the angelic figure does not seem to have come from Doyle's pencil, on a first glance. But the sentiment is his throughout, glowing with Leigh Hunt's sunny inspiration.

It is no discredit to the artist that he should be at his best with Linton's strong and skilful hand for partnership, any more than it lessened Doré's praise that he should be interpreted by H. Pisan and S. Pannemaker, those consummate masters of a school of engraving which has now withdrawn before the inroad of "process." One can only call such an artist a very fortunate man, for that occasion.

Doyle illustrated "Piccadilly Papers," by Lawrence Oliphant, and like its author, who chose to set up as Preacher, does not quite succeed in his attempt to be serious. The theme of a man tempted to suicide, and loathing the vision of the bubble Reputation and the Race for Wealth, is a strong theme in the hands of a strong man, but in "Piccadilly" it merely evolves as a fancy. Leech, or even "Phiz," would have made it impressive. Tenniel, in those Titanic days of his when he drew the 'Pythagorean,' would have produced a great work. Rethel, author of "Der Tod als Freund," would have produced a *very* great work. But gentle Doyle's pretty drawings are no more in grim earnest than the "Piccadilly Papers." To accomplish the bitter tragedy of Vierge, Rops, and Mèryon, one must have some vitriol in one's composition.

Still, though not vitriolic, Doyle has once or twice accomplished tragic drawings of noble pathos. In Dickens's "Cricket on the Hearth" (1846), the last design, illustrating the very painful misunderstanding between two good people, is extremely impressive. The sorrow

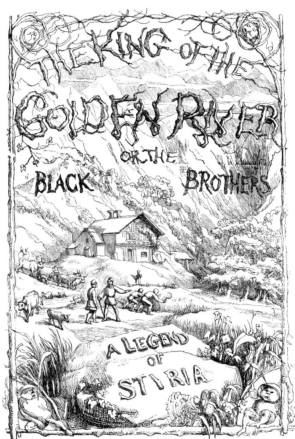

Title-Page. By R. Doyle.
From "*The King of the Golden River*" (1851). *By John Ruskin.*
By permission of Mr. George Allen.

is genuine—despite the fanciful figures, in which Doyle has excelled even his usual grace,—the carrier and his wife sit in real misery about each other. To look at the honest man's face is to understand that there is some sorrow of which one may die, if it endure very long. And the figure of the woman is full of silent eloquence too. Plainly she is inocent, yet plainly she is wretched. All the past happiness of these two cannot bring their hearts together just now.

One cannot often find a work of Doyle's so simply complete as this, perhaps one should not expect it. He can generally be sufficiently in sympathy with his author, if not required to be strenuous, grim, or realistic. Realism was impossible to one who had never had certain harsh experiences, such as the grinding-mill of the Schools and the heavy pounding of the Struggle for Fame and bare Life, such as Vierge and Mèryon endured—and which crushed the latter.

No, one must not separate Doyle too far from his style, which belongs to graceful fancy, not to awkward fact; you must not take him from his proper sphere of decoration, and set him to work at realism with its tones and values. Give him a gracious idea to put into decorative fancy, and he did it with a refinement peculiar in its simplicity. At the end of John Forster's "Life of Goldsmith" is a very remarkable example p. 249). The stately statue of the childish but greathearted author stands in the centre. Around are the varied incidents of his chequered life; his setting forth, poor and unknown, to trudge to London; his moments of sorrow in his lonely garret; his grave conversation with Johnson, to which Reynolds with his ear trumpet attends critically; his wanderings, his debts, his death, —the Wreath of Thorns is woven around them all, even round the feet of the great central Figure. But the figure rises away out of the thorns of this world, and stands serene, with laurels arching its noble head— Laurels and Sunlight.   LEWIS LUSK.

Doyle's classical, comic and historical styles were united in his preliminary
ink sketch for Punch, *Volume VI, January - June 1844.*
Private collection.

NOTES

Chapter I

1 *Art Journal,* March 1868, p.47.

2 The exact date of John Doyle's arrival in London varies from 1817 (Nordon) to 1821 (DNB). John Doyle and his family lived in London in 1825 at 60 Berners Street, 1827 at 14 Mannings Place, Lambeth, 1829 at 23 Euston Cresent, 1835 at 5 Brill Terrace, Somerstown, c1840 at 17 Cambridge Terrace, Hyde Park.

3 John Doyle to Robert Peel, 1 January 1842 (British Library). For a full discussion of HB's work see Graham Everitt, *English Caricaturists and Graphic Humorists,* 1893 edition, pp.235-276.

4 The road, just off the Edgware Road, still exists, the house being on the east side of Sussex Gardens, although the original numbering has not survived.

5 Michael Baker, editor, *The Doyle Diary,* 1978, p.81.

6 Arthur Conan Doyle, *Memories and Adventures,* 1924, p.21.

7 Dalziel Brothers, *Record of Fifty Years Work,* 1901, p.56.

8 Richard Doyle to John Doyle, 1 January 1843 (Pierpont Morgan Library).

9 See *Dick Doyle's Journal,* 1885, entry for 6 August.

10 Quoted in *Sir Arthur Conan Doyle Centenary,* 1959.

11 John Doyle to Sir Robert Peel, 1 January 1842 (British Library).

12 Richard Doyle to John Doyle, 12 November 1843 (Pierpont Morgan Library).

13 Quoted in Everitt, *op.cit.* p.287.

14 For a discussion of these sketchbooks see Lionel Lambourne, "Two Books Full of Nonsense", *Burlington Magazine,* May 1978, pp.290-291.

15 Henry Doyle to John Doyle, 26 November 1843 (Pierpont Morgan Library).

16 John Doyle to Sir Robert Peel, 1 & 22 January 1843 (British Library).

17 Charles Doyle to John Doyle, 3 undated letters c1843 (Pierpont Morgan Library).

18 See collection of letters Henry Doyle to John Doyle, 1840-45 (Pierpont Morgan Library).

19 Richard Doyle to John Doyle, 23 July 1842 (Pierpont Morgan Library).

20 Richard Doyle to John Doyle, 27 August 1843 (Pierpont Morgan Library).

21 Richard Doyle to John Doyle, 16 April 1843 (Pierpont Morgan Library).

22 Richard Doyle to John Doyle, 6 August 1843 (Pierpont Morgan Library).

23 Everitt, *op.cit.* p.391.

24 See *Dick Doyle's Journal,* 1885, entry for October.

25 Richard Doyle to John Doyle, 19 March 1843 (Pierpont Morgan Library).

26 Richard Doyle to John Doyle, 14 May 1843 (Pierpont Morgan Library).

27 Richard Doyle to John Doyle, 27-28 August 1843 (Pierpont Morgan Library).

28 Richard Doyle to John Doyle, undated [June 1843] (Pierpont Morgan Library).

29 Richard Doyle to John Doyle, undated [September 1843] (Pierpont Morgan Library).

30 Richard Doyle to John Doyle, 27 September 1842 (Pierpont Morgan Library).

31 Richard Doyle to John Doyle, 16 April 1843 (Pierpont Morgan Library).

32 Richard Doyle to John Doyle, 7 January 1843 (Pierpont Morgan Library).

33 Richard Doyle to John Doyle, 27 March 1843 (Pierpont Morgan Library).

34 Richard Doyle to John Doyle, 8 & 16 August 1843 (Pierpont Morgan Library).

35 Richard Doyle to John Doyle, 8 August 1843 (Pierpont Morgan Library).

Chapter II

1 M.H.Spielmann, *The History of Punch,* 1895, p.454.

2 Richard Doyle to Bradbury, undated (private collection).

3 Richard Doyle to John Doyle, 29 October 1843 (Pierpont Morgan Library).

4 Richard Doyle to John Doyle, 17 December 1843 (Pierpont Morgan Library).

5 Spielmann, *op.cit.* p.49.

6 Richard Doyle to Charles Doyle, undated [c1849] (Lausanne).

7 See Edwin W.Morris, editor, *Letters of Thomas Carlyle to his Brother Alexander,* 1968.

8 *The Month,* March 1884, pp.309-310.

9 Richard Doyle to Charles Doyle, undated [c1849] (Lausanne).

10 The Queen's etchings were "Esmeralda" and six other sketches after Richard Doyle dated 8 January 1845; see *The Printseller,* 1903, p.508. For Walter Crane's early career see Isobel Spencer, *Walter Crane,* 1975, p.21.

11 Pierre Nordon, *Conan Doyle,* 1966, p.10.

12 Richard Doyle to Charles Doyle, undated [c1849] (Lausanne).

13 Gordon Ray, editor, *Letters of Thackeray,* 1955, Volume II, p.537.

14 *Ibid.* p.164.

15 Quoted in *Sir A.C.Doyle Centenary,* 1959.

16 Thackeray to John Euston Cooke quoted in *Appleton's Magazine,* September 1879.

17 Ray, *op.cit.*II, p.374.

18 Richard Doyle to F.Elliot, undated [c1848] (New York Public Library).

19 For reproductions see C.P.Johnson, *The Early Writings of W.M.Thackeray,* 1888; also *The Century Magazine,* XXV, p.596. The British Museum owns four Doyle pencil sketches of Thackeray.

20 Lewis Lusk, *The Art of Richard Doyle,* unpublished MS, p.91 (Lausanne).

21 Quoted in *Sir A.C.Doyle Centenary,* 1959.

22 Richard Doyle to Charles Doyle, December 1849 (Lausanne); for reproductions see F.G.Kitton, *Charles Dickens by Pen and Pencil,* 1891, pp.63-65. The British Museum owns three Doyle pencil sketches of Dickens.

23 Quoted in part by J.D.Carr, *Arthur Conan Doyle,* 1949, p.13; typed copy Lausanne.

24 Walter Dexter, *The Letters of Charles Dickens,* 1938, Volume I, p.647.

25 Quoted recently in Norman and Jeanne Mackenzie, *Dickens, a Life,* 1979, p.194.

26 See Thackeray's "An Essay on the Genius of George Cruikshank", *Westminster Review,* June 1840.

27 *The Morning Chronicle,* 26 December 1845.

28 Richard Doyle to Charles Doyle, December 1849 (Lausanne).

3 Richard Doyle to Annette Doyle, September (sic) 1850 (Lausanne).

4 *Ibid.*

5 Quoted in Nordon, *op.cit.* p.11; John Doyle to T.Cubbitt, 12 December 1849 (British Library).

6 *Art Journal,* March 1868, p.47.

7 John Doyle to Lord John Russell, 20 June 1850 (Victoria & Albert Museum); see also chapter 4 notes below.

8 Carr, *op.cit.* pp.11-12; Richard Doyle to Charles Doyle, December 1849 (Lausanne); Baker, *op.cit.* p.56.

9 Quoted in Dalziel Brothers, *op.cit.* p.61; letter now in private collection.

10 Richard Doyle to F.M.Evans, 15 February 1848 (sic) (Punch archive).

11 Anne Pollen, *John Hungerford Pollen,* 1912, p.280; see *Dick Doyle's Journal,* entries for 2 & 5 November; Doyle added, "I wonder whether he knew how I restrained myself from buying ginger beer at every cart and shop down that very street some two months ago."

12 Richard Doyle to Charles Doyle, undated [c1850] (Lausanne).

13 Everitt, *op.cit.* p.390.

14 See Marion Lockhead, *John Gibson Lockhart,* 1854, pp.283-284; Richard Doyle to Mark Lemon, undated [late 1850] (Punch archive).

15 Spielmann, *op.cit.* p.456.

16 *Quarterly Review,* December 1854.

17 Ray, *op.cit.*IV, pp.322-323.

18 Richard Doyle to Messrs. Dalziel, undated [c1851] (Huntington Library).

19 Dalziel Brothers, *op.cit.* pp.62,59.

20 Richard Doyle to Edward Dalziel, undated [c1850] (private collection).

21 *Ibid.*

22 John Ruskin, *Praeterita,* Volume II, p.116.

23 Fred Kitton, Supplement to *Charles Dickens by Pen and Pencil,* 1890, p.65.

24 Ray, *op.cit.*II, p.767.

25 Dalziel Brothers, *op.cit.* p.61.

26 Richard Doyle to Annette Doyle, September (sic) 1850 (Lausanne).

27 Richard Doyle to Charles Doyle, undated [c1851] (Lausanne).

Chapter III

1 Ray, *op.cit.*II, p.614; for reproductions see C.P.Johnson, *op.cit.*pp.xiv,64.

2 Richard Doyle to Charles Doyle, December 1849 (Lausanne).

Chapter IV

1 Ray, *op.cit.*II, pp.773,312.

2 Dickens to Mrs Watson, 7 December 1857; for a discussion of this phenomena see Mark Girouard, *The Return to Camelot, Chivalry and the English Gentleman,* 1981, pp.200f.

3   Richard Doyle to Charles Doyle, summer of 1850, 24 April 1856 (Lausanne).

4   Nancy Mitford, *Ladies of Alderley,* 1967, I, p.284, II, p.4.

5   I am grateful to Penelope Fitzgerald for pointing this out to me; for a discussion of the Doyle-Blanche Stanley relationship see her article, "Notes on the Fairy Pictures of Richard Doyle", *World Review,* December 1950, pp.64-67.

6   Richard Doyle to Charles Doyle, undated [early 1853] (Lausanne).

7   Richard Doyle to Charles Doyle, undated [c20 January 1854] (Lausanne).

8   Ray, *op.cit.* III, p.231.

9   Ray, *op.cit.* III, p.251.

10 John Doyle to Richard Owen, 31 May [n.y.] (British Library).

11 Ray, *op.cit.* III, pp.300, 304.

12 Quoted by Nordon, *op.cit.* p.12.

13 Ray, *op.cit.* II, p.823.

14 Mrs George Jones to her sister, quoted in Gordon N.Ray, "The Newcomes", *Thackeray,* 1968, p.153; for a discussion of the Newcomes collaboration see Viola Hopkins Winner, "Thackeray and Richard Doyle", *Harvard Library Bulletin,* April 1978, pp.193-211.

15 Lusk MS (Lausanne).

16 Ray, *op.cit.* III, pp.372, 375, 384.

17 Lusk MS, pp.75-76.

18 Quoted in Mary Lutyens, *Millais and the Ruskins,* 1967, p.107.

19 Lewis Lusk in *Art Journal* 1902, p.251.

20 See P.G.Hamerton, *Etching and Etchers,* 1868; Burne-Jones's article reprinted in *The Bibelot,* 1898, pp.321-359.

21 Ray, *op.cit.* III, pp.350-351.

22 Richard Doyle to Lord Aberdeen, 27 April 1854; Lord Aberdeen to Richard Doyle, 4 May 1854 (British Library).

23 Nancy Mitford, *The Stanleys of Alderley,* 1939, Volume II, pp.95, 54.

24 Dalziel Brothers, *op.cit.* p.66; the proof engravings now in Victoria & Albert Museum.

Chapter V

1   Richard Doyle to Charles Doyle, 24 April [1856] (Lausanne).

2   William Holman Hunt, *Pre-Raphaelitism and the Pre-Raphaelite Brotherhood,* 1905, Volume I, pp.273-274.

3   Spielmann, *op.cit.* p.457.

4   Diana Holman Hunt, *My Grandfather and I,* 1969, p.82; also Holman Hunt, *op.cit.* p.275.

5   Richard Doyle to Charles Doyle, undated [May 1850] (Lausanne).

6   See Robert B.Martin, *Tennyson, The Unquiet Heart, A Biography,* 1980, p.401, which also uses the drawing as a frontispiece.

7   Reproduced in Hallam Tennyson, *Alfred Lord Tennyson,* 1897, Volume I, p.365.

8   I am grateful to Professor Robert Martin for this information.

9   Richard Doyle to Frederick Locker, 10 April [18] 77 (Harvard Library).

10 Charles E.Hallé, *Life and Letters of Sir Charles Hallé,* 1896, pp.129-130; the illustrated catalogue is now in the Victoria and Albert Museum.

11 See the *Exhibition Handbook of Paintings,* Manchester Guardian, 1857, pp.12-14.

12 Hallé, *op.cit.* pp.251-252.

13 Hallé, *op.cit.* pp.175, 161.

14 Richard Doyle to Macmillan & Co., 23 letters dated December 1857 - December 1858 (New York Public Library).

15 See Edward C.Mack and W.H.G.Armytage, *Thomas Hughes,* 1952, pp.109-110.

16 The log is in the National Library of Scotland; Richard Doyle to Charles Doyle, undated from Keir, Sterling (Lausanne).

17 Richard Doyle to Annette Doyle, undated [c1855] (Lausanne).

18 Richard Doyle to Charles Doyle, undated [c1851] (Lausanne).

19 Richard Doyle to Charles Doyle, 28 September [n.y.] (Lausanne).

20 Richard Doyle to Charles Doyle, 26 November 1851 (Lausanne).

21 Richard Doyle to Charles Doyle, 26 August 1856 (Lausanne); see appendix for list of Charles Doyle illustrations.

22 Richard Doyle to Charles Doyle, 18 September [n.y.] (Lausanne); for examples of Charles Doyle's paintings see Robert W.Wark, *Charles Doyle's Fairyland,* Huntington Art Gallery catalogue, 1980.

23 Richard Doyle to Charles Doyle, undated [c1853] (Lausanne).

24 Carr, *op.cit.* p.15.

25 Richard Doyle to Charles Doyle, undated [c1851] (Lausanne).

26 Nordon, *op.cit.* p.6.

27 Dr Patricia Thomson quotes in new edition *In Fairyland,* 1979, p.64.

28 *Sir A.C.Doyle Centenary,* 1959, p.12; also quoted by Lusk, *op.cit.* p.26.

29 Richard Doyle to Lady Gordon, 22 March 1851 (Huntington Library).

30 Richard Doyle to Mrs Brookfield, 16 February [n.y.] (private collection).

31 Lusk, *op.cit.* p.87; also Daria Hambourg, *Richard Doyle,* 1948, p.23.

32 Charles E.Hallé, *Notes from a Painter's Life,* 1909, pp.147-148.

33 Holman Hunt's remark quoted by Lusk, *op.cit.* p.96.

34 Daphne Du Maurier, editor, *The Young George Du Maurier,* 1951, pp.126-127.

35 Lady Jeune, *Lesser Questions,* 1894, pp.40-41.

36 Richard Doyle to Lord Rippon, 17 December [1864] (British Library); Richard Doyle to John Everett Millais, 9 January [1865] (Huntington Library).

37 Richard Doyle to Frederick Locker, 2 December [1857] (Harvard Library).

38 Richard Doyle to Frederick Locker, 3 December [1864] (Huntington Library).

39 Richard Doyle to Frederick Locker, 1 March 1865 (Huntington Library).

40 The twenty drawings (nineteen watercolour, one in pencil) now in Grolier Club, New York City; see Richard Doyle to Frederick Locker, 28 March and 3 June [1865], also undated [June 1865] (Huntington Library).

41 Richard Doyle to Macmillan, June [1865?] (Huntington Library).

Chapter VI

1 Richard Doyle to Charles Doyle, undated [c1855] (Lausanne).

2 Lusk, *op.cit.* p.82.

3 Morton Cohen, editor, *Letters of Lewis Carroll,* 1979, pp.119-120.

4 *Blackwood's Magazine,* April 1885, pp.485-488.

5 Henry Chorley, *Autobiography,* 1873, Volume II, p.227.

6 See Jeremy Maas, *Victorian Painters,* 1969, p.150; also Beatrice Phillpotts, *Fairy Paintings,* 1978.

7 *Blackwood's Magazine, op.cit.* p.489.

8 Richard Doyle to Frederick Locker, 24 June 1865 (Huntington Library).

9 J.A.Harland and T.J.Wilkinson, *Legends and Traditions of Lancashire,* 1873, pp.265-270.

10 Richard Doyle to Frederick Locker, 6 May 1871 (Harvard Library).

11 Thomas Keightley, *The Fairy Mythology,* new edition 1850, pp.109-111.

12 Longman's *Notes on Books,* n.d. [c1869] (University of California Library).

13 Geoffrey Grigson, editor, *William Allingham's Diary,* 1967, p.201.

14 Ralph Nevill, editor, *Life and Letters of Lady Dorothy Nevill,* 1919, p.199; see also Lady Nevill, *Under Five Reigns,* 1912.

15 Richard Doyle to Gladstone, 26 May 1869 (British Library).

16 At least three Doyle fans are known, the second with cherubic clown stealing apples disturbed by a policeman (private collection); third depicting the Seven Ages of Shakespeare (private collection).

17 See Girouard, *op.cit.* p.207.

18 Hallé (Notes), *op.cit.* p.113.

19 Henry Doyle to Rt.Hon.Austin H.Layard, 6 December 1874 (British Library).

20 Carr, *op.cit.* p.25.

21 Conan Doyle, *Memories, op.cit.* pp.10, 30.

22 *Pall Mall Magazine,* 1899, quoted by Lusk, *op.cit.* pp.102-103; see also Frederick Locker-Lampson, *My Confidences,* 1896, p.370.

23 Adrian Conan Doyle wrote "quite untrue" on Lusk's MS, p.89.

24 *The Triumph of Innocents,* painted 1876-85, is now in Walker Art Gallery, Liverpool; for Holman Hunt's devil story see G.H.Fleming, *That Ne'er Shall Meet Again,* 1971, p.329.

25 Richard Doyle to Mrs Richmond Ritchie, [c27 February 1879] (author's collection).

26 Richard Doyle to Mrs Holman Hunt, 31 January, 24 March [1880] (Huntington Library); Richard Doyle to Frederick Locker, 15 July 1880 (Harvard Library).

27 Carr, *op.cit.* p.44; Conan Doyle *Memories, op.cit.* p.27.

28 See Arthur Conan Doyle, *Pheneas Speaks,* 1927, p.33; for the Cottingley fairies see Arthur Conan Doyle, "An Epoch-making Event – Fairies Photographed", *Strand Magazine,* Christmas 1920, the photographs published in *The Coming of the Fairies,* c1922. For recent news of the fakes see *The Times* (London), 18 March, 4 April 1983.

29 *The Athenaeum,* 31 January 1885; also *Blackwood's Magazine,* April 1885.

30 *The Month,* March 1884, pp.315-316.

31 Georgiana Burne-Jones, *Memorials of Edward Burne-Jones,* 1904, Volume II, p.138.

32 J.H.Pollen introduction to *Dick Doyle's Journal,* 1885, p.xii.

Epilogue

1 Quoted in Hambourg, *op.cit.* p.30; Leslie Linder, editor, *The Journal of Beatrix Potter,* 1966, pp.56-57.

2 James Doyle to unnamed, 19 February [1884] (New York Public Library).

3 Nordon, *op.cit.* p.12.

4. Hamerton *op.cit.*; also quoted by Everitt, *op.cit.* p.392.

5 Everitt, *op.cit.* p.382.

6 Lusk, *op.cit.*

7   Pollen, *op.cit.* p.xii.

8   *The Month, op.cit.* p.318; also Hambourg, *op.cit.* p.27.

9   Holman Hunt, Pre-Raphaelitism, *op.cit.* I, p.274.

10   See John Lewis, *William Heath Robinson,* 1973.

11   Joseph Pennell, *Modern Illustration,* 1895, p.83.

12   Spielmann, *op.cit.* p.458.

13   Lusk, *op.cit.* p.39

14   William Michael Rossetti, *Some Reminiscences,* 1906, Volume I, p.206; also Hallé (Notes), *op.cit.*

APPENDICES

A

BOOKS ILLUSTRATED IN PART OR WHOLLY BY RICHARD DOYLE

Note: The following list of books with illustrations by Doyle was compiled from the abbreviated sources given above, and arranged chronologically when works were done, with dating discrepancies noted in parenthesis. Bindings and variant editions are noted only when books have been seen. Except where noted, all refer to first editions.

JUVENILE WORK

1836
Homer for the Holidays by a Boy of 12 [Richard Doyle]
London: Pall Mall Gazette Extra, No.33, 1887 (BL,ENG)
Title and 15 comic plates by Doyle done 1836, with extracts from Pope's translation (unbound, oblong 4to) (price 1s)
(18 original watercolours is Ross County Historical Society, Chillicothe, Ohio).

1840
The Tournament [at Eglinton] or The Days of Chivalry Revived
London: J.Dickinson [1839?] (VAM) 1840 (Hambourg, Pollen), afterwards London: Fores
6 lithographed plates loose, with title design on cover all by Doyle (oblong folio) (original edition 50 copies, at least 150 printed).

Fores National Envelopes
Series of 10 illustrated envelopes by James and Richard Doyle
London: Messrs Fores, at their Sporting and Fine Print Repository, 41 Piccadilly
Nos.1-6 published 1 September 1840, No.8 on November 9-10, No.9 end of November, No.10 early December. (cf.E.B.Evans, *A Description of the Mulready Envelope,* London, 1970, pp.161-176.)
Lithographed envelopes coloured and plain, lithographed by J.R.Jobbins, printed by J.Graf. (average size 3¾ x 5½"). Titles by Richard Doyle – No.2 Musical, No.3 Dancing, No.6 Coaching, No.8 Civic (with James), No.9 Military, No.10 Christmas. (cf.James Doyle entry below).

Dick Doyle's Journal A Journal kept by Richard Doyle in the year 1840. Introduction by J.Hungerford Pollen
London: Smith, Elder & Co. 1885 (BL, ENG)
Facsimile edition of manuscript now in BM; half-title, wood-engraved portrait frontispiece, facsimile pictorial title, letterpress title, 8 page introduction, 152 page facsimile with illustrations
Bound in buff cloth, gilt embossed designs by Doyle (4to) (price 21s)
2nd edition, 1886; American edition New York: Scribner & Welford 1886 (NU)
New edition with introduction and notes by Christopher Wheeler, London, Edinburgh: British Museum Publications, John Bartholomew & Co. 1980.

Dick Doyle's 'Comic Histories', with The Startling Story of Tommy and the Lion
London: Pall Mall Gazette Office 1885
12 illustrations with text below of early project for John Doyle, first published as *Scenes from English History* (cf.below); second later cautionary tale 12 illustrations captioned by Doyle for his story (oblong 4to).

Scenes from English History by the late Richard Doyle
London: Pall Mall Gazette Office 1886 (BL,ENG)
Lithographed portrait frontispiece, pictorial border to title-page reusing Eglinton Tournament border, text chromolithographed after James Doyle design, 12 chromolithographed plates and tailpiece by Doyle at 16, 1840 (as *Comic Histories*) printed from drawings on stone by T.Sadler by Messrs Hanhart
Bound in yellow boards with black design based on a Doyle plate on cover (oblong 4to) (price 7s 6d).

1842
Jack the Giant Killer by Richard Doyle
London: Eyre & Spottiswoode [1888] (BM) 1888 (ENG)
Facsimile 48 page manuscript written, drawn and watercoloured by Doyle in 1842. 55 watercolour illustrations colour lithographed within different historical borders
Bound in grey pictorial cloth with crimson lettering (NU), pale blue with black lettering (BL), cover design based on Doyle illustration (4to) (price 5s).

Beauty and the Beast a Manuscript translated by Adelaide [Doyle] and illustrated by Dick [Doyle]. Introduction by C.Ryskamp
New York: Pierpont Morgan Library 1973
Facsimile of illustrated story done about 1842; 36 pages handwritten text including pictorial title and dedication, 35 black and white illustrations, pictorial borders on first and last text pages (4to).

A Grand Historical Allegorical Classical and Comical Procession of Remarkable Personages Ancient Modern and Unknown Dick Kitcat Pinxt. Author of the Tournament
London: T.McLean 1842 (NU)
60 lithographed illustrations coloured by hand; cover design of historical figures by Doyle, card wrappers (oblong 8⁰) (4 original watercolours in NYPL) A panoramic christening procession for the Prince of Wales based upon Doyle's 1840 drawings for the Princess Royal.

PUNCH PERIOD WORK

1843
The Fortunes of Hector O'Halloran and his man Mark Antony O'Toole by W.H.Maxwell
London: Richard Bentley; Dublin: John Cumming; Edinburgh: Bell & Bradfute [1842-43] (BM)
27 etched illustrations by John Leech, 5 etched plates by 'Dick Kitcat' (Doyle)
Other editions: W.Tegg 1850; 1853; c1875 (NU) (ENG).

1844-46
CHARLES DICKENS CHRISTMAS BOOKS

The Chimes by Charles Dickens
London: Chapman & Hall 1845 (published Christmas 1844) (BL)
Frontispiece and title designs by Maclise , 11 illustrations by Leech, Stanfield, 4 by Doyle, wood-engraved by F. Becker, Groves, Linton, G.Dalziel, Gray, red cloth gilt, 175 pages (sm 8vo) (price 5s).

The Cricket on the Hearth by Charles Dickens
London: Bradbury & Evans 1846 (published Christmas 1845) (BL)
Frontispiece, pictorial title by Maclise, 12 illustrations by Stanfield, Leech, E.Landseer and 3 by Doyle, wood-engraved by Thompson, G.& E.Dalziel, T.Williams, Swain, Groves, red cloth gilt, 174 pages (sm 8vo) (price 5s).

The Battle of Life by Charles Dickens
London: Bradbury & Evans 1846 (published 19 December 1846) (BL)
Frontispiece, pictorial title by Maclise, 11 designs by Maclise, Stanfield, Leech and 3 by Doyle, wood-engraved by Thompson, G.& E.Dalziel, T.Williams, Green, red cloth gilt, 175 pages (sm 8vo) (price 5s).

LATER EDITIONS

Christmas Books by Charles Dickens
London: Chapman & Hall 1869 (BL) 1870 (BL stamp)
10 illustrations by Doyle to *The Chimes, The Cricket on the Hearth,* and *The Battle of Life.* 465 pages (8⁰)
Bound in red cloth, black and gilt lettering.

Christmas Books by Charles Dickens
London: Chapman & Hall, New York: C.Scribner & Sons 1910 (NU)
65 illustrations by Landseer, Leech, Maclise, Tenniel, Stanfield, Doyle, F.Stone.

1846
Almanack of the Month by Gilbert à Beckett
London: Punch Office 1846
12 monthly parts with preliminaries for 2 half-yearly volumes, 180 wood-engraved illustrations and initials, cover design all by Doyle, with pictorial paper wrappers, (sm 8vo). Discontinued after 1 year.

The Fairy Ring A New Collection of Popular Tales. Translated from the German by Jacob and Wilhelm Grimm by John Edward Taylor
London: John Murray 1846 (BL)
Frontispiece, title vignette, 10 plates and cover design all by Doyle, wood-engraved by G.& E.Dalziel, W.Green, W.J. Linton
Bound in blue boards (8vo).

The Illustrated London Almanack see periodicals below

1847
A Jar of Honey from Mount Hybla by Leigh Hunt
London: Smith, Elder & Co. 1847 (BR,Hambourg) 1848 (VAM)
Frontispiece, 26 pictorial initials and vignettes wood-engraved by W.J.Linton and E.Dalziel, decorated boards cover design by Owen Jones (8vo).

1848
Selections from the Rejected Cartoons with descriptive letterpress and critical remarks
London: T.McLean & Fred Syrett 1848 (NU, Hambourg)
Pictorial title and 15 lithographed plates by Doyle, based upon the Westminster Hall cartoon competition, satirizing Maclise, Pugin and other styles, 36 pages red cloth gilt (folio)
(5 plates redrawn from *Comic Histories,* cf.1840 above).

The Gallantee Show
London: Bradbury & Evans 1848 (NYP)
Pictorial advertisement announcing publications, 2 pages, illustrations by Doyle and Leech (8vo).
(NYP copy inscribed "Strictly Private" in Dicken's hand).

The Life and Times of Oliver Goldsmith by John Forster
London: Bradbury & Evans 1848 (BL)
1 Doyle illustration, "The Author's Present and Future", 40 others wood-engraved after designs of Stanfield, Maclise, Leech, R.J.Hamerton
2 volume edition 1854, new 1 volume edition 1855 (BL).

L'Allegro and Il Penseroso by John Milton
London: Art Union of London 1848 (BL)
30 wood-engraved designs of which 1 is by Doyle (No.XV), engraved by C.T.Thompson, remainder by H.O'Neil, J. Absolon, F.Goodall, E.H.Corbould, K.Meadows, H.K. Browne, J.Tenniel, J.Gilbert, cloth-backed printed boards (4to).

1849
Fairy Tales from all Nations by Anthony R.Montalba [Anthony Whitehill]
London: Chapman & Hall 1849 (BL)
12 wood-engraved plates and 12 wood-engraved illustrations by Doyle, cloth bound (8vo)
2nd edition: *Famous Fairy Tales of All Nations,* 1872 (Lusk), 8 plates, title-page vignette and 9 other illustrations on 5 plates all from 1st edition; sold as separate parts (cf.1871-72 entry below)
3rd edition: *The Doyle Fairy Book,* London: Dean & Son 1890 (BL) with the original 12 plates and 12 illustrations from 1st edition, and 12 plates from the *Juvenile Calendar* (cf.entry below), and 1 vignette by Crowquill, with memoir and introduction by member of Folklore Society
Bound in red cloth, black and gilt embossed design by Doyle (8vo)
4th edition: 1893 (BL) identical to 3rd.

The Enchanted Doll by Mark Lemon
London: Bradbury & Evans 1849 (BR) 1850 (title date)
Wood-engraved pictorial frontispiece and title, 21 illustrations, initials and decorations all by Doyle
Bound in boards, miniature editions London: Wells, Gardner, Darton & Co. 1899 (S), 1903 (BL) Republished as *Fairy Tales by Mark Lemon,* London: Bradbury & Evans 1868 (BL); also John Slark n.d. 1 decorative subtitle, 1 pictorial initial dropped, 2 new initials with 2 by Charles Bennett (included Bennett's drawings to "Chronicles of the Three Sisters")
Bound in blue and green cloth (8vo).

The Lover's Stratagem and other Tales by Heinrich Zschokke
London: John & Daniel Darling 1849
Numerous illustrations including 30 wood-engraved illustrations engraved by W.J.Linton after designs probably by the Doyle family: 1 signed DD, 1 RD, 3 others all probably by Richard; 2 signed CD (Charles Doyle?); 5 signed JD (James Doyle?); 9 signed HD (Henry Doyle?); the remainder unsigned but probably most by Henry on stylistic grounds, decorated boards (8vo).

Manners and Customs of ye Englyshe Drawn from ye Quick by Richard Doyle. To which he added some extracts from Mr Pips hys Diary contrybuted by Percival Leigh
London: Bradbury & Evans 1849 (VAM, BR) 1850 (BL)
40 wood-engraved plates and decorated title by Doyle from his *Punch* series 1849, republished 2 volumes in 1 (oblong 4to) (price 6s)
New editions: London: Bradbury & Agnew & Co. 1876 (price 12s 6d); revised edition as *God's Englishman.* Introduction and edited by Michael Sadleir, London: Avalon Press & John Bradley 1948
French edition: *Les Mouers et les Coutumes des Anglais en 1849,* London: Bradbury 1851 (ENG) a small version of original (4to) (price 15s).

Juvenile Calendar and Zodiac of Flowers with descriptions by Mrs T.K.Hervey [later Montague]
London: Sampson Low & Son 1849 (BR)
Pictorial title and 12 illustrations by Doyle wood-engraved by E.& G.Dalziel, Smith & Cheltenham
Bound in scarlet cloth, gilt stamped title and design by Doyle (8v0) (price 5s) 2nd edition: 1855 (BL, NU), (cf.1871-72 entry below).

The Book of Ballads edited by Bon Gaultier [Sir T.Martin]
London: William S.Orr & Co. 1849 (BL) 1851 (BR)
A new edition of the 1845 original illustrated by Crowquill, here with new ballads illustrated with 61 wood-engravings, 16 designed by Doyle engraved by the Dalziels, also by Crowquill, Leech, tailpieces by K.Meadows, cloth gilt (8vo)
2nd edition: 1855 (Lusk) [1855?] (BL)
3rd edition: 1857 (Lusk); 13th edition: Edinburgh: W.
Blackwood 1877, 1 drawing dropped, 7 additional Doyle illustrations, bound in blue cloth gilt embossed title; later edition London: W.Blackwood & Sons 1903 (NU).
(This extremely popular book went into numerous editions with minor changes to the text.)

1849-50
Rebecca and Rowena A Romance upon Romance by Mr M.A.Titmarsh [Thackeray]
London: Chapman & Hall 1849 (BR) 1850 (BL)
Frontispiece, pictorial title, 7 plates and 2 small vignettes by Doyle, wood-engraved by the Dalziels
Bound in pink boards, also issued hand-coloured (BL).

1850-51
The Story of Jack and the Giants
London: Cundall & Addey 1850 (BR) 1851 (NU,Hambourg)
Wood-engraved frontispiece, pictorial title, 6 plates, 27 illustrations and initials all by Doyle wood-engraved by the Dalziels
Bound in red cloth, gilt design from contents on upper cover (4to) (2s 6d plain, 4s 6d coloured) (Proofs on China paper Huntington; another set for title, 7 plates M.Heseltine)
New edition: London: Griffith & Farran 1858 (cover probably not by Doyle).

The King of the Golden River, or The Black Brothers A Legend of Stiria by John Ruskin
London: Smith, Elder & Co. 1851 (BL) (published 21 December 1850)
Wood-engraved frontispiece, pictorial title, 22 initials and illustrations by Doyle, wood-engraved by C.T.Thompson, the Dalziels, H.Orrin Smith, I.Thompson, C.S.Cheltenham, H.D.Linton
Bound in yellow boards, 2 designs on upper cover subsequently used internally (8vo)
2nd edition 1851; 3rd edition 1856 with frontispiece altered (nose of South West Wind conventionalized); 6th edition 1863 bound in orange cloth with gilt design by Doyle; 7th edition Sunnyside, Orpington, Kent: George Allen bound in dark green with gilt design; also 1884 edition (BL); 10th edition Orpington: George Allen 1892; American edition: New York: John W.Lovell & Co. [1885] (NU)
(Story also serialized in A.Mee's *Children's Encyclopedia*).

POST PUNCH WORK

1851
An Overland Journey to the Great Exhibition showing a few extra articles and visitors
London: Chapman & Hall 1851 (ENG, BL)
16 sections of panorama illustrations by Doyle, wood-engraved by the Dalziels
Bound in sage green boards (oblong 8vo) (3s plain, 5s handcoloured)
Reissued by Chapman & Hall as *Richard Doyle's Pictures of Extra Articles and Visitors to the Exhibition* [1852?] with new title, contents page, cover design, the panorama as 8 double-page plates, bound in blue boards.

1854-55
The Newcomes Memoirs of a most respectable family edited by Arthur Pendennis, Esq. [Thackeray]
London: Bradbury & Evans 1854, 1855 (BL)
Originally published in 24 monthly parts September 1853 – August 1855, yellow printed paper covers; bound in 2 volumes with etched frontispiece, pictorial title, total 50 etched plates and titles 118 wood-engraved initials, vignettes by Doyle, cloth (8vo)
American edition: New York & London: Harper & Bros. 1899 (NU)
(Original sketches, colour drawings in NYP).

The Foreign Tour of Messrs Brown, Jones and Robinson by Richard Doyle
London: Bradbury & Evans 1854 (BR) 1855 (BL)
Wood-engraved pictorial title, 174 illustrations and text by Doyle, engraved by the Dalziels and T.Williams
Bound in blue cloth gilt stamped (4to)
Later edition: London: Bradbury & Agnew [1878] bound in red cloth, gilt letters and black embossed illustrations; also London: George Routledge & Sons and American edition: New York: E.P.Dutton & Co. 1904 (BL).
American pirates: *The Laughable adventures of Messrs Brown, Jones and Robinson!* Showing where they went and how they went, what they did! And how they did it, with

nearly 200 most thrilling comic engravings, New York: Garrett, Dick & Fitzgerald 185-? (NU), smaller edition of 48 pages (24⁰); also New York: D.Appleton & Co. 1860, 1867, a lithographic facsimile of original, by American Photo-lithographic Co., N.Y.; other editions 1871, 1877 (all NU)
American parody: *American Tour of Messrs Brown, Jones and Robinson* being the history of what they saw and did in the US, Canada, and Cuba. By Toby, New York: D.Appleton & Co. 1872, 1873, 1874 (NU, UCLA) 74 illustrated pages (4to) (price 21s)
English parody: *Foreign Tour of the Misses Brown, Jones and Robinson* being the history of what they saw and did at Biarritz and in the Pyrennes, London: Bickers & Son [1885?] (inscription date 1888) (printed by Cowells Anastatic Press).

Poetical Works by Letitia Elizabeth Landon
London: Longman, Brown, Green & Longmans 1855
2 volumes with 2 Doyle title vignettes in each, cloth (8vo).

1857
Merry Pictures by the Comic Hands of H.K.Browne, Crowquill, Doyle, Leech, Meadows, Hine and others
London: W.Kent & Co. (later D.Bogue) 1857 (BL)
42 pages of comic illustrations, Doyle's unsigned, all wood-engraved by E.Evans, W.O.Mason, Vizetelly, G.Dalziel
Bound in pictorial boards cover design by Crowquill (oblong folio) (price 12s).

1858-59
The Scouring of the White Horse or The Long Vacation Ramble of a London Clerk by the Author of 'Tom Brown's School Days' [Thomas Hughes]
Cambridge, London: Macmillan & Co. 1859 (BL, stamped Nov.1858)
Wood-engraved double-page pictorial title, 18 illustrations and initials all by Doyle, engraved by W.J.Linton
Bound in dark blue cloth, embossed gilt design border (8vo) (price 8s 6d); also special presentation binding (16mo)
Reprinted 1859, 3rd edition 1889.

Sunday Employment, Sunday Enjoyment by Mrs Upcher Cousens
London: Dean & Son [c1859]
Frontispiece design in colour wood-engraved adaptation from Doyle's *Juvenile Calendar* (cf.1849 entry) (8vo).

The Adventures of a Sunbeam and other Tales in Verse by Eliza Grove
London: Dean & Son [1859]
Title border design by Doyle taken from *Juvenile Calendar* (cf.1849 above) but with month and text cut away (sm 4to).

1862
A Chaplet of Verses by Adelaide Procter
London: Longman 1862
Wood-engraved title vignette by Doyle, (8vo).

Puck on Pegasus 1862, see 1869 entry

1863-64
Bird's Eye Views of Society taken by Richard Doyle
London: Smith, Elder & Co. 1863 (ENG) 1864 (BL)
Wood-engraved pictorial title, series of 16 illustrations and related pictorial initials and text all by Doyle, originally published in *The Cornhill* (cf. periodicals section) engraved by the Dalziels, half-roan, title reprinted on upper cover (oblong folio) (price 15s)
Reprinted as *The Bird's Eye Views of Modern Society* [c1885?] 16 plates without text.

The Adventures of a Watch by Julie Gouraud
Dublin: James Duffy [1864]
Wood-engraved frontispiece of watchmaker, and pictorial title by Doyle, decorated cloth gilt (8vo).

1865
A Selection from the Works of Frederick Locker (Moxon's Miniature Poets series)
London: Edward Moxon 1865 (BL)
Wood-engraved title vignette, 18 wood-engraved illustrations some incorporating titles of poems, all by Doyle, wood-engraved by Swain and W.T.Green, decorated cloth gilt (8vo)
2nd edition 1868; special edition for Cosmopolitan Club 1874 (Lusk)
(Original pencil sketches now in Grolier Club, N.Y.; proofs in collection M.Heseltine).

An Old Fairy Tale Told Anew in Pictures and Verse by Richard Doyle and J.R.Planché
London: George Routledge & Sons [1865] (BL) (preface dated Nov.1865)
Wood-engraved frontispiece, 18 illustrations by Doyle, 1 reduced version of text illustration used as title vignette, engraved by Dalziels, having originally commissioned the drawings mid 1850
Bound in brown cloth, embossed and gilt cover design (4to)
2nd edition: London, New York: George Routledge & Sons 1868 (NU), printed on better quality paper, new plain brown cloth binding gilt stamped.

1868
The Visiting Justices and The Troublesome Priest or Irish Biddy in the English Gaol. An Easter Carol for 1868 too well founded on fact
London: Richard Bentley 1868 (BL)
9 illustrations by Doyle, paper printed boards (4to).

Fairy Tales by Mark Lemon 1868, cf. *The Enchanted Doll* 1849

Puck on Pegasus by H.Cholmondeley-Pennell
London: George Routledge 1869 (BL) 1862 (Hambourg)
New revised and enlarged edition probably of 1862 edition, with 1 Doyle plate, "A Tailpiece" (dragons) wood-engraved by Swain, other plates by Leech, Tenniel, Millais, Noel Paton, Phiz, Portch, M.E.Edwards
Bound in dark green cloth, embossed and gilt artists' signatures on cover (8vo)
5th edition: London: Chatto & Windus (VAM);
6th edition: London: John Camden Hotten 1869 (BL);
8th edition: London: Chatto & Windus 1874.

Burlesques, Novels by Eminent Hands illustrations by W.M.Thackeray and Richard Doyle
New York: Caxton Publishing Co. [18-?] (NU) 1869 (Lusk) (8vo).

1869-70
In Fairyland a Series of Pictures from the Elf World with a Poem by William Allingham
London: Longmans, Green, Reader & Dyer 1869 (ENG) 1870 (BL) (published Christmas 1869)
Wood-engraved pictorial title, 16 plates with 36 colour wood-engraved illustrations and 3 initials, all wood-engraved and colour printed by Edmund Evans after Doyle's designs originally captioned by him
Bound in dark green cloth embossed gilt cover design by Doyle (folio) (price 31s 6d)
Reprinted edition: 1874 (price 15s) (ENG)
Revised edition: *The Princess Nobody. A Tale of Fairy Land* by Andrew Lang
London: Longmans, Green & Co. 1884 (BR, BL)
Reuse of Doyle's colour illustrations with new Lang text; omits 5 illustrations, cuts down the remainder (double-page plate IV in 9 original sections here scattered throughout); total of 25 colour and 30 brown ink drawings, 1 repeated as pictorial endpapers, 56 pages total
Bound in cloth-backed pictorial boards with "The Fairy Queen" in colour on cover (4to)

New edition: with Allingham poem and Lang story combined, introduction and essay,
London: Michael Joseph, Webb & Bower 1979, 1983.

1870
Piccadilly A Fragment of Contemporary Biography by Laurence Oliphant
Edinburgh, London: William Blackwood & Sons 1870 (BR, BL)
8 wood-engraved plates and cover design after Doyle designs engraved by Swain
Bound in green cloth, embossed and gilt design by Doyle
2nd edition 1870; another edition 1874 (BL)
(proofs in collection M.Heseltine).

1871-72
Dean & Sons series of gift books with 1 colour lithographed frontispiece and several black and white wood engraved illustrations usually engraved by the Dalziels and C.T. Thompson, originally published as the four separately paginated sections of the 1872 Montalba *Fairy Tales from all Nations* (cf.1849 entry). The 4 titles arranged by appearance are:
Rose-red & Snow-white with other Famous Fairy Tales. New Edition
London: Dean & Son [1871] (BL) 1872 (Lusk, BL, NU)
Bound in red cloth, black and gilt embossed border to colour plate inset on cover (8vo) Later edition 1882.
The Enchanted Crow and other Famous Fairy Tales
London: Dean & Son [1871] (BL) 1871 (Hambourg)
Bound in sienna, embossed gilt and colour plate inset on cover (8vo).
Fortune's Favourite and other Famous Fairy Tales
London: Dean & Sons [1871] (BL)
Bound in purple cloth with embossed gilt and colour plate inset on cover (8vo).
The Feast of the Dwarfs and other Famous Fairy Tales
London: Dean & Son [1871] (BL stamp Jan.1872)
Bound in dark green cloth, embossed gilt and colour plate inset cover (8vo).

1875
The Attractive Picture Book
London: Griffith & Farran [c1875]
Numerous wood-engraved illustrations from various sources including 19 by Doyle from *Jack and the Giants* (cf. 1850-51 above), cloth-backed printed boards (oblong folio).

1876
Higgledy-Piggledy by E.H.K.Knatchbull-Hugessen (Baron Brabourne)
London: Longmans, Green 1876 (Osborne)
Wood-engraved title vignette, 8 plates by Doyle
Green cloth binding (8vo); another edition 1877 same spine but ornamental cover design.

Sad Story of a Pig and a Little Girl written by Madeline Wyndham
Private Printed: Walker & Cockerell [1901] (BL stamp Jan.1902)
Facsimile of 12 page story with 9 Doyle ink sketches done at Isel Hall, Cumberland October 22 1876
Bound in heavy blue paper wrappers, printed on rag paper (8vo).

1878
*Benjamin Disraeli, Earl of Beacons*field, KG in upwards of 100 Cartoons from the collection of Mr Punch
London: Punch Office 1878 (BL)
Reproduces Doyle's cartoon "Gulliver and the Brobdingnag Farmers", no.11 (4to).

POSTHUMOUSLY PUBLISHED WORK

A number of juvenile books were published after Doyle's death but listed here by dates when they were done, in the juvenile section above.

1884
The Princess Nobody see *In Fairyland* 1869-70 above.

1885
Dick Doyle's Journal and *Comic Histories* see 1840 entries above.

1886
Scenes from English History see 1840 above.

1887
Homer for the Holidays see 1836 above.

1888
Jack the Giant Killer see 1842 above.

The Early Writings of Thackeray by Charles Plumptre Johnson Elliot Stock 1888 (BL)
Illustrated with Doyle drawings reprinted from early work.

1890
The Doyle Fairy Book see *Fairy Tales from All Nations* 1849 above.

The Enchanted Princess by Dorothea S.Sinclair (Author of 'Sugar Plums')
London: Dean & Son [c1890] (S)
9 illustrations by Doyle; 1 reused from *Juvenile Calendar*, 8 from Montalba's *Fairy Tales from all Nations* (cf.1849 entries above), here published with illustrations by Arthur Hitchcock (8vo).

1897
The Queen and Mr Punch The Story of a Reign told by Toby, M.P.
London: Bradbury, Agnew & Co. [1897] (BL)
Preliminary vignette and final tailpiece by Doyle, others by Leech, Tenniel, Sambourne
Bound with pictorial wrappers (4to).

1901
Sad Story of a Pig see 1876 entry.

The Brothers Dalziel a Record of Fifty Years
London: Methuen 1901 (reprinted 1979)
4 designs from Doyle books engraved by the Dalziels.

1902
Songs of Childhood by W.J.de la Mare ("Walter Ramal")
London: Longmans & Co. 1902 (Osborne)
Boards (8vo)
Doyle's "Fairies under a Tree" drawing as frontispiece.

Mrs Caudle's Curtain Lectures by Douglas W.Jerrold
London: R.Brimley Johnson [1902] (BL)
25 Doyle illustrations and initials originally in *Punch* January-November 1845 (8vo).

1903
John Bull's Year Book edited by Arthur à Beckett
John Bull Press 1903
Various illustrations including 16 by Doyle originally in *Almanack of the Month* (cf.1846 above) (8vo).

1907
Pictures by Richard Doyle
London, Glasgow: Gowans & Gray 1907 (BL)
Reprints Doyle's "Bird's Eye Views", "Manners and Customs", and 4 pages of "Brown, Jones and Robinson", 64 pages (Humorous Masterpieces series No.6) (4to).

1909
Mr Punch's Pageant
London: Leicester Galleries 1909
Illustrations by various *Punch* artists including 2 by Doyle (published with souvenir catalogue of exhibition in limited edition) (sm 4to).

B

PERIODICALS ILLUSTRATED BY RICHARD DOYLE

Note: entries are arranged chronologically.

Fraser's Magazine
1842-44 ornamental border possibly by Doyle, from a 32 page book list (Harvard Library).

Punch
2 cover designs, comic initials, full-page cartoons and almanack designs over 7 years, totalling about 1000 drawings wood-engraved by Swain.
1843: 1 small drawing, 5 full-page borders, title-page only for *Punch Almanack.*
1844: 100 small drawings, 8 full-page cartoons, cover design for *Punch,* done January.
1845: 153 small drawings including initial letters, 9 full-page cartoons, includes the Mrs Caudle's Lectures series, January-November; also first full-page border designs for *Punch Almanack.*
1846: 110 small drawings and initials, 16 full-page cartoons, borders for *Punch Almanack.*
1847: 128 small drawings, 11 full-page cartoons, borders for *Punch Almanack.*
1848: 131 small drawings, 17 full-page cartoons, borders for *Punch Almanack* (also issued separately in coloured and uncoloured editions).
1849: 129 small drawings and initials, 10 full-page cartoons, (this year includes his second cover design, January, and the series "Manners and Customs of ye Englyshe" 12 March - 23 December); also border designs for *Punch Almanack.*
1850: 177 small drawings and initials, 22 full-page cartoons, "Punch's Holidays", Extra Number, August; and (includes "Manners and Customs" new series 9 February - 28 September; and full-page series "Pleasure Trips of Brown, Jones and Robinson" July-November), borders for *Punch Almanack.*
1857, 1862 (4 small drawings), 1864 (published designs from old stock, Doyle having resigned *Punch* late 1850).

The London Illustrated Almanack
12 designs by Doyle for monthly calendar headings, wood-engraved by Linton, Vizetelly, Dalziels, E.Evans, published by the *Illustrated London News* office, 1848 (folio, printed wrappers).

Illustrated London News
Doyle did various designs here including monthly calendar headings for their Almanack (cf. above); and "St Valentine's Day", illustrating a poem by William Bough, 15 February 1851, p.136, a full-page series of vignettes with postman presenting valentine to a woman, wood-engraved by Smith & Cheltnam.

The Ladies' Companion at Home and Abroad 1849-50
Weekly magazine "edited by Mrs Loudon", assisted by the most eminent writers and artists".
1849: Doyle headpiece on title-page, 5 Doyle illustrations to articles by Tom Taylor and others, wood-engraved by the Dalziels.
1850: half-page drawing, "The Fireside Fairy" to illustrate "The Princess of Babylon and the Cedar Peacock", initial 'T', 6 other illustrations.

Once a Week
Cover design c1859? (see Christie's sale catalogue 19 July 1983, No.29).

The Cornhill
Bird's Eye Views of Society series, 16 fold out illustrations, Doyle initials and text, April 1861-October 1862:

1861: "At Home", "A Juvenile Party", "A Morning Party", "A State Party", "A County Ball", "A Charity Bazaar", "The Picture Sale", "At the Sea-side", "A Popular Entertainment".
1862: "Dinner Down the River", "Belgravia out of Doors", "After Dinner", "Rotten Row in the Season", "At Home – Music", "Science and Art Conversazione", "The Smoking Room at the Club".

POSTHUMOUSLY PUBLISHED MAGAZINE ILLUSTRATIONS

The Studio
1897-98 Special Number, "Children's Books and their Illustrators", p.19 (brief book list).
1923-24 Special Number "British Book Illustration Yesterday and Today, 2 colour plates of Doyle paintings.

Art Journal
1902: half-page reproduction of "The Arrival at Cologne" from Brown, Jones and Robinson, p.95.
1907: half-page reproduction of "Manners and Customs of ye Englyshe – New Series No.1 "Ye Serpentyne duryng a hard frost. Ye Publycke upon it" (originally published in *Punch* 1850), here p.59.

C

WORK EXHIBITED BY RICHARD DOYLE

ROYAL ACADEMY
1868 - The Enchanted Tree (No.727)
1871 - The Haunted Park (No.629)

MESSRS FOSTERS, LONDON
A group of watercolours, c1862

GROSVENOR GALLERY
12 watercolours exhibited May 1878:
On the Road to Glenquoich, Inverness-shire (No.172)
Manners and Customs of Monkeys (No.173, now in VAM)
On the River Derwent, Cumberland: "The rooks were blown about the skies", Tennyson's *In Memoriam* (No.175)
The Witch Drives her Flock of Young Dragons to Market (No. 176, engraved version in *Puck on Pegasus,* 1861; cf.1885 entry below)
The God, Thor, drives the Dwarfs out of Scandinavia by throwing his Hammer at Them (No.177)
The Laddie Bourne, Invergarry, Inverness-shire (No.178)
Miss Blanche Egerton (No.179; cf.1885 entry below)
Rose-red and Snow-white, from Grimm's *Fairy Tales,* (No.180, reproduced *Grosvenor Notes,* July 1878, p.51)
Under the Dock Leaves – An autumnal evening's dream (No.181, now in BM, also called The Fairy Glen in *Art Journal* 1902, p.250)
The Old Library, Longleat, Wiltshire (No.182)
Fish out of Water (No.183, reproduced in *Grosvenor Notes,* July 1878, p.52, cf.1885 entry below; depicts sailors from H.M.'s ship Galatea "keeping the ground" on the occasion of the entry into London, after the marriage of the Duke and Duchess of Edinburgh)

12 watercolours exhibited May 1879:
"Peace or War?" (Elves urging Frogs to fight) (No.226, cf.1880 and 1885 entries)
In the Park, Rentcombe, Gloucestershire (No.227, cf.1885 entry)
Isel House, Cumberland, from the River Derwent (No.228, now in National Gallery, Dublin)

The Rock at Cortachy, Forfar (No.229)
The Good Fairy Returning from the Christening of the 'Sleeping Beauty' (No.230)
Waterfall at Drumlawrig, Dumfrieshire (No.231)
The Pied Piper of Hamelin (No.232, reproduced *Grosvenor Notes,* July 1879)
The River Nith from 'The Duchess Walk' (No.233)
An Adventure in the History of Athenatius Gasker (No.234)
A View on Warncliffe Chase, Yorkshire (No.235)
View of Raby Castle, Durham (No.236)
The Princess plays Chess with the Dragon for her Liberty (No.237)

4 watercolours exhibited May 1880:
Design for a frieze – Birds and Fairies Playing Leap-frog (No.238)
A View of Isel, Cumberland (No.239)
The Battle of the Elves and Frogs (No.240)
On the River Derwent (No.241)

2 watercolours 1881:
The Sailor and Monkeys; a Story of Imitation (6 watercolour chapter illustrations described in *Grosvenor Notes,* 1881, Nos.244-249)
The Truimphal Entry of the Queen – "Now she's coming!" (No.251, possibly 'The Triumphal Entry, a Fairy Pageant' in the National Gallery, Dublin)

2 watercolours 1882:
A Welsh Legend – "One peculiarity of the Cambrian fairies is, that every Friday they comb the goats' beards to make them decent for Sunday" (No.268, 2 versions known, one in the BM; cf.1885 entry below)
In the Park at Studley Royal, Yorkshire (No.269, now in National Gallery, Dublin)

5 watercolours 1883:
The Home of Charlotte Brontë (No.322, cf.1885 entry below)
The Altar Cup in Aagerup (No.328, cf.1885 entry)
The Schwein-General in Nassau (No.330)
Portrait of Lady Mary Leveson Gower (No.333, cf.1885 entry)
Dame Juliana Berners teaching her Young Pupils the Art of Fishing (No.334, cf.1885 entry, *Grosvenor Notes* 1883 for accompanying text)

Over 70 frames of watercolour, pen and pencil sketches January 1885:
(reviewed in *The Athenaeum* 3 January, 1885, p.22, and 31 January 1885, p.160) those lent by Annette Doyle given (AD)
Story of Tommy – The Little Boy Who Didn't Care and Was Gobbled Up by a Lion. (12 drawings in 3 frames, Nos.217-219, cf.book section *Tommy and the Lion,* 1885) (AD)
Designs for *Punch* title-page and political caricatures (Nos.220-221) (AD)
Portrait Sketches of Mr Charles Hallé and Signor Manuel Garcia playing chess, and other drawings (No.222, lent by Charles Hallé)

Henry VIII and Catherine Parr (No.223) (AD)
Studies of birds, (watercolours, No.224) (AD)
4 watercolours of women and children (No.225) (AD)
A Child's Dream of Fairyland, and The Youthful Ulysses (No.226) (AD)
4 watercolours of fairies and witches (No.227) (AD)
Pen and ink designs for book illustrations (Nos.228-230) (AD)
A Child's First Steps, a portrait group (No.231) (AD)
An Enchanted Tree (No.232, cf.RA entry 1868, lent by Miss Emmerson-Tennant)
The Goat Legend (No.233, cf.1882 entry above) (AD)

The Witch Drives her Flock of young Dragons to Market (No.234, cf.1878 entry above) (AD)
Ariel (No.235) (AD)
The Enchanted Forest (No.236) (AD)
Churchyard in Devonshire (No.237, "This is the last drawing executed by the artist") (AD)
Knights Crossing a Bridge (No.238, cf.BM version "On the Way to War") (AD)
A Fairy Flight (No.239) (AD)
A Witch and young Dragons (No.240, cf.1878 entry above, lent by Hon.Mrs Lionel Tennyson)
St Christopher (No.241, lent by Mrs Hallé)
Beauty and the Beast (No.242, lent by Mrs Hallé)
Castle Howard, Yorkshire (No.243) (AD)
Ariel (No.244, cf.Nos.251, 261; lent by Mrs Thackeray Ritchie)
The 'Dame Blanche' of Normandy – "She sat upon a wooden bridge, and would not allow any one to pass unless he went on his knees to her." (No.245, cf.No.271 below, lent by Duke of Norfolk, E.M.)
Miss Blanche Egerton (No.246, cf.1878 entry above, also No.297) (AD)
Elves and Fairies (No.247, lent by Marquis of Ripon)
Fish out of Water – Sailors from H.M.'Galatea' keeping the ground on the entry into London, after their marriage, of the Duke and Duchess of Edinburgh (No.248, cf.1878 entry above, lent by A.J.Balfour, MP)
A Northern Stream (No.249) (AD)
The Triumphal Entry of the Queen – "Now She's Coming!" (No.250, cf.1881 entry above, now owned by National Gallery Dublin, lent by James Doyle)
Ariel (No.251, lent by Lady Henry Somerset)
The Lady Mary Leveson Gower (No.252, cf.1883 entry above, lent by Earl Granville, KG)
Isel Hall (No.253, cf.Nos.284, 313, 317, 335 below) (AD)
The Altar Cup in Aagerup, from Keightley's *Fairy Mythology* (No.254, cf.1883 entry above, also No.294; lent by James Doyle)
Snails and Fairies (No.255, lent by Mrs Manning)
Madonna and Child (No.256, lent by Charles Hallé)
An Adventure in the History of Athanatius Gaskar – "I have contented with the cranes on the banks of the Scamanda, having nothing to defend myself with but an old cotton umbrella." (No.257, lent by Viscount Powerscourt)
The Goat Legend (No.258, cf.1882 entry above, lent by James Doyle)
A Moonlight Scene (No. 259, cf.plate in *In Fairyland,* 1870, lent by James Doyle)
Fairy Rings and Toadstools (No.260, lent by Richard Popplewell Pullan)
Ariel (No.261, lent by Benson Rathbone)
Battle of Elves and Frogs – "This event took place, it is supposed, in pre-historic times, or it might have been added to 15 decisive battles in the world – making 16." (No.262, cf. No.288, lent by Lord Carlingford)
Haworth Rectory: the Home of Charlotte Brontë (No.263, cf.1883 entry above, lent by Miss Balfour)
Study of Rocks (No.264, lent by Marquis of Ripon)
The Hon.W.E.Leveson-Gower (No.265, lent by Earl Granville, K.G.)
The Princess Plays Chess with the Dragon for her Liberty (No.266, lent by Mrs Manning)
The Toilet of Titania (No.267, lent by George Holt)
Battle of Elves and Crows (No.268, lent by Lord Carlingford)
A Ruined Castle (No.269) (AD)
Night in Fairyland (No.270, lent by Basil Rathbone)
The 'Dame Blanche' of Normandy – "The Dame Blanche requires him whom she thus meets to join her in a dance." (No.271, cf.245 above, lent by Duke of Norfolk, EM)
The Lady Griselda Ogilvy (No.272, lent by Countess of Airlie)
The Eagle's Bride (No.273) (AD)
The Dragon of Wantley (No.274, at least 2 versions

known; in National Gallery Dublin, and BM) (AD)
The Sleep of the Fairy Queen (No.275) (AD)
The Knight and the Jötun (No.276, cf.version in VAM collection, lent by H.Virtue Tebbs)
A Mermaid (No.277, lent by H.Virtue Tebbs)
Fairy and Owls (No.278, lent by James Doyle)
An Elf Baby (No.274, lent by James Doyle)
Calm Weather (No.280) (AD)
Manners and Customs of Monkeys (Darfur, Africa) (No. 281, now in VAM, lent by Sir Julian Goldsmith)
A Flight by Night – Bats and Elves (No.282, lent by James Doyle)
Under the Dock Leaves – An autumnal evening's dream (No.283, cf.1878 entry above) (AD)
Isel Hall (No.284, cf.version National Gallery, Dublin, lent by Hon.Percy Wyndham)
Through the Trees (No.285) (AD)
The Laddie Bourne – Invergarry, Inverness-shire (No.286, cf.1878 entry above, lent by A.J.Balfour, MP)
The Pied Piper of Hamelin (No.287, cf.1879 above, lent by A.H.Christie)
Peace or War? Elves inciting Frogs to Fight (No.288, cf.No.262, lent by Charles Lloyd Norman)
Fairy Rings (No.289) (AD)
The Haunted Park (No.290, cf.RA 1871, No.316 below; lent by Lady Goldsmith) This version depicts "two country children passing through an avenue of lime trees leading to an old red mansion-house, see the ghosts of former inhabitants enjoying a picnic in the woods".
A Scottish Loch (No.291) (AD)
An Old Bridge (No.292) (AD)
St George and the Dragon (No.293) (AD)
The Altar Cup, from Keightley's *Fairy Mythology* (No.294, cf.No.254, also 1883 entry above; lent by Sir Julian Goldsmith)
The Fairy Chariot (No.295, lent by James Doyle)
The Wraith (No.296) (AD)
Miss Blanche Harriet Egerton (No.297, cf.No.246, also 1878 entry above, lent by Admiral the Hon.Wilbraham Egerton)
Musical Fairy Giving a Singing Lesson to the Little Birds (No.298, see plate *In Fairyland*, lent by Charles Hallé)
Queen Elizabeth and Melville (No.299, lent by Benson Rathbone)
The Scandinavian god, Thor, Drove all the Dwarfs out of the Country by Throwing his Hammer at Them (No.300, cf.1878 entry, also No.320) (AD)
The Ruins of Fountains Abbey in the Park, Studley Royal (No.301, lent by Marquis of Ripon)
Small Sketch for the Altar Cup (No.302, cf.254, 294) (AD)
An Intruder (No.303) (AD)
The Good Fairy Returning from the Christening of 'The Sleeping Beauty' (No.304, cf.309, lent by George Holt)
The Staircase at Dorchester House (No.305, lent by Rt.Hon.Sir William Harcourt)
View of Balcarres [Canada] (No.306, lent by H.Sedgewick)
Library at Longleat (No.307, cf.1878 entry above, also No.311) (AD)
Landscape with Rooks (No.308, lent by the Hon.Mrs Percy Wyndham)
The Fairy Godmother of the 'Sleeping Beauty' (No.309, cf.No.304, lent by A.H.Christie)
Through the Trees (No.310) (AD)
The Library at Longleat (No.311, cf.No.307) (AD)
Deer Park – Autumn (No.312, version in National Gallery, Dublin) (AD)
Isel Hall (No.313) (AD)
The Enchanted Tree (No.314, cf.RA 1868 entry, lent by Lord Aberdare)
Dame Juliana Berners Teaching her Young Pupils the Art of Fishing – "Dame Juliana Berners was Prioress of the Nunnery of Sopwell, and the authoress of the famous work on fishing published at St Albans 1486" (No.315, cf.1883

entry above, lent by Lord Aberdare)
The Haunted Park (No.316, cf.RA 1871 entry, lent by Marquis of Ripon)
Isel Hall from the Derwent – Evening (No.317, lent by Lady Elcho)
Stirrup Cup – "If the Knight drinks from the cup offered him by the 'wild woman', he becomes insensible, and is led off into the mountains." Keightley's *Fairy Mythology* (No.318) (AD)
A Rocky Path (No.319) (AD)
God Thor Drives his Enemies from Scandinavia by Throwing his Hammer at Them (No.320, cf.1878 entry above, also No.300, lent by Duchess of Cleveland)
Fairy Rings and Toadstools (No.321, lent by F.Stroud)
The Return of the Dragon Slayer (No.322, lent by Lord Egerton of Tatton)
The Devil's Stone, Cortachy (No.323, lent by the Countess of Airlie)
Study of Rocks (No.324) (AD)
Raby Castle (No.325, cf.No.331) (AD)
In the Park, Studley Royal (No.326, now in National Gallery, Dublin) (AD)
Eastnor – Autumn (No.327, lent by the Marchioness of Tavistock)
The Altar Cup (No.328, cf.1883 entry above, also Nos. 254, 294, lent by Benson Rathbone)
The Lady Rita Leveson Gower (No.329, lent by the Earl of Granville, KG)
Yew Tree – Whittingham (No.330, lent by A.J.Balfour, MP)
Raby Castle (No.331, cf.No.325) (AD)
Study for a Larger Picture (No.322) (AD)
Lord Leveson (No.333, lent by Earl of Granville, KG)
The Schwein-General of Nassau (No.334, cf.1883 entry above, lent by Miss E.Baring)
Isel Hall (No.335)(AD)
The Home of Charlotte Brontë (No.336, cf.1883 entry, lent by R.H.Hodgson)
The Return of the Dragon Slayer (No.337, lent by J.Dykes Campbell)
Witch and Young Dragons (No.338, lent by Lord Coleridge)
Two Portraits (No.339) (AD)
View of Christchurch Bay, from a Gallery (No.340, lent by Henry Reeve, CB)
First Steps (No.341) (AD)
Series of 20 drawings presenting humorous incidents of Greek, Roman and Saxon history (Nos.342-349, cf.*Comic History,* 1885) (AD)
Comic illustrations from Homer's *The Iliad* (No.350, cf.*Homer for the Holidays*) (AD)
3 Sketches at the Manchester Art Treasures Exhibition, 1857 (No.351, cf.VAM collection, lent by Charles Hallé)
6 Ornamental Friezes in Caricature (No.352, cf.BM collection) (AD)
The Irish Famine – The Knight and the Goblin: 2 pen drawings (No.353, cf.VAM collection of drawings) (AD)
Portrait (No.354) (AD)
A sheet of 5 humorous sketches (No.355, lent by Charles Hallé)
A Window in Cheltenham and other sketches (No.356, cf.BM collection) (AD)
Guy Fawkes and 5 other sketches (No.357, cf.*Manners and Customs,* No.36, pen and ink sketches) (AD)
"Contiguous to a Melancholy Ocean" and other sketches containing portraits of Carlyle, Thackeray, Disraeli, Lord Brougham (No.358) (AD)
2 Designs for cartoons in *Punch* (No.359) (AD)
6 designs for *Punch* – Marshall Pelissier and others (No.360) (AD)
Series of fanciful designs in pencil and watercolour (Nos. 361-366) (AD)
8 drawings representing scenes in London life by an intelligent Japanese (Nos.367-368, cf.National Gallery of

Scotland collection) (AD)
Design for *Punch* cartoons (Nos.369-370) (AD)
Humorous sketches (No.371, lent by Charles Hallé)
7 frames containing 23 watercolour drawings, humorous illustrations of the History of England, intended to represent the rejected cartoons for Westminster Hall (Nos.372-378, cf. *Rejected Cartoons*, 1848)
Leap-Frog, a frieze (No.379, cf.BM collection) (AD)
Fairy Rings (No.380, lent by Benson Rathbone)
Elves and Fairies at Play (No.381, lent by Benson Rathbone)
Edward the Black Prince and the King of France (No.382, cf.*Scenes from English History*, 1886, no.5) (AD)
Proof impressions of designs for *Punch* title-page (No.383) (AD)
Sketches, portraits of Lord Tennyson, Lord John Russell, etc. (No.384, cf.BM collection) (AD)
Frame of 6 sketches, illustrations to Sir Walter Scott and humorous designs (No.385) (AD)
4 tinted illustrations to *The Grand Steeplechase of June 17th, 1839*, at the Hippodrome, Notting Hill (No.386, done at age 14, lent by Mr Mayne)
Dick's Journal (No.387, now in BM) (AD)
Dick's Nonsense (Nos.388-390, 3 sketchbooks, now in VAM)
A Treatyse of Fysshynge wyth an Angle (No.391, unpublished manuscript) (AD)
An Album of original drawings (No.392, lent by Mrs Manning)
Sketch portrait of the late W.M.Thackeray (No.393, cf. portrait drawings in BM) (AD)

ESTATE SALE, CHRISTIE'S 7 JUNE, 1886
124 lots included the following pen and ink drawings and watercolours exhibited for the first time:
King Stork and the Frogs (No.85, pen drawing)
Portraits of Children (No.92, pen drawings)
Study for The First Step (No.96, cf.GG 1885, nos.231, 341)
4 subjects of English Life (No.99, pen drawings done at age 12 or 13 cf. drawings in VAM)
A Child's Dream of Fairy Tales (No.114, watercolour)
Titania's Toilet (No.115, cf.GG 1885, no.267; watercolour)
The Pet Bears (No.116, watercolour; cf.pen drawing Huntington)
A Fix (No.118, watercolour)
The Battle of the Crow's Nests (No.119, watercolour)
Study for The Enchanted Tree, Studley Royal (No.120, watercolour; cf.RA 1868, GG 1885, No.314)
Study in the Park, Studley Royal (No.121, watercolour)
The Stolen Kiss (No.122, now in BM, watercolour)
Fashions (No.123, watercolour)
Design for *The Talisman* (No.124, watercolour)
Butterflies (No.125, cf.*In Fairyland*, 1870, watercolour)
A Tree Fight (No.127, watercolour)
On the Hills and On the Sea (No.128, watercolour)
A Scene in a Park (No.131, watercolour)
Jealousy (No.132, watercolour)
A Scotch Loch – from nature (No.133, watercolour)
The Biter Bit (No.134, watercolour)
A Lady's Muff (No.135, watercolour)
The Rt.Hon.Robert Lowe taking an oar (No.136, pencil and watercolour)
A Portrait of a Child (No.141, watercolour)
Groups of Mothers and Children (No.143, 4 in one frame, watercolours, cf.Fitzwilliam Museum collection)
A Mother and Child, and A Puzzled Traveller (No.144, watercolours)
Mermaids and a landscape (No.145, watercolour)
Puck (No.147, watercolour)
The Guardian Angel (No.148, watercolour)
The Knight and The Enchanted Cup (No.151, watercolour)
Raby Castle (No.152, watercolour, another version No.160)

On the Road to Invergarry (No.154, watercolour)
An Old Bridge near Fountains Abbey (No.155, watercolour)
Cortachy Castle (No.157, watercolour)
Sketches in the Highlands (No.161, watercolours)
Calm Weather (No.163, watercolour)
A Rocky Pass, Wharncliffe Chase (No.164, watercolour)
Dunstanborurgh Castle (No.165, watercolour)
A Comic Alphabet (No.179, 7 frames)

Various sketches and designs for published books, proofs for *Bird's Eye Views, Manners and Customs, The Newcomes, Rebecca and Rowena, Brown, Jones and Robinson, Punch, In Fairyland.*

BOOKS AND PROJECTS SOLD WITH COPYRIGHT
Book of Designs (No.180, pen and ink, dated 1840)
The Book of Nonsense (Nos.181-182, 2 volumes)
More Nonsense (No.183)
Reynard the Fox, from the German, illustrated (No.184)
Jack the Giant-killer (No.185, 1842, published 1888)
Beauty and the Beast (No.186, published 1973)
A Grand Historical, Allegorical, Nonsensical Procession of the Princess Royal (No.187, published version in 1842 was a variation)
The Corsair, illustrated (No.188, unfinished, now in Fitzwilliam Museum)
Royal Academy catalogue 1850, illustrated (No.189)

D

UNPUBLISHED OR INCOMPLETE BOOK WORK BY RICHARD DOYLE

Dick Kitcat's Book of Nonsense; A Book Fuul (sic) *of Nonsense* 1842; and *More Nonsense*: 3 books of humorous and fanciful sketches (GG 1885, no.388; Estate sale 1886, nos.181-183; now in VAM). *A Treatyse of Fysshynge wyth an Angle*: (GG 1885, no.391). Comic illustrations to Homer's *Iliad*: 19 sketches (GG 1885, no.350; Estate sale 1886, no.90) (cf.*Homer for the Holidays*). Illustrations to Sir Walter Scott: 6 pen and colour drawings (Estate sale 1886, no.91). *The Merchant of Venice*: drawn at age 12 or 13 (Estate sale 1886, no.97). *Reynard the Fox*: from the German (Estate sale 1886, no.184). 'The Corsair' by Byron, drawn by Doyle in his 16th year, incomplete (Estate sale 1886, no.188, now in Fitzwilliam Museum). Designs for Victor Hugo's 'Le Beau Pécopin' 1842, coloured sketches (Estate sale 1886, no. 197, with text in English and French, possibly translated by Adelaide Doyle) one French page in VAM, others in private collection). Comic Friezes: series of social satires in 1 frame and 1 volume, incomplete (Estate sale 1886, no.105). Series of 20 drawings presenting humorous incidents of Greek, Roman and Saxon History (GG 1885, nos.342-349). The Grand Steeplechase of June 17, 1839 at the Hippodrome, Notting Hill: 4 tinted illustrations done aged 14 (Estate sale 1886, no.386; now in National Gallery, Dublin). *The Impressions of a Japanese Visiting London*: proposed series of sketches (Estate sale 1886, no.79, cf.drawings in National Gallery Scotland). *A Comic Alphabet*: 7 frames (Estate sale 1886, no.179). *History of Belgium*: several separate designs made c1839, mentioned by Pollen, p.viii. "Don't Care - A Tragedy in Eight Acts": title and 9 pen sketches similar to *Tommy and the Lion (private collection, cf.book section above).*

E

WORK BY THE DOYLE FAMILY

JOHN DOYLE 'HB' (1797-1868)

Paintings:
Royal Academy
1825 - Turning out the Stag (No.218)
1826 - Portrait of a Gentleman (No.577)
1827 - Portrait of a Gentleman (No.618)
1830 - Portrait of a Gentleman (No.794)
1831 - Portrait of a Lady (No.770)
1835 - Portrait of a Lady (No.862)

Prints and Books:
(The largest collection of pencil studies and prints are in the BM and VAM.)
The Life of a Race Horse, 1822, 6 prints
Political Sketches of HB, 1829 – published in book form, London: T.McLean, 1841, 1844 (with an illustrative key)

Posthumous Publications:
William Cobbett, a study of his life by E.I.Carlyle. London, 1904 (with 4 caricatures by HB)
The Seven Years of William IV, a reign cartooned by John Doyle by G.M.Trevelyan. London, 1952.

JAMES WILLIAM EDMUND DOYLE (1822-1892)

James began his artistic career with Richard on 2 juvenile works: the Fores envelopes, and *Scenes from English History* (cf.Richard book list)

Fores Envelopes
10 comic envelopes done with Richard about 1840 for Messrs Fores, lithographed by J.R.Jobbins, printed by J.Graf. James's work appeared on 4, possibly 5: No.1 Courting, No.4 Hunting, No.5 Racing, No.8 Civic (with Richard), and probably No.7 Shooting (cf.Richard Doyle book list above)

Books:
He was employed as writer of literary criticism for the Catholic paper, *The Tablet,* c1849, and published 2 monumental works illustrated with his own drawings.
A Chronicle of England, B.C.55-A.D. 1485 written and illustrated by J.E.D.[oyle] London: Longmans, 1863-64. (81 colour illustrations wood-engraved and colour printed by Edmund Evans)
The Historical Baronage of England showing the succession, dignities, and offices of every peer from 1066 to 1885. By James Doyle. London: Longmans & Green, 1885-86. (1,600 illustrations in 3 volumes; large paper edition of 120 copies, 1885; small version with new title-page, 1886)

Paintings, drawings:
He was also a painter and draughtsman, whose works included 2 designs after Sir Walter Scott subjects for the walls of the Royal Summer House, Buckingham Palace, which had been selected by the Queen and Prince Albert, c1850s; The Duke of Wellington's Horse, led by his Groom at the Funeral, 1852, large lithograph.

Prints after paintings:
A Literary Party at Joshua Reynolds's, stipple engraving by William Walker with D.G.Thompson, published by Owen Bailey 1848, republished 1851, declared to the PSA in an original edition of 325.
Breakfast of Poets at Samuel Rogers's, planned as companion to above December 1849, published ? by McLean.
Caxton Showing Proofs from his Printing Press to the Abbot of Westminster, mezzotint by William Walker, published 1851 (BM,VAM)

Petrarch, Chaucer & Froissart, mezzotint by Herbert Davis, published by Henry Graves 1862, declared to PSA, edition of 70 (attributed to John Doyle (sic), after a painting for John Field, completed c1852).

HENRY EDWARD DOYLE, RHA (1827-1892)

Paintings:
Royal Academy
1858 – His Eminence Cardinal Wiseman (No.794)
Royal Hibernian Academy, Dublin
(Elected ARHA, 1872 and RHA, 1874)
1867 - The Annunciation (watercolour)
1877 - Percy Fitzgerald
- Viscount Monck

Portraits:
Richard Doyle (oil sketch, National Gallery, Dublin)
John Doyle (chalk portrait, National Portrait Gallery, London)
John Ruskin (pencil)
Cardinal Wiseman (print, proof 1856)

Mural Designs:
1864 - Chapel decorations to the Dominican Convent, Cabra, near Dublin
'The Last Judgement' mural paintings for transept of Roman Catholic Chapel, Lancaster.

Book and Magazine Illustrations:
Illustrations to Telemachus, c1840 (admired by Prince Albert)
5 small initial designs for wood-engravings in *Punch,* 1844-46
Contributed caricatures to *The Great Gun,* 1845.
Pictorial Half Hours with the Saints [with] 12 illustrations of the principal Festivals of the Year. By Henry Doyle, etc. 1865 (BL)
Cartoonist on *Fun,* 1867-69, generally diminutive full-length portraits with large heads, signed with a hen or "Fusbos"
An Illustrated History of Ireland from the earliest Period, By M.F.C., with historical illustrations by Henry Doyle. London: Longmans, 1868 (BL)
Catalogue of the Works of Art in the National Gallery of Ireland edited by Henry Doyle, 1890.

CHARLES ALTAMONT DOYLE (1832-1893)

Paintings:
Royal Scottish Academy
10 exhibition watercolours and drawings exhibited 1862, 1874, 1875, 1877, 1880, 1887. These include "The Kyle Cattle-market, Sutherlandshire" (lent by his employer, Robert Matheson), and "Prestor John's Promenade", both exhibited in 1874.
Brook Street Galleries, London
"The Humourous (sic) and the Terrible", exhibition of drawings and studies by the late Charles Doyle, 31 January - 13 February 1924. This was organised by Sir Arthur Conan Doyle and reviewed substantially in the press. The 124 items were mostly for sale, priced from £4 to £35, with all copyrights "strictly reserved":
1) A Presentation 2) Scotch Lowlands (with reverse) 3) Arthur's Seat 4) Caught 5) Explaining the Horse Chestnut to a Horse 6) Children of the Sun (figures bow to a dandelion with weasel overlooking) 7) Have a Weed? (with reverse) 8) Two Old Gossips 9) Tam o'Shanter 10)Homewards 11) Beauty and the Beast 12) Elves 13) Water Lilies 14) The Drowning Seaman's Vision 15) The Nile Lily 16) Hospital Visitors (angels round a bed) 17) Joy Riding 18) Pipe-Dreams 19) The Haunted Room 20) Shade of Achilles 21) Meditation 22) Procession in Faerie 23)

Ducks (with reverse) 24) The First Born 25) Don't be so cross 26) Fairy Pages (island scene with 2 figures) 27) Cupid's Catch 28) The Fairy Student 29) After the Harvest (lent by J.Henry Ball, relative of Henry Doyle) 30) The Professor of Agriculture 31) The Last Journey 32) Walpurgis Nacht 33) The Ghost House (fairy escape scene) 34) Was that a Gun? 35) A Messenger 36) The Blind Piper 37) Old Pals 38) The Death Coach (four horses drawing coach filled with huddled ghosts, against starry sky) 39) A Serenade 40) Bracket Accomodation for Three 41) A Hell-Blast 42) The Saving Cross (young girl clutching a Celtic cross in a graveyard, tormented by sinewy demons) 43) Duddingstone Loch 44) Light and Shade 45) Enter the Sultan 46-47) Queer Cards (set of 12 child-like designs) 48) Fairies Envying the Family going to Church (hung in Sir Arthur's home, according to his daughter) 49) The Dancers 50) Her Majesty 51) Clouds 52) A Monster (a ferocious weasel) 53) A Fairy Lover (fairy on a tree) 54) The Mating of Flowers 55) Before the Harvest 56) The Aerial Express 57)The Death of Winter 58) A Seachange Rare 59) The Fairy Piper 60) The Plant Bearer 61) Cupid Angling 62) A Joyride 63) The Fairies' Cook 64) Froggie would a wooing go 65) Nature Spirits (lent by J.Henry Ball) 66) Flower Spirits 67) The Fairy School 68) The Harvest Home 69) Queen Titania (lent by J.Henry Ball) 70) The Salmon Leap 71) Sketches in Fairyland 72) The Roaring Game 73) The Piper 74) When Swallows Homeward Fly 75) The Breaking Wave (man in deep water clinging to ship's spar) 76) The Forest Glade 77) Studies of Fairies (lent by J.Henry Ball) 78) The Fun of the Fair 79) A Fairy Meeting (group of fairies in cornfield, one speaking from a threshing machine) 80) Young Neptune 81) The Sportsman's Train 82) Eavesdroppers (love-making in a cornfield, troops of fairies) 83) The Fairies Christmas Tree (fairy figures on tree) 84) Windy Day 85) The Tamer 86) Playmates 87) A Tug of War 88) Going Home 89) Flower Elves 90) A Sun Worshipper 91) A Phantasy 92) A Study in Colour 93) Pussie 94) The Angry Cat 95) The Fairy's Omnibus (mouse with fairies on its tail) 96) The Fairy Queen 97) The Mermaid 98) Cricket 99) The Sick Cow 100) The United Kingdom 101) Fellow Students 102-103) The Months 104) The Uninvited Guest 105) Football (possible unpublished etching see below) 106) Curling (black and white pen drawing) 107) Humorous Studies 108) Winter 109) Rivals 110) A Misunderstanding 111-117) Three Pigs went to Market (drawings for Waterson Nursery book, see below, priced £35) 118-120) The Rogue's Progress 121) Her Pet 122) A Procession 123) When the Nurse is Sleeping 124) A Peace-Maker (cat and dog)
Other drawings and watercolours are now in collections of the University of Texas, and largest collection in Huntington Art Gallery, San Marino California, also National Gallery of Scotland, British Museum (prints), National Gallery, Dublin, the Conan Doyle collection, Bibliotheque Cantonale, Lausanne; and Conan Doyle family members' collections.

Prints:
"The Mummelsee and the Water-Maidens", oval wood-engraving (BM)
Set of 4 unpublished etchings: Football, Blindman's Bluff, Croquet, The Slide (copper plates sold 27 June 1889)

Sketchbooks, letters:
The Doyle Diary edited by Michael Baker, London 1978
Letters illustrated to John Doyle, Pierpont Morgan Library
"The Adventures of the last Abencerrage" early illustrated historical romance (unpublished)
Sketchbooks in Huntington Art Gallery

Magazine Illustrations:
Diogenes c1850-54
The Illustrated Times, 1856-60
Good Words, 1860 (his drawings here "call for no particular comment", according to Gleeson White, *English Illustration, the Sixties*, 1897)
London Society, 1862-64, the illustrations to "A Shy Man", 1864 (were "some of his best drawings", according to White), "Curling" to "The Bonspiel", 1870, p.74
The Graphic, 1877

Book Illustrations:

Travels of Mungo Park in Africa to discover the Source of the Niger New Illustrated Edition by Charles Doyle. Edinburgh: A.& C.Black, 1859 (Advert)
Coelebs the Younger in Search of a Wife or the Drawing-room Troubles of moody Robinson, Esquire. Illustrated by C.A.Doyle. London: J.Hogg & Sons, [1859] (BL) 7 full-page engraved illustrations and title design by Doyle, bound in red cloth, gilt stamped.

Men who have Risen a Book for Boys. Illustrated by C.A.Doyle. London & Edinburgh: J.Hogg & Sons, 1859 (BL). 8 black and white engraved illustrations, bound in red cloth, gilt stamped.

The Life and Surprising Adventures of Robinson Crusoe by Daniel Defoe. Illustrated by C.A.Doyle. Edinburgh: A.& C.Black, 1859 (BL). 4 full-page illustrations and title vignette wood-engraved by F.Borders. ("An edition of 1859, published by Longmans (sic), is a rather special curiosity, less for the quality of its illustrations, which is not very high, than for the fact that they were the work of C.A.Doyle... This seems to have hung fire and its price was reduced in 1861." Muir, p.22).

Friendly Hands and Kindly Words illustrated by C.A. Doyle. [1860] (BL). Copy destroyed in BL, catalogue also lists 1868 edition (see below).

The Pilgrim's Progress by John Bunyan. Illustrated by C.A.Doyle. London: James Hogg & Sons, [1860] (BL). 12 black and white engraved illustrations, bound in brown leather gilt stamped.

The Queens of Society by Grace and Philip Wharton. Illustrated by Charles Altamont Doyle and the Brothers Dalziel. London: James Hogg & Sons, 1860 (BL). 2 volumes of 16 illustrations, 9 by Doyle. Also an 1867 edition.

The Long Holidays, or Learning without Lessons by H.A.Ford. Illustrated by C.A.Doyle. London: James Hogg & Sons, [1861] (BL) (VAM). 8 full-page wood-engraved illustrations by Doyle, engraved by F.Borders; bound in magenta cloth, gilt stamped.

The Story of Herbert Lovell, or Handsome is who Handsome Does a Book for the Young. By the Rev.F.W.B. Bouverie (author of Life and its Lessons). With Illustrations by C.A.Doyle. London: James Hogg & Sons, [1862] (BL). 8 full-page illustrations within arched borders, engraved on wood by E.D.Evans; bound in mauvre cloth gilt stamped.

The Diverting History of John Gilpin showing how he went farther than he intended, and came safely home again. Illustrated by C.A.Doyle. Edinburgh: William P.Nimmo, 1866 (1865, BL). 7 full-page colour illustrations by Doyle; bright green paper wrappers with brown printed title.

The Book of Humorous Poetry with illustrations by Charles A.Doyle. Edinburgh: William P.Nimmo, [1867] (BL). 7 full-page illustrations by Doyle wood-engraved by Williamson; bound in red cloth, gilt stamped.

Friendly Hands and Kindly Words: Stories illustrative of the Law of Kindness; The Power of Perseverance; and the Advantages of Little Helps. With 21 illustrations by C.A.Doyle and others. London: Virtue & Co.; New York:

Virtue & Yorston, 1868 (BL) (cf.1860 entry above). 2 full-page illustrations by Doyle, his wife's portrait as a beggar op.p.108; bound in brown leather gilt stamped.

Mistura Curiosa being a Higgledy Piggledy of Scot, English, Nigger, Golfing, Curling, Comic, Irish, Serious and Sentimental Odds and Ends of Rhymes & Fables by F.Crucelli. With illustrations by Charles Doyle and John Smart. Edinburgh: Maclachlan & Stewart, 1869 (BL). 58 small wood-engravings and process cuts by Doyle; bound in green leather, gilt stamped.

Brave Men's Footsteps a Book of example and anecdote in practical life, for young people. By the editor of *Men who have Risen* (cf.1859 entry above). Illustrated by C.A. Doyle. London: Henry S.King & Co., 1872 (BL). 4 black and white illustrations; bound in red cloth, gilt stamped. Also an 1873 edition (BL).

Our Trip to Blunderland, or Grand Excursion to Blunderland and Back by Jean Jambon (Rt.Hon.John Hay Athol Macdonald, afterwards Lord Kingsbridge). With 60 illustrations by Charles Doyle. Edinburgh & London: William Blackwood & Sons, 1877 (BL) ("second thousand"); 1878 ("15th thousand"). 20 full-page and 40 vignettes by Doyle wood-engraved by the Dalziels; bound in bright blue cloth, gilt stamped.

Waterson Nursery Library Series:
A series of large paper-cover colour toybooks (1 shilling paper, 2 shillings cloth) published by George Waterson & Sons, 56 Hanover Street, Edinburgh, and 9 Rose Street, New Gate Street, London. Generally 12 pages with 6 full-page colour illustrations.
1) *Three Naughty Little Boys* New edition. Illustrated by Charles A.Doyle. (1878) (ENG).
2) *The Two Bears* illustrated by Charles A.Doyle and William S.Black. 1880 (BL).
3) *How the Three Little Pigs Went to Market, and the Old One Stayed at Home* (A tragic yet strictly moral story). With Music. c1880 (Advert).
4) *Three Blind Mice* with Mewsic and Words from an Early Edition. Illustrated by C.A.Doyle. 1883 (BL).

European Slavery or Scenes from Married Life by Celphane Rose. Illustrated by Charles Doyle. Edinburgh: Andrew Elliot, 1881 (BL) 1882 (BL stamp). 6 full-page wood-engraved illustrations by Doyle, engraved by Paterson.

Remollescences of a Medical Student by J.A.Sidney. Illustrated by Charles Doyle, 1886 (BL).

A Study in Scarlet by Arthur Conan Doyle. Ward Lock & Co. 'Shilling Shocker', 1888. 6 black and white engraved illustrations by Charles to a story originally published in *Beeton's Christmas Annual*, 1887.

INDEX